D0856139

GRAND fINALES

A Neoclassic View
of Plated Desserts

GRAND finALES

A Neoclassic View
of Plated Desserts

BY TISH BOYLE AND TIMOTHY MORIARTY

EDITORS OF *CHOCOLATIER* MAGAZINE

PHOTOGRAPHY BY JOHN UHER

JOHN WILEY & SONS, INC.
New York • Chichester • Weinheim • Brisbane • Singapore • Toronto

Copyright © 2000 by John Wiley & Sons, Inc. All rights reserved.

Published simultaneously in Canada.

Library of Congress Cataloging-in-Publication Data:
A neoclassic view of plated desserts: grand finales/[compiled] by
    Tish Boyle and Timothy Moriarty; photography by John Uher.
            p.   cm.
        Includes bibliographical references and index (p.).
        ISBN 0-471-29313-X (alk. paper)
        1. Desserts. 2. Pastry.   I. Boyle, Tish. II. Moriarty, Timothy,
    1951-
    TX773.G684 2000
    641.8'6—dc21
    98-50537
    CIP

Book design by Vertigo Design, NY.
Printed in the United States of America.
10 9 8 7 6 5 4 3 2 1

contents

recipe contents

preface

This is the third volume in the *Grand Finales* series. These books present the recipes and plate designs of some of America's most talented pastry chefs.

A plated dessert is a dessert that is prepared at the last minute, upon the individual order of the customer. The pastry chef assembles several components, most of which were prepared that very day, and artfully arranges them on the plate. Staff members working for the chef are expected to duplicate the presentation as closely as possible. A plated dessert usually consists of the main item (the item that is described on the menu) plus a garnish and a sauce, but the chef has the freedom to expand or mix and match this roster, within the boundaries of economics, flavor, and common sense. A plated dessert can include several components (sauce, ice cream, cookies, sugar) that present contrasts in texture (crunchy and creamy) and flavor (sweet and acidic), and if there can be a warm item to contrast with cold, so much the better. A plated dessert can be as complex or as simple as the chef's sensibility allows. The trend toward plated desserts—and away from dessert cart, slice or scoop of ice cream, or single item desserts—was first seen in Europe and in culinary competitions in the late 1980s. American chefs in the appropriate settings and with the necessary budgets have been presenting these desserts since approximately 1990.

Because plated desserts are compositions, they lend themselves to many different visual approaches. In *Grand Finales: The Art of the Plated Dessert,* we classified the visual presentations of American plated desserts into nine categories, using schools of the visual arts as a frame of reference. Impressionist desserts use abstract and literal forms to convey an image or feeling; Architectural desserts are strongly vertical; Performance Art desserts move or involve action by the diner in some way. And now, Neoclassic desserts.

For this volume, we challenged 27 pastry chefs to create desserts within the confines of the definition of neoclassic desserts as outlined in *Grand Finales*—that is, a dessert that features a classic dessert as a major component, though that component may contain a contemporary variation; this variation may entail a slight alteration of the classic recipe, or it can involve a change in the accepted presentation of the dessert.

As was noted in the first volume of the series, neoclassic is a broad term. In fact, most desserts qualify. "If you look at what people are doing, there is usually one element that is a classic," points out Martha Crawford, department chair of the International Baking and Pastry Institute at Johnson & Wales University. Most of the recipes in this volume, then, are accessible to most professionals, and are time-proven, best-selling menu items. They are never out of place, never out of style. A bit more show business goes into their planning and presentation, but after all, as Todd Johnson, pastry chef at the Ritz-Carlton Hotel in Naples, Florida, puts it: "When a customer spends that kind of money, there's nothing wrong with putting on a show."

T.M.

"Napoleon, Napoleon

He was a big galoot

Now he's just a piece of cake

And nobody gives a hoot."

— DITTY SUNG TO YOUNG
ANN AMERNICK BY HER MOTHER

Introduction

NEOCLASSICS AND THE KITCHEN

Nick Malgieri recalls ordering apple pie in a chic restaurant. "What I got were segments on a plate," says the director of the pastry program at Peter Kump's New York Cooking School. "It was chunks of apple and irregular shards of puff pastry. The apples were well sautéed, the pastry was fine—it was all there, but it was scattered over the plate. It was a beautiful plated dessert but it was by no means a piece of pie, and the word pie was not even in quote marks on the menu. I was disappointed as a customer. I wanted a piece of pie. Not every dessert is the Chrysler Building. Paraphrasing Freud, sometimes a cigar should be a cigar."

The classics are the foundation; ask any chef. They will always be there. They are the basis for most, if not all, of what follows. In other areas of our culture (literature, drama, music) people may pay lip service to the classics, but in pastry the classics are more than relevant—they are crucial. And they still sell.

"Anyone who is in school should be concentrating on doing the classics very well," says Michael Hu, pastry chef and consultant in New York. "St. Honoré, tarte Tatin, pont neuf—done well, they are great and they are a great learning tool. Everything comes full circle; it will always come back to the classics."

"But classics have to be updated, reevaluated, and be relevant to what we do nowadays," says Malgieri. "This is why we make individual portions—it makes it relevant. Portions are rather small. A serving today, rather than an eighth of a large cake, is more

Norman Love

CORPORATE PASTRY CHEF,
Ritz-Carlton Hotel
Company, Naples, FL

BORN: December, 1959,
Philadelphia, PA

TRAINING/EXPERIENCE:
various restaurants,
bakeries and country
clubs; Sheraton,
InterContinental and
Mayfair hotels; Caribbean
Cruise Lines; pastry shop,
Mougins, France; Beverly
Hills Hotel; Ritz-Carlton
Hotel, St. Louis, MO

"A fear-driven kitchen is not tolerated any more, even in Europe. We are creating our own environment in the kitchen. There is an American environment, and I think that environment is very healthy. There is a line between a fearful environment and one that is directed by someone who is a perfectionist, who demands quality continuously and never deviates from that. He or she has a certain expectation and strives to actually go beyond that expectation. This does not come with love and kisses. It does require some reprimanding, constant attention, and a constant push from the top. But the result is incredible. Something is going right. We have an explosive industry, great culinary movements, and that is created by the effort from within."

like a fifteenth. We approach the classics with a fresh outlook."

In talented hands, this fresh approach is not a violation of the classic approach. "The classic tarte Tatin was done as a whole nine-inch tart," concedes Michael Hu, "but you can do it as an individual serving and not lose the integrity of it. In fact, you probably are able to serve it fresher in a restaurant situation, and much truer to the way it was originally served. And then you can create your own garnish or your own twist." Ann Amernick, pastry chef and owner of Amernick in Wheaton, Maryland, is no great fan of elaborate presentation, but she does appreciate a clean presentation, even in a dessert that is notoriously untidy. "A crumble, for example," she says. "Rather than seeing it just dumped on the plate, I'd like to see it encased in a ramekin, very clean, with the crumble on top."

But there are limits to how much you can clean up a classic, as Nick Malgieri discovered. "All things have to work in flavor, texture, and appearance," he says. Stanton Ho, executive pastry chef of the Las Vegas Hilton, agrees. "If you're going to serve apple pie, serve it like grandma used to make," he says. "It would be a gamble, in my opinion, to serve it in a nontraditional way, or reconstructed version."

Thus, some classics lend themselves to a floor-to-ceiling "reconstruction"—in the recipe, in the presentation—and others do not. To do a classic well is "to meet the expectations," says Jill Rose, executive chef at Urban Horizons Food Company in the Bronx, New York. "But you want to exceed them. Take them in the direction you want to go, keeping in mind what the customer wants. In crème brûlée you give them what they expect, but you personalize it too. You try to maintain a relative balance."

It is in this grey area that pastry chefs live every day. The classics are the foundation, yet they need to be updated. The chef needs to make a consistent product, but in order to express himself—and to avoid boredom—he needs to experiment. And the balancing act

Pat Coston

EXECUTIVE PASTRY CHEF,
Mercer Kitchen,
New York, NY

BORN: May 6, 1971,
Oklahoma City, OK

TRAINING/EXPERIENCE:
Ernie's Restaurant,
Moose's, Aqua, The
Cypress Club, all in San
Francisco, CA; Picasso,
Las Vegas, NV

continues in the day-to-day life of the kitchen: a pastry chef needs to balance his or her time between turning out an excellent product and also setting aside time to teach.

In this examination of the role of the classics on the menu and in the kitchen we will also focus on the role of education in the professional kitchen. How does a classic become a classic if not through education? Whether in a medieval guild, a nineteenth-century Parisian patisserie, or a modern hotel kitchen, it is time spent between master and apprentice.

For the purpose of this book, the "classics" are primarily the finished desserts (cakes, cookies, custards, pies, tarts, etc.) of European and North American origin—recognizing that other parts of the world have their own classics. "A classic has to have a certain degree of age in order to have withstood the test of time," says Nick Malgieri. "And it has an intrinsic value. It makes sense." The term also refers to the building blocks that comprise the finished desserts—linzer dough, sponge cakes, joconde, japonaise, pâte à choux, puff pastry, short dough, ladyfingers, meringue, pastry cream, curds, sauces and fillings, nut pastes, streusel toppings, ganache. The building blocks tend to blend into the actual finished products—not only can meringue, mousse, sorbet, ice cream, shortbread, gingerbread, and macaroons stand alone or support a main component, but we live in an age when a brownie can form the core of an ice cream dessert and crème brûlée can be found at the interior of an individual cake serving. Then there are the classic classics—strudels, cobblers, florentines, pithiviers, madeleines, éclairs, battenburg, rum balls, all the fruit and custard tarts, tarte Tatin, linzer tart and cookie, bavarians, charlottes, terrines, soufflés, bread puddings, turnovers, fritters, pumpkin pie, vacherins, coupes, Black Forest Cake, Boston Cream Pie, Diplomat Cake, Dobos Torte, Paris-Brest, Mont Blanc, Springerle, Bûche de Noël, Baked Alaska, Cherries Jubilee, Othello, St. Honoré, and so on and so forth. A menu with no end. "If it hasn't survived, there's probably a reason for it," says Chris Broberg, pastry chef of Lespinasse in New York.

When you ponder all of the variety of items that can be made, then factor in breads, decorative work in chocolate, and sugar and marzipan, it becomes too great a mountain to climb.

That is where education comes into play.

"Teaching is all about improving. The more I show someone, the more I can rely on him or her, and the more I can work on new things and develop as a pastry chef myself. If we can do this type of dessert—daring and architectural to look at but with clean flavors—for 200 covers a night, everyone benefits."

James Foran

PASTRY CHEF,
Silk's, Mandarin Oriental
Hotel, San Francisco, CA

BORN: June 6, 1969,
New York, NY

TRAINING/EXPERIENCE:
Johnson & Wales
University, Pastry Arts;
Restaurant Lafayette,
Drake Hotel, Sign of the
Dove, both in New York;
Abiqui, Vertigo, Bruno's,
all in San Francisco, CA

"I first knew that I had a knack for this when I started tasting things in my mind, without actually tasting it in fact, while planning a dessert or menu. Sometimes the flavor of the finished product will be different than I imagined it, but it's still a good process. Trying to come up with flavor combinations that work is a creative form, so there are lulls, moments with pad and pencil, trying to realize these ideas. It's not so much an attempt to create something new, as it is to do something that feels right at the time."

PROKITCHEN 101

It may surprise some culinary students that even when they graduate an exhaustive, quality program, they are only beginning their education as a professional. Even educators acknowledge this.

"What you have to cultivate in students is humility," says Nick Malgieri. "We try to impress upon them that they are not pastry chefs when they finish our baking program, but they are ready to start at the bottom. We teach the basics," he says of his program at Peter Kump's. "We teach vocabulary, which is important, and some of the procedures. We prepare them for an entry-level position. Then we try to give them an idea of what the pluses and minuses are of starting at the bottom."

"I like to think that when a student comes out he is disciplined," says Martha Crawford of her program at Johnson & Wales, "but in no way is he ready to be a manager or executive." Their two-year course is not geared for that, but they are planning a four-year program that might hit the mark.

Executive-level chefs, in general, are quite aware that a new person in his or her kitchen—whether a student or someone with some experience—cannot be expected to be brilliant, day one. "Everyone deserves to have a period of training, a chance to learn what the job entails and to perform parts of the job correctly," declares Malgieri. "Even someone who has experience deserves that. Otherwise, if you get weird results, who do you blame? If you don't show them, they can't be responsible for the results."

Malgieri remembers receiving a visit from a chef from France, a chef renowned for his skills. "I was showing the chef the shop, this and that, and the chef says, 'Can you show me how you make this brioche dough?' Everyone has gaps in their knowledge."

"Everyone has different ways of doing things," adds Daniel Jasso, the advanced bakeshop instructor at Western Culinary Institute in Portland, Oregon. So if new blood in the kitchen is taking time coagulating, so to speak, "It isn't just a matter of readiness for a pressure working kitchen, it's also methods," points out Jasso. "Each chef will have a different way of doing pâte à choux—should it have milk, should it have salt, should it have

Lincoln Carson

PASTRY CHEF, Picasso, Bellagio Hotel, Las Vegas, NV

BORN: March, 1969, Beirut, Lebanon

TRAINING/EXPERIENCE: pastry program, Johnson & Wales University; Le Pactole, Le Bernadin, Peacock Alley (Waldorf-Astoria), Luxe, Four Seasons Hotel, Cascabel, La Côte Basque, all in New York; The Highlands Inn, Carmel, CA

sugar, should it use water only, should it use butter, should it be thicker, and so on."

And sometimes, it's just a different world: "I have been in a kitchen where I asked them to make pastry cream, and they couldn't," affirms Jemal Edwards, a pastry chef based in New York. "Sponge cake, same thing. And this is an established kitchen. You have to wonder, how much knowledge do your people have? What went on here before? Sometimes, you don't want to know. And sometimes you're amazed what is accepted by the buying public. Sometimes the answer is, before you came mixes were used, bases were used, or the chef had no use for what you consider basic to a pastry kitchen."

Happily, contemporary pastry chefs are quite willing to teach, even under the pressures of a working kitchen. It is, they say, part of the job. "You have to be able to teach, otherwise how can your staff produce the work that you expect?" says Norman Love, corporate pastry chef for the Ritz-Carlton Hotel company. "Give them a reason for learning. You take the time, five minutes, or two minutes, every day, show a technique, an idea, a do or don't. Is it practical? I think so. Even employees that are with you a long time have a right to learn continually. Unfortunately, there are people in this business who are content to learn just their own job. But for those that have the eagerness to want to grow in this business, you as a chef should assist them in doing that."

It wasn't always so, and there are exceptions.

Keegan Gerhard, pastry chef of Dean & Deluca in Charlotte, North Carolina, recalls a chef in Chicago who, when he found out that Jacquy Pfeiffer and Sebastien Canonne were visiting his kitchen, hid all of his sugar work, tools, and plans. What, we wonder, did that chef think he knew about sugar that would stump or amaze these two? Gerhard recalls other chefs who deliberately would not share what they knew. "That doesn't work in pastry," says Gerhard.

"People who hide things are a bit insecure," says Susan Notter, corporate pastry chef of Albert Uster Imports in Gaithersburg, Maryland.

Most chefs take seriously the responsibility of passing on what they know. "As a chef you have two main responsibilities," says Norman Love. "Most obvious is to produce a

"I take a lot of pride in some of the ideas that I come up with, and I usually feel that it's something new. But it's ridiculous to think that someone else hasn't thought of the same thing in their spare time. It's food. There's only so much you can work with. It's been done before by someone, possibly simultaneously—as we get new products, we have new ideas to work with."

John Degnan

EXECUTIVE PASTRY CHEF, The Lodge at Koele, HI

BORN: 1965, Rockaway Beach, NY

TRAINING/EXPERIENCE: New York City Technical College; Patisserie Lanciani, Pierre Hotel, Rainbow Room, Ritz-Carlton, Sea Grill, Omni Berkshire Hotel, all in New York

"There is more experimentation in fine dining restaurants, in general, because if you as a customer are in the mood for a culinary experience, you're not going to go to a down-home restaurant, where you know the menu. In general the younger clientele do experiment more, and they tend to buy. Restaurants today are not just about the food; they're about the energy, the people that go there, the wines, the desserts."

wonderful product every day. The second is to help the people who work for you reach their individual goals. This is done by creating a work environment that people want to come to. It's your responsibility as the leader. You create that environment by giving them a reason to learn, giving them an environment that is clean and professional, where they can be with their friends, have relationships with them inside of work and out. Most important, give them an opportunity to learn. And this creates a motivated, stimulating environment."

To those just out of school or just entering the field, "I like to teach the fundamentals of the pastry shop," says Marshall Rosenthal, executive pastry chef at the Reno Hilton Hotel in Reno, Nevada. "They have knife skills and know how to make tart shells. Now you teach them organization, sanitation, decorating, and the basics of buttercreams, doughs, and so on. But it all depends on their attitude, the enthusiasm. I will spend my time if they have this attitude, but I'm not going to beg somebody."

LESSONS LEARNED

Cue the music, a dirge, as Sebastien Canonne, co-owner and instructor at The French Pastry School in Chicago (and a most accomplished pastry chef) recalls the sadsack first days of his pastry education—this, mind you, after Cannone had graduated first, *first,* in his class in culinary: "I was a cook when I arrived at Lenôtre. I came from a cooking background and we didn't do so much refined stuff—decor and designs. It was not so precise. Pastry is a completely different ball game. They first made me do rosettes. I couldn't get it. It took me all day. I was in the corner and people were looking at me like, 'My friend, get a life. You have two left hands. You can make a lot of money with that. Join a carnival. Open a booth—the man with the two left hands!' The first day, I was so frustrated. When you're young, it's cruel. You're fourteen, you can't do a rosette. It hurts. But before I went home, I bought tubes of toothpaste. And I piped rosettes and rosettes and rosettes. Then I practiced with piping bags. I began to write okay, so I began to pick up speed . . ."

Most chefs' educations are not filled with such drama. For the most part, the process is invisible. So much work is done, so much time passes, then, one day, the chef (pastry

Jean Marc Viallet

EXECUTIVE PASTRY CHEF, Ritz-Carlton Huntington Hotel & Spa, Pasadena, CA

BORN: May 24, 1962, Livry-Gargan, France

TRAINING/EXPERIENCE: Ferrandi Culinary School, Paris; pastry shops, Paris; Clement's, Paris Island, Ixtapa; Maxim's Airport, Paris; Meridien, Newport Beach; Four Seasons, Newport Beach; Hyatt Regency, Dallas; Atlanta Hilton Towers; Beverly Hilton, Beverly Hills, CA

cook/assistant) looks up from the stainless steel table and realizes that much has been learned, many skills have been acquired. Still, certain mentors, moments, or lessons stand out.

Ann Amernick credits Patrick Musel and Roland Mesnier as particularly influential on her approach and skills. "Roland said to me: 'The first thing you must learn when you go into a kitchen is to know your oven, because if you don't, nothing will come out. Is it fast, is it slow, does it cook hot, is it uneven, how do you adjust?' That was something I never forgot. It was so basic, but people don't think about it."

Kim O'Flaherty, assistant pastry chef at the Four Seasons Hotel in New York, names Christophe Toury and Keith Jeanminette as two chefs who impressed her. "When they were creating a new item, they would make it, try it, and ask themselves, what can I do to improve it? They would make it again, improve, then improve again, again and again, four or five times. Too many chefs rush the process," says O'Flaherty. "Once you finish one menu, you should start experimenting with the next menu. Give yourself time. That's one of the things they taught me."

"The old style of apprenticeship is over with, but we Europeans have difficulty managing the way Americans manage. The old way was, 'Do this or get out of here; the door is over there.' Now you tell that to someone, and you can be sued. The apprenticeship was hard but helpful. It was a way of life. There was respect for the chef. You never discussed what the chef said. Even if it was wrong, that's what you did."

"Walter Schreier [of the Culinary Institute of America] was incredibly influential," says Heather Ho, pastry chef at Boulevard in San Francisco. "His lectures were all about simplifying, simplifying. Making your life easier. Looking at pastry in a practical, pragmatic way. Every base recipe—a custard, a crème anglaise, a genoise—can be broken down into simple ratios. And that way, you will be able to look at a recipe and be able to tell if it will work or not. I can work recipes out in my head. If someone comes to me and says, why isn't this working? I can tell them."

Todd Johnson, executive pastry chef of the Ritz-Carlton Hotel in Naples, Florida, was working savory in a hotel where "a young pastry chef was more interested in drinking than pastry." In time, that unfortunate young man was replaced by a German pastry chef, Herman Niebaum, who was 72 years old at the time. "As soon as Niebaum took over," says Johnson, "I saw a dramatic difference in the pastry. I transferred to his department. I soon found that he was more than just interested in my performance in the pastry shop and how we made him look to management and the customers. He was interested in the whole person."

PASTRY CHEF, Masa's,
San Francisco, CA

BORN: August 11, 1963,
Castro Valley, CA

TRAINING/EXPERIENCE:
California Culinary
Academy; Blue Fox,
Mandarin Oriental Hotel,
Ritz-Carlton Hotel, all in
San Francisco, CA

"I've always had confidence in my abilities, mostly because I become obsessed—almost to the point where I eat, sleep, and drink pastry. Even when I'm supposed to be relaxing, I'm thinking about dessert plates. I believe that if you don't do that, you're dead in the water. As Sandy Koufax said, practice doesn't guarantee you everything, but without it you don't stand a chance. It's the same with pastry. There's so much competition, everyone is always one-upping the other guy."

Many chefs, including Tom Worhach of the Four Seasons in Palm Beach and Nick Malgieri, credit Albert Kumin as being a major influence. "Albert wanted to nurture pastry chefs," says Malgieri. "I worked with him for the opening of Windows on the World in '76. It was great working in a high-volume place that was also high quality. To see the degree of organization you needed to have, and the commitment to flavor and freshness.

"Joe Baum once said of Albert Kumin that he could make two hundred dozen kaiser rolls with one hand while he was making an elaborate sugar basket with the other," continues Malgieri. "I think that is what he imparted to people: that you've got to know finesse and how to do the beautiful things, but you have to know how to produce too. Do it in quantity. He was not afraid of large-volume production work; he was perfectly comfortable with it, and he saw no dichotomy or contradiction in the quality of large-volume work. I don't think he thought that it had to be inferior to small-batch work. He approached everything with the same degree of care. His manner in the kitchen was strict," Malgieri adds. "He liked to take a break, have a conversation—it was not drudgery, but when you were working you were working, and if something was wrong you heard about it."

Keegan Gerhard offers Jacquy Pfeiffer as a man from whom he learned a great deal. "His primary concern is pastry. That's all he cares about," asserts Gerhard. "If you don't care about pastry, or don't know about it, you can't be around him. On our days off we went to hardware stores and looked for tools to work with chocolate. In a grocery store, he'd look and say, 'that light cover would make a great mold.' Jacquy is like the Pied Piper. He just does pastry all day. He doesn't care if you help or not, or watch or not, or do or don't. If you do, you'll get involved. When you're around that focus, not to mention that skill level, you can't help but become enthusiastic."

Some chefs can recall a specific moment or a learned technique that, once mastered, spurred them to continue their training or to persevere in a difficult industry. Several chefs say that when they first learned how to work chocolate, especially tempering, it was a critical, timely boost in morale. A pivotal moment for Marshall Rosenthal was when he began to

John Hui

EXECUTIVE PASTRY CHEF, Caesar's Palace, Las Vegas, NV

BORN: August 25, 1957, Hong Kong

TRAINING/EXPERIENCE: City College of San Francisco, Hotel Restaurant Management; Saint Francis Hotel, Hyatt Regency, Fairmont Hotel, all in San Francisco; Westin Maui; San Francisco Marriott; Cottage Bakery (vice president)

see the value in, and have the ability, "to make good lines, make things as perfect as you can. Make it delicate and not heavy. Have as much finesse as you can. Even if it's a piece of fruit, make it perfect." Martin Howard, a pastry chef and consultant in New York, recalls a moment of clarity in his training, involving finishing cakes. "There's a moment when it suddenly comes to you—the leveling off of the top of the cake. Working with a palette knife, it's the move in the air, then coming across the top of the cake. Beginners tend to go around it, make a dome of it. Piping borders, same thing. It's not something you get right away, then suddenly . . ."

Other epiphanies are more psychological than physical.

"There were a few defining days where I turned the corner or, as I say, got on the bus," says Pat Coston, pastry chef at The Mercer Kitchen in New York. "I come from a very rigid background, a lot of screamers. And there were a few days when you were virtually given an ultimatum. I became a subscriber. I started to understand the food, the technical aspect, then how to convey what I do to my staff. Down the road, two or three months later, I realized I had grasped something, and now it was time to move forward."

"My first kitchen experience was with a chef who would hide things from everyone else. He would never show you anything. He would give you the wrong recipes, and force you to figure it out for yourself. In a sponge batter, he would change some of the ingredients, and then blame you, ask you, what did you do wrong? If you made a batch and it didn't turn out, you might lose thirty or forty cakes. It made him look good, he thought."

"What I learned was not settling. It's never good enough. You can always make it better," says Lincoln Carson, pastry chef at Picasso in the Bellagio Hotel in Las Vegas. "And more importantly, I learned focus—to look at the whole with energy and dedication." Carson now tries to pass on this philosophy of focus: "I tell people who work for me: visualize in your head what it is you're attempting to achieve—the end product. If you can see that end result every step of the way, each step will have a purpose. You can cut down on wasted, unnecessary movement, wasted time, sloppy plates, burnt cookies—whatever it is."

CLASSIC MISTAKES

James Foran, pastry chef at Silk's in San Francisco, describes the feeling of horror when you've just discovered your mistake: "You can't destroy it, you can't serve it. You just

Stanton Ho

EXECUTIVE PASTRY CHEF, Las Vegas Hilton Hotel, Las Vegas, NV

BORN: April, 1952, Honolulu, HI

TRAINING/EXPERIENCE: Kapiolani Community College (University of Hawaii), culinary program; Ecole Lenôtre, Paris; various hotels and resorts, Hawaii

"Some people in a pastry kitchen are not proficient with flavors and tastes, but their skills are in management, accounting, keeping the numbers in line. Others are more 'people' chefs; they can gather a group of people, no matter the skill level, and get them to work for them. There are a number of characteristics and skills that can lead a person to become a good executive pastry chef."

wait, like a deer in the headlights, to get caught or something."

Norman Love describes the remedy: "You lift the paper liner out of the can, dump your mistake in it, and quickly take the trash out the back door. Of course everybody does that. Everybody makes mistakes. That's how you learn. How do you hide it from the chef? Very carefully."

"It was a Sunday afternoon," Pat Murakami, the chef and owner of Ambrosia Fine Foods in Sacramento, recalls. She is recounting an experience at a restaurant long ago. "We're doing four million dinners. I put a squirt bottle down on the stove, and it melts, and I can't get the sauce out of the tip, it's oozing all over. And it's an exquisite reduction; there isn't a lot of it around. Everyone is tapping their toes, waiting for my plate . . ."

"When I was first training, I was in charge of the puff pastry," says Marshall Rosenthal. "I was working at night and made the whole batch with salt instead of sugar. They asked me, did you do that? I said no. I got a hot cake pan in the ass for that—literally. That was the punishment."

Kim O'Flaherty relates an epic tale of pastry kitchen mistake cover-ups. It is a true story, confirmed by more than one chef in this volume: "I knew a guy who screwed up a dough and put it in the back of his car, then went back to work," says O'Flaherty. "And it proofed, filling up the whole back of his car. He worked the overnight shift, so in the morning, with the dough proofed, he decided to drive home and get rid of it there. He had a little car, like a Pinto, and the bag had proofed so much, he couldn't see out the back. It was while he driving over a bridge that he decided to get out of the car, pull the dough out and throw it away, into the water. But he couldn't get the bag out of the car so he took out his knife and started stabbing the bag. Unfortunately, someone caught him on film, this stabbing motion and a big bag going over the bridge into the water. They called the police on him, said they saw him kill someone, and gave the police his license plate. The police came. He was new to this country and didn't speak English, so he couldn't explain what happened. He ended up spending two months in jail." A tragedy? Not at all. "He eventually married the lawyer who represented him," says O'Flaherty.

The moral of the story? Mistakes can be turned to advantage. Pastry history confirms it, and so does Marshall Rosenthal: "There are certain ways to hide things," he says. "Sometimes I will forget to put gelatin in something, and a cake that was supposed to have gelatin in it between layers is so bagged out, all of a sudden it turns into a mousse dessert in a glass. You take the cake off and put it in a glass and pipe something over it.

"When you're working with ice cream, this sort of thing happens all the time," Rosenthal continues. "I was making Baked Alaska. I put it in the freezer, and the freezer some time later went into defrost. When they took them down to a banquet and took the lids off the plates, all the Baked Alaskas were in a pool, a floating meringue. It was oeufs à la neige all of a sudden."

Mistakes are part and parcel of any learning experience. But try telling that to an executive chef who's watching a disaster forming in his kitchen.

Stan Ho is among the chefs who will, for the sake of education, allow an employee to make a mistake—"though I want to define that mistake," he adds. "If it's a crucial party or function, I will correct that problem. But if it's just regular operation, yes, I will let that individual make the mistake, partially to show them that mistakes are done."

"I will allow mistakes, even if it means throwing six sheetcakes in the garbage," admits Pat Coston. "I don't enjoy doing it, but sometimes you have to let them realize it on their own. If someone showed no promise, though, I would step in, because in the end it would hurt the whole team. If I have to redo the work I am paying someone to do, it is inefficient. Then, nobody wins."

"It depends on the magnitude of the mistake," says Jemal Edwards. "If they're going to make one that is irreparable, I will step in. In restaurants, there is a cost issue. If someone is about to waste six pounds of chocolate by breaking a ganache that you maybe won't be able to bring back, then, yeah, I'll step in."

At Peter Kump's, as in any academic setting, the issue of whether to let a student make a mistake is different. "If he or she is in the final stages of something, you want to head them off," says Nick Malgieri. "If they're about to make a major mistake, make them

Patricia Murakami

CHEF AND OWNER, Ambrosia Fine Foods (Specialty Baking and Distinctive Catering), Sacramento, CA

BORN: November 28, 1951, New Brunswick, NJ

TRAINING/EXPERIENCE: Contra Costa Community College; American River College; Red Lion Inn, Sacramento, CA; Domaine Chandon, Yountville, CA; Chinoise East/West

"Philippe Jeanty was the executive chef at Domaine Chandon at the time I worked there, and what I admired in him and learned from him was his fanaticism for perfection. No plate went out without its being perfect. It didn't matter if the customer had to wait, or what was at stake—every plate, absolutely perfect, no matter how long it took or how much effort. Day in and day out."

Daniel Jasso

ADVANCED BAKESHOP INSTRUCTOR, Western Culinary Institute, Portland, OR

BORN: January 13, 1967, Frankfurt, West Germany

TRAINING/EXPERIENCE: Western Culinary Institute (graduate); freelance catering; Montana Blackfoot Catering, Missoula, MT

"The trend today is to lighten classic desserts, trim the fat and calories. But when people come to eat in a restaurant, it is often because it's an event of some kind. In that sense, why not have fat and sweetness? As long as it's not an everyday occurrence, why not splurge and enjoy?"

understand what is about to happen. People learn a lot better if they're in the process of doing something."

Sebastien Canonne is another who lets a mistake happen, because, again, it is in a classroom setting. Not only does he let a mistake happen, "I plan it sometimes," he says. "The idea is, okay, it didn't work, we can fix it, no big deal. Because down the road, it will happen. You must teach them, it's okay, it can be fixed. Pastry is a science. There is always a reason why something doesn't work." What about when he was running the kitchen at the Ritz-Carlton? "No. We didn't have time to allow mistakes."

FROM TREE BARK TO SILICON: CLASSICS ILLUSTRATED

Mistakes have played a crucial part in the evolution of classic desserts. As Nick Malgieri surmises: "A chef may have been making fritters and made a mistake and thought, maybe if I put some jelly in it nobody'll notice. And the jelly doughnut is born." Such things do happen, but, in fact, they are only one factor among many in the development of the classics. "A lot of things happen for reasons of economy and practicality than a chef really wanting to make something better, or a romantic mistake," he says.

"Pastry history is a natural evolution, evolution being accident and endless experimentation," agrees Markus Farbinger, of the Green Mountain Chocolate Company in Waterbury, Vermont. "In trying for perfection, we try a little change, one small thing at a time." He cites mousse as an example. From its origins as simply melted chocolate, whipped cream and perhaps butter, "Eggs were introduced just to make it richer and to emulsify. Then they discovered that when they whipped it up, they introduced air. Then they started separating the eggs, and introduced even more air, and they got a different product. Then at some point—perhaps spurred by Lenôtre and Thuries—they began to introduce gelatin into mousse, to stand it up as a component, to incorporate it as an ingredient. Now we are adding less gelatin, and on and on. It all boils down to the basic techniques, the basic mixing methods, and how they can be applied."

As dictated by necessity, adds Nick Malgieri. "They made pastry out of puréed lentils during World War II," he observes. "You do what you can with what you have."

A NEOCLASSIC VIEW OF PLATED DESSERTS

Didier Goller

EXECUTIVE PASTRY CHEF, Ritz-Carlton Hotel, Palm Beach, FL

BORN: February 1, 1964, Bagneux, France

TRAINING/EXPERIENCE: apprenticeship, CFA Versailles; Waterside Inn, England; various pastry shops, France; Palace Hotel, Wengen, Switzerland; Club Med, Vittel, France; pastry shops for the President of Brazil and the King of Morocco; La Renaissance, Scarsdale, NY; Colony Beach and Tennis Resort, Long Boat Key, FL; The Hilton at Short Hills, NJ

Sadly, the origins of many of the desserts we consider classics and their component parts (hold the lentils, please) are shrouded in mysteries created by rival kitchens and a confusion of cute folk tales. For example, it is said that Baked Alaska was created, at least in part, by a doctor studying the heat conduction properties of meringue. But Nick Malgieri's understanding is different, and not so folksy: "I read that Baked Alaska was invented in the nineteenth century at the Hôtel de Paris. It was originally called Norwegian Soufflé Omelette. Back then, sweet soufflé omelettes were very popular, though they are not done anymore. These sweet omelettes had a loaf shape. The word Norway for this particular one was used to denote the cold interior—it looked like a standard sweet soufflé omelette, but you cut into it and it had ice cream in it. Meringue was a corruption, a development from that."

"When you're sixteen years old and you're working ten, twelve hours a day, it's difficult. Sometimes they would curse you, scare the hell out of you. Back then, it was hard to understand why this was necessary. Even today, I still don't like it, but at least I realize it was for the good—they were pushing me to become better and better. I was tougher on kids in my shop ten years ago than I am now. I wish I was tougher. It is good for them, and you want to be sure the job is done right."

The evolution of baking and pastry classics is, then, a story of necessity, technology, abundance, scarcity, commerce, fashion, and mistakes interacting on several planes. For the most part, however, it is a matter of minute deviations, incremental developments over time. And as always, history is written by the so-called winners. "My view is very Eurocentric," admits Markus Farbinger. "All of us who are European or European-trained view the history of pastry that way. After all, who defined cooking? The French. Because they were able to organize a profession more effectively, they are the last word. But we must remember that people cook all over the world, and they have done so for thousands of years—in the Middle East, Asia, Africa," he adds. "The truth is, Europe does not have the finest cooking, and we borrow from other cultures too."

For Farbinger, it is a mistake to think that the discipline of pastry evolved from cooking, from the Chef. In his mind, pastry chefs evolved from bakers. "To be specific, it comes from the growing of grain, then the baking on open fires. From the open fire came the closed fire, then the oven.

"Six thousand years ago, some early Europeans used tree bark as a mold," Farbinger continues. "They would rough out a form from tree bark, fill it with dough as a liner, and

Keegan Gerhard

EXECUTIVE PASTRY CHEF, Dean & Deluca, Charlotte, NC

BORN: December 2, 1963, San Bernardino, CA

TRAINING/EXPERIENCE: Commander's Palace, New Orleans; Hotel Boulderado, Boulder, CO; Peabody Hotel, Memphis, TN; George's at the Cove, La Jolla, CA; Pirets French Bistro, San Diego, CA; Sheraton Hotel and Towers, Chicago; Charlie Trotter's, Chicago; Waldorf-Astoria Hotel, New York; Ritz-Carlton Hotel, Naples, FL

"I was very competitive all my life, and when I started in the culinary business, I looked for someone who was very passionate. I found him, and then some, in Charlie Trotter. I'll say this about Charlie: Hardass that he is about a lot of things, he will help any-one—give them recipes, help them find any purveyor he can. He believes that you can only have a great restaurant in an environment of other great restaurants. He gets in-volved in the neighborhood. He will have his people clean up the garbage two blocks from his place, because 'this is our neighborhood and we will have an impact here.' I love that idea."

bake it. They made a shell out of paste, filled it with fruit and drizzled honey over it." Honey was also used to help mark special ceremonies or holidays, some four to five thousand years ago; it was incorporated into bread to create a ceremonial cake. It was, says Farbinger, such religious observations that helped propel baking beyond the basic loaves.

Leavening was discovered by the ancient Egyptians. Grains of the ancient world needed to be toasted before threshing, which made leavening chemically impossible. It is known that the Egyptians, by approximately 400 B.C., had developed a wheat that could be threshed raw. Then accident set in most probably: bakehouses and alehouses were one and the same at the time, and such an arrangement is a breeding ground for airborne yeast spores; it is probable that some yeast spores settled on some dough that was waiting to be baked. This bread would rise, even slightly, and be more flavorful. Attempts to reproduce this would lead to experimentation. Another possible explanation is that ale instead of water was used to mix dough, the results were intriguing, and history took its course. It is estimated that the ancient royal Egyptians were served as many as 40 different breads and pastry varieties—flatbreads as well as raised breads, formed into conical shapes or plaited, incorporating honey, milk, and eggs.

Pastry and breads were also enjoyed by the nobles and commoners of ancient Rome; and since there were no utensils, breads served as scoop, vessel, and nourishment.

"But I believe that gingerbread is the first pastry, the first product elevated beyond bread," says Farbinger. Gingerbread's origins, like so many others, is unclear, but by the time of the guilds, it was a distinct product. Europe of the Middle Ages saw the emergence of the guilds, with different responsibilities that were clarified by law. And each guild had its own by-laws—very strict procedures for who was admitted, for training apprentices, for qualifications for various levels like journeyman and so on, and for how the product was made: ingredients, proportion, procedures. The size and weight of the finished product was strictly monitored. "It was very much like our education system now," says Farbinger. "They would present a series of objectives, like little study units. There were strict procedures for the making of marzipan, ice cream, bon-bons, pralinées, gingerbread, and even how to keep accounts.

"Every shop was—and still is—very secretive," continues Farbinger. "Their recipes and procedures were protected by the guilds. You didn't give them away to anyone outside the guild. This is why there is so little documentation about the history of pastry at the time. Still today," he adds, "Americans are very open and pragmatic, while Europeans are generally more secretive."

Oddly enough, the disciplines of gingerbread-making and candle-making were linked, and still are, to some extent, in Austria. The pastry maker emerged from that discipline. "Around 1650, the sugar bakers split from the gingerbread makers, by decree," says Farbinger. "The gingerbread makers were by this law only allowed to make 'dark' baked goods using mostly rye and honey. The sugar baker was only allowed to make a 'light' product, using refined sugar and wheat. In that same year, the chocolate maker guild was formed."

An obvious important development at this time was the appearance of sugar. "Honey is not a structure, it only has a sweetening effect," points out Farbinger. "Sugar is a building material, like flour; it gives a product structure. That was a major breakthrough and led to baking as we know it today—baking, cakes, products that are tall; not flat bread, not gingerbread."

Sugar has been produced for thousands of years. Farbinger points out that Alexander the Great may have brought sugar back to Europe from his conquests. The original home for cane sugar was India, but even Indian royalty did not have it at their disposal. European colonial production of sugar was begun around 1770, but supplies were disrupted by wars and banditry. Around 1800, from the European point of view, the supply was stabilized. Quickly, the price fell, and it was generally available.

Of course, European royalty and nobility were the primary beneficiaries. There was a patissier in the kitchens of European royalty who made desserts, ice creams, and so on. "Among royalty, what was popular was ices, because they were luxurious and difficult to

Todd Johnson

PASTRY CHEF, Ritz-Carlton Hotel, Naples, FL Owner, Creative Culinary Tools, Naples, FL

BORN: June 19, 1959, Cincinnatti, OH

TRAINING/EXPERIENCE: The Culinary Institute of America; La Maisonette, Cincinnati; Grand Hotel, Mackinack Island, MI; The Rellim, St. Petersburg, FL; Chateau Robert, Marcel's French Bakery, both in Ft. Myers, FL

"What separates the people who rise to the top from the people who don't is their skills with people more than their skills with pastry. You have to devote time to manage people. If you can have tremendous talent with pastry, you might make it in a small restaurant. But in a hotel situation, you have to have people skills."

Thomas Worhach

EXECUTIVE PASTRY CHEF, Four Seasons Hotel and Resort, Palm Beach, FL

BORN: March, 1952, Danville, PA

TRAINING/EXPERIENCE: The Culinary Institute of America; Hotel Bel Air, Los Angeles; Ritz-Carlton Hotel, Houston; Ritz-Carlton Hotel, Philadelphia; Mansion on Turtle Creek, Dallas

"An executive chef at a hotel is still a hands-on chef. I prefer it that way. If your people see you working hard, they are more likely to try hard. But much of the job involves trying to put out fires. Everybody is always in a hurry, and often the first things they forget are the basic methods they learned in school—how to fold, how to scrape the bowl. Under pressure, it's the simple things that people forget to do. That's why I tell students not to be in so much of a hurry—they need to remember the basics."

prepare," says Malgieri. "Everything is exciting when you can't have it," agrees Farbinger. Bread bakers did not live at court, mostly because the ovens were huge and hot and dangerous. They were in a separate place, called the bakehouse. "Bread bakers were protected by law," says Farbinger. "There could be only so many bakers and millers per square mile. They lived and worked outside, and delivered the product to court."

Vigorous trade with far-flung corners of the world brought not only sugar but other ingredients and skills to Europe's pastry kitchens. "A lot of the items we think of as European fancy pastry originated or were developed from their initial Arab identities in France, Spain, and Italy in the early Renaissance times, the late fifteenth century," says Nick Malgieri. These three cultures were, over the centuries, joined by exchanges through marriage, trade, and the rise of the merchant class. "From the Middle East came white sugar, citrus fruits, candied fruits, peaches, apricots, spices, and almond paste," says Malgieri. "By the middle of the nineteenth century, the stage was set for an explosion." A renaissance.

This renaissance in patisserie began to take form around 1850. "It brought more elaborate cooking to a wider segment of the population," says Malgieri. "Before that it had only been the nobility. Now more people were enjoying fancier food. The reason that a lot of this progress codifying and development of fancy food occurred in the nineteenth century is due to the technological advances leading to the Industrial Revolution. In the late eighteenth and early nineteenth centuries, food went public. Restaurants, pastry shops, and the original take-out stores called cookshops all came on the scene during that time. It was the heyday of the pastry shop. Ladurée, for example, opened in 1863.

"There was a lot going on, and a public willing to buy this," continues Malgieri. "Development began to increase incrementally. Ideas were spawned and borrowings took place from far afield—other countries and cultures. It was fusion, nineteenth-century style. All the great pastry shops had their specialties—one place known for its brioche, another known for its St. Honoré, and so on." The competition among these shops was fierce.

More than money, pride was at stake. "Chefs want to create desserts that are unique and exciting," says Farbinger. "We want to be recognized for our skills. It is a basic need."

Custard tarts were much in demand, "hundreds of different things, especially made out of and filled with almond paste," says Malgieri. "Meringues, nut pastes, fillings and doughs, shaped tartlets. That was the golden age of pastry cream—it was used as all kinds of fillings, it was served hot and cold, it was gelatinized. There was no refrigeration, and a lot of people died from eating spoiled pastry cream. That's how chiboust was developed—cooked meringue was added to cold pastry cream, which made it safer. Lenôtre was the popularizer of chiboust." Also popular was anything made from pâte à choux and any kind of out-of-season fruit, though fruit desserts were not common at all. "The introduction of fruit is a recent one in pastries, post World War II," says Farbinger.

Bill Hallion

PASTRY CHEF, The Renaissance Vinoy Resort, St. Petersburg, FL

BORN: October 20, 1960, Camden, NJ

TRAINING/EXPERIENCE: Bakeries, New Jersey; pastry program, Baltimore International Culinary Institute; Adam's Mark, Philadelphia; The Renaissance, Nashville, TN

"Teaching is definitely part of this job. A half hour or an hour a day spent with one person or several—even that little amount of time helps. Over a period of time the body of knowledge grows, the confidence grows, and they catch on. Heck, it doesn't make any sense to criticize someone's work if you haven't spent any time teaching them."

The ovens were wood- or coal-burning, of course. Says Malgieri, "The way they used to gauge the heat of the oven, the way it is expressed in cookbooks before thermostats is this: they would put a piece of paper in the oven, and they would see the paper turn color. They would write the instructions as, bake this cake in an oven of straw-colored paper, or bake it in an oven of light brown-colored paper. It was an attempt to establish a standard temperature before thermometers. Before that, they would throw something in and see what happened."

"A lot of early ice cream was made in brine, which held a low temperature. It was a predecessor of refrigeration," says Malgieri. Buttercream was developed in the mid-nineteenth century, but it too had evolved over time. "The way it originated, the only way to keep cakes fresh before Saran Wrap and refrigerators, was to seal the cake in a thin layer of butter, in order to preserve it," says Malgieri. "At some point it occurred to someone to put a little sugar in it and keep it on the cake when it was served."

In America, it wasn't using what was rare, but rather what was abundant, that generated classics. Easy to make, easy to eat, that was the American way, says Meridith Ford, a food writer and instructor in baking and pastry at Johnson & Wales University.

Jacquy Pfeiffer

CO-OWNER AND IN-STRUCTOR, The French Pastry School, Chicago, IL

BORN: February, 1961, Molsehim, Alsace, France

TRAINING/EXPERIENCE: Apprenticeship, Jean Clauss'; various pastry shops and hotels in France, Saudi Arabia, and California; pastry chef for the Sultan of Brunei, Borneo; Hyatt Regency Hotel, Hong Kong; Fairmont Hotel and Sheraton Hotel and Towers, Chicago

"I remember thinking, during my pastry training in France, 'If I can survive this, I will never be in fear again.' A kick in the rear doesn't give you talent, but it does give you discipline. Many chefs are talented, but they don't have the discipline to send the same dessert out two days in a row. They lose focus. You must combine talent and discipline. And you must endure difficulties in learning, because, truly, it is a beautiful profession—the things you can do with the products of nature. How many people have this chance? That's what should keep you in focus."

A lot of the country rustic desserts were designed to use whatever was around. "Pies were basically meat extenders," says Ford. "But when the colonists settled in the New World in the 1600s, somehow or other, native ingredients being a prime factor, sweet pies were created. In New England, they started making sweet pies out of what was readily available—pumpkin and molasses, which was one of the only sweeteners they had. Later, the Indians showed the settlers how to tap trees. That's how chess pie and pecan pie were born; syrup pies were only using what was abundant." Ford lists as American classics apple brown betty, bread pudding, buckles, cobblers, crisps, apple pandowdies, grunts, Indian pudding, shoofly pie, brownies, and chocolate chip cookies. "Bread pudding is European in origin but we took hold of it," says Ford. "Our spoon desserts, rustic desserts, or country desserts are almost like extenders."

American classics of southern origin developed along a different path, says Ford. "Much of the culinary heritage of the South stems from the lingering fascination with the European aristocracy, through the vigorous importation of clothing, design, spices, and other culture as well as an influx of influential chefs, many of them from France, escaping the Revolution," she says. "Particularly in the large port towns—New Orleans, Charleston, Savanna—the French influence began to seep in, also because the people of these towns were wealthier than their New England and frontier counterparts. Some of the classics generated at the time—Lady Baltimore and Lord Baltimore cakes—take their names from aristocracy."

Hard upon the renaissance in European pastry shops of the mid-nineteenth century was the Industrial Revolution. "Everything we know, say, and do stems from the Industrial Revolution," says Nick Malgieri. "And the way we eat is pretty much post-World War I. That's when the twentieth century really began." He sees this era as a turning point in all areas of the culture, culinary included. "That's when a lot of the streamlining began to take place. The banquets, the 36-course meals, all that began to disappear. What happened in the '20s—dress, manners, haircuts—everything was diminished, simplified. The same thing happened with food. The three-course meal made its debut. One dessert rather than many desserts was served."

Kitchen staffs began to shrink, and consolidate. "In the big hotels, you had a glacier who made the ices, a patissier for desserts, boulanger for bread, viennoser who made some brioches, a sucrer who made sugar pieces, and only sugar pieces," says Nick Malgieri. Some of this elaborate staffing lingered for a time, but after World War II, labor costs went up, and that style of kitchen brigade was no longer viable.

It is the rising cost of labor, still very much an issue today, that has influenced the development of pastry in our time. "Skills, technology, and efficiency have become more important," says Farbinger. "In the old days, a boy cranking a churn handle was middle-level skill, and this was the learning curve of an apprentice. There could be 20, 80 ingredients and a huge team of people to form these ingredients into pièces montées. Labor was not an issue. Today, labor is expensive."

Malgieri cites millefeuille as a pastry example. "To make various refinements on that to a certain degree was fairly easy," he says, "but to do that nowadays in a delicious non-insane way, it just gets harder and harder."

It seems that pastry has not evolved much since the mid-nineteenth-century renaissance. There are many reasons for this: the limits imposed by baking science, the familiarity of ingredients and equipment, even mundane reasons such as the rising cost of labor. So much was new back then, so much was being learned; think of it as a funnel that narrows, strangling possibility. "The further you go along the evolution of pastry and desserts, the more variation that is developed, and the more genius and talent is needed to go beyond it," says Malgieri. "The first geniuses,

Martha Crawford

DEPARTMENT CHAIR, International Baking and Pastry Institute, Johnson & Wales University, Providence, RI

BORN: June 20, 1962, Philadelphia, PA

TRAINING/EXPERIENCE: The Culinary Institute of America; Country Epicure; Desserts International, Exton, PA

"Gunther Heiland taught me technique, to be sure, but what he really taught me was an attitude; he tried to instill in me to always strive for perfection. If you stopped working on something and said, 'It's okay, it's done,' he would walk away and not say anything. But he always made you look to the next level. Whenever and whatever you did, nothing was ever perfect. You were always challenging yourself to go to the next level. As a whole person, if you do everything like that, it seeps into your work. I feel like he's still looking over my shoulder, but there's nothing wrong with that. I'm still pushing. I'm never happy with mediocre."

Marshall Rosenthal

EXECUTIVE PASTRY CHEF, The Reno Hilton, Reno, NV

BORN: September, 1959, Baltimore, MD

TRAINING/EXPERIENCE:
Various patisseries and bakeries, Baltimore area; Hyatt Hotels; Royal Sonesta, Boston; Renaissance Harborplace Hotel, Baltimore; Trump Taj Mahal Hotel and Casino, Atlantic City, NJ

"I find that people just getting into the business place too much emphasis on how much they're going to get paid and how many hours they're going to work, instead of what they need to learn. Of course the money is important—to repay school loans for one thing—but you have to be in this for the long haul. You can't look too closely at the money, because when you calculate how many hours you put in to earn it, it doesn't seem like much. You need to keep your focus on enhancing your skills. The more you know, the more you grow, the more you're worth, the more you make."

Escoffier and Carême, made a great contribution on codifying it. But it was easier for Picasso to be Picasso in the 1900s than it is for the person in 2000 to do the same."

STREAMLINE—AND SELL, SELL, SELL

Many of the spurs to innovation in pastry remain the same today as they have been for centuries—new equipment, the need to have one's work recognized, exotic ingredients, the simple urge to tinker, experiment, to create something rare and fabulous. These spurs are joined by one more: the need to lighten the classics, to adjust for the way we eat today.

"Dense desserts in large portions—that's the way it was," Sebastien Canonne says, "and that's the way I like it," he adds. "But lifestyles are not the same anymore. Back then people worked heavy work, outside, construction. Afterwards you would need a millefeuille. But now after a three-course meal you will want a light millefuille. The style of life became different so the style of food needed to become different."

Some chefs in this book expressed the hope that, by experimenting, they might come up with a dessert that will be considered, in future, a classic. But most are more modest in their aspirations. "The goal is to keep the true flavor, the natural flavor of each product, to use it in a classic way, but update with the new equipment, new techniques," says Canonne. "Not to take shortcuts, but find efficient ways to produce it better, faster, lighter."

The goal of neoclassicism, in Canonne's view, is to update the look of classics that are just fine as they are—poached pear, for example—and to lighten those that are out of step with the times—millefeuille, for example. "Maybe instead of pastry cream with 300 grams of sugar per kilo you'll use 150 because it's enough, says Canonne. "And maybe you will lighten the pastry cream with sweetened whipped cream but with stabilizers so that later it doesn't collapse."

Susan Notter

CORPORATE PASTRY CHEF, Albert Uster Imports, Gaithersburg, MD

BORN: July 17, 1961, Birmingham, England

TRAINING/EXPERIENCE: South Guild College of Further Education, Leicester, hospitality course; Manor Oven Pastry Shop, Melton Mowbrey; Konditorie Heinmann, Cologne; Konditorie Bachmann, Switzerland; Confiserie Honold, Zurich; International School of Confectionery Arts, Zurich and Gaithersburg

"New equipment doesn't change the recipes, but it might change the procedures," agrees Michael Hu. He mentions as examples the spreader, a device that allows the chef to spread greater amounts of dough, and many other products that facilitate large batch production: "Meringue powder, atomized glucose, cocoa butter in pellet form, chocolate in pistilles, of course," enumerates Hu. "A lot of people say, 'I will never have instant this or that in my kitchen,' but there is a place for it. Some of the stabilizers, and cold and hot processed pastry cream—a lot of this is not used as the basic ingredient but as a fortifier, for doing huge batches. A good example is chiboust cream. It's basically light pastry cream. If we do a banquet for a thousand, I'll still make a pastry cream the old way, but when I lighten it, instead of using gelatin as a binding ingredient I will use the pastry cream powder. And it enhances the flavor."

"I know a lot of people can name five different types of exotic fruits, but can you name five different apples and what they're used for? Which is best for a pie, which is best poached? We should always strive for more flavor, of course, but also texture in desserts. The trend is away from the baby food puréed items."

"We are getting better starches, instant starches, the chocolate pastilles, fruit purées," lists Martha Crawford. "Some people say you have to purée your own fruit, and I say, why? I give my students the option, but I feel that it saves me time to do other things. We're learning to cut time when we can cut time."

Of course, when something is gained, something else is lost. Ironically, the new equipment produces new pressures. "The pressure put on a shop to produce and reduce workforce is partially due to equipment," says Michael Hu.

And some chefs fear that basic skills might erode due to new equipment: "hand skills, like piping and even preparing a piping bag," says Hu. "Writing 'Happy Birthday' on a birthday cake is a talent that is being lost to transfer sheets."

Chefs will naturally experiment, if not to meet changing expectations, then to meet a challenge within themselves. This presents the dilemma, the balancing act that must be performed: trying to stay cutting-edge and creative, for their own sake and the sake of good business for their venue, while trying to give customers what they want. "Every dish doesn't have to be an education, especially the dessert," says Chris Broberg. "You want the guest to be comfortable. You have to balance the rigidity of following the classics with being inventive enough to meet your needs or interesting enough for a jaded clientele."

EXECUTIVE PASTRY CHEF, Ritz-Carlton Hotel, Chicago, IL

BORN: Richmond, VA

TRAINING/EXPERIENCE: Baking and Pastry Program, The Culinary Institute of America (first graduate); catering company, Connecticut; Cafe Didier, Washington, DC; Lespinasse, New York

"In a kitchen, you have to assemble a team of people that will work together. Sometimes you can feel it—whether it's a new situation for you or there have been changes recently, and the people just don't mesh. Then it's up to the chef to build that team. If two people don't get along, you have to help them make it work, or make a change. When you hire someone, you have to consider, will he or she fit in? You have to take your best guess. The strength of a kitchen is everyone working together."

"You can get bored if you just make classics," says Heather Ho. "You want to inject fun and levity into your work." But, says Ho, there can be a limit to how much fun a chef can have: "I enjoy looking at an architectural dessert, but I wouldn't want to eat one because I know what needs to happen to make them stand up straight—the amount of gelatin that goes into a lemon curd to make it stand up straight. It's not as good, as creamy, as tart and luscious as it could be—why would anyone want to eat that? But there has to be a middle ground—not just classics and not just eclectic. Desserts don't sell well if the menu is all over the place."

What sells in one market may not sell in another, most of our chefs agree, which places another limit to experimentation. "In major cities where there's more variety of restaurant and an educated diner, the customers are more apt to experiment," says Norman Love, a man that has logged considerable travel.

Norman Love mentions Sachertorte, baba au rhum, and crème caramel as desserts that are often requested in his hotels, nationwide. "Charlottes, éclairs—people relate to that," he says. "These are not experimental diners. They won't order cherry soup with licorice ice cream, but they will order something they can identify with."

"Philadelphia is very conservative. Customers here don't like to experiment very much," says Suzanne Silverman, executive pastry chef for the Main Street Restaurant Group in Philly. She enumerates some of her hits and misses: "Chocolate chile cake didn't work, neither did tequila bread pudding. It hurts your ego a little bit when you make all these beautiful things and they don't sell, but I try these odd little things now and then. What I have learned is, most anything chocolate sells."

Washington, D.C., is another big town with a reputation for a conservative palate. "Anything that's not ice cream or chocolate or apple or lemon, I can't sell it," says Ann Amernick. "In New York you can sell anything. Not so much here."

Jill Rose, who was pastry chef at Lespinasse, also in Washington, D.C., for several years, does not agree that capital customers have a collective dull palate. "I've been sur-

Sebastien Canonne

CO-OWNER AND IN-STRUCTOR, The French Pastry School, Chicago, IL

BORN: October, 1968, Amiens, France

TRAINING/EXPERIENCE: Apprenticeship, École Hotelière, Normandy; apprenticeship, Gaston Lenôtre; La Côte St. Jacques, Burgundy; Beau Rivage Palace, Geneva; Hotel Palace Euler, Basel; St. Germain, The Ritz-Carlton Hotel, both in Chicago, IL

prised," says Rose. "I grew up in that area, and I thought I was familiar with their tastes. But we did a chef tasting menu, and I reserved my most adventuresome desserts for that menu, and I was shocked to find that when I was experimenting and going far out, those would be the desserts that would sell the most." As an example, Rose cites a shaved ice dessert with mixed melon and Midori syrups, candied mung beans and coconut milk. "We called it a melon granité with whatever. That is a big part of it—the name that you give it should soften it, give them something they can relate to, but at the same time pique their curiosity." Rose balances the exotic menu with tried-and-true items: crème brûlée ("which we serve with biscotti") a selection of ice creams and sorbets with a marinated berry compote, and soufflés, always.

Even in a culinary theme park like San Francisco, there is a conservative clientele. "Some of the things that excite me the most don't sell very well. It tends to dampen my enthusiasm," laments Keith Jeanminette of Masa's in San Francisco. "Other places in town are much more successful with items like that. The clientele that I serve is less inclined to experiment. I need to find a happy medium between what excites me and what I can sell."

"I was first in my class in cooking. Then I tried pastry because I always loved it and I went from first in my class to last. It was very frustrating. So I worked hard. Hard work will always pay, but work cleverly, otherwise you are just banging your head against the wall. What opened my eyes is when I worked in smaller shops— they were always working one step ahead and ten backwards. I saw that it is possible to work hard like a moron. It is better to learn the better way right away, and work cleverly. Every day people are finding a better way."

"Soufflés." says John Degnan, the executive pastry chef at The Lodge at Koele in Hawaii. "You put it on the menu, it sells, it sells, it sells."

"All classics sell well," in John Hui's experience. The executive pastry chef of Caesar's Palace in Las Vegas, lists his best-sellers: "Sacher torte, linzertorte, baba au rhum."

"Charlottes and bavarians are classics that are overlooked and underrated," says Daniel Jasso.

"Fruit crisps." says Heather Ho, "because it's basic. People love it, and it changes from season to season. You can play with a lot of different textures."

Martin Howard has great success with chocolate chip cookies and brownies, as themselves or used as components in desserts. "People know them and love them," he says.

Brian Schoenbeck

PASTRY CHEF, Westin River North, Chicago, IL

BORN: July 24, 1963, Chicago, IL

TRAINING/EXPERIENCE: Joliet Junior College, Joliet, IL; Johnson & Wales University, Providence, RI; The Drake, The Ritz-Carlton, The Park Hyatt, The Fairmont, The Art Institute of Chicago, all in Chicago

"I've always loved baking. My dad loved to bake so, even as a kid, it was something I liked to do, and it's ended up being a great career for me. Every day is different, you meet great people, and there's a lot of creativity. Of course, because it's not routine, it's also not nine to five. The hours can get a little tough, especially when you're married and you have a family. But you can't get into it because of the money. You have to love it."

Ann Amernick notes that ice cream is a classic no kitchen can do without—with chocolate sauce handy as well. She also mentions tarts. "Chocolate torte is a best seller—a big, rich piece, with warm ganache over it," she says. "When I was at Citronelle, I did a brownie, but we didn't call it that. I did the brownie so that I could do a napoleon and other European classics. Americans need to try other things. I did a cranberry panna cotta that is so good, such a burst of flavor. It just didn't sell. I did a goat cheese cake. I couldn't call it goat cheese on the menu of course, but it's so delicate, just a little bit of sourness. It didn't sell. Same with baba au rhum. It didn't sell. Then I put rum raisin ice cream on it, chocolate sauce over it and walnuts, and it sold. A recipe of Marian Burros that I loved and changed just a little—sour cream dough, paper thin and flaky, with apricot jam and walnuts and raisins—is incredible, and I couldn't sell it for anything. We called it walnut raisin strudel, then faux strudel, then walnut raisin rugelach."

Amernick adds that it is important for pastry chefs to stay in contact with the waitstaff. "You need to stay on their backs," is how she puts it. "They're willing, but they forget. Go to them, give them a taste, tell them, 'You should try to sell this thing.'"

FORGOTTEN AND UPCOMING

In an age of restless experimentation, it seems that every possible exotic ingredient, odd flavor combination, and avant-garde texture has been tried by some chef, somewhere. "I don't think there's much that's being neglected," agrees Jemal Edwards. "There are so many pastry chefs doing so many things." But the buying public—that is a different matter. Chefs sometimes champion a particular dessert, whether a personal favorite or as gesture to educate the clientele. As often as not, such offerings are defeated in the marketplace.

Suzanne Silverman wonders why Americans don't see the value in the "plain pastries that are seen in Paris, with a very thin fruit layer or purée. Fruit and custard, perfectly done. French pastry amazes me. It's so beautiful outside, and it's almost a surprise inside."

Floating Island is the dessert Heather Ho wishes Americans would take to their bosom. Why? "The idea of poached meringue in milk," she says. "It's kind of funky." Ho cites another example, likewise funky: "Indian pudding is the most heinous thing you've ever seen. It looks like hell on a plate. I wish someone would come up with a way to serve it that is more appealing."

Kim O'Flaherty cites figs and chestnuts as ingredients that are welcome in desserts, but are not popular in the States. Michael Hu can name another: "We have a problem with candied fruits. Fruitcake is a joke in America. But in France they have great fruit and they candy it so well. I love it when it's done well."

In perhaps the quintessential example of chefs' creative facet and business facet at war: they express weariness with desserts that are everywhere, difficult to innovate—in other words, desserts that sell so well they cannot be removed from the menu. Perfect examples are crème brûlée and tiramisù. Soufflés, another guaranteed seller, many chefs wish they could retire for a while. Another: "Those chocolate spheres. You see them everywhere," says Kim O'Flaherty. "I like a mousse," agrees Nick Malgieri, "but it's overdone. Not everything has to be mousse."

Michael Hu is disdainful of the classic, buttercreamy wedding cake with its inevitable syrupy sponge cake. "Boring, no imagination," he complains. "You are directing your energy toward things that don't matter. There are a whole lot of other things you can do that are great."

Since imported ingredients play such an important role in Western pastry history, are there perhaps other ingredients or whole desserts from foreign cultures that Americans might enjoy, if given half a chance? Sticky rice, says Chris Broberg. "Cooked with coconut milk and served with mango," he adds. "It's an Asian dessert I've seen more of."

Jill Rose is also enthusiastic about Asian components. "There are classic Indian, Chinese, and Japanese desserts that Americans are unaware of. We may dislike certain textures or approaches, but there are certain things we can gain from it, flavor combinations we can gain from." One example from India are reduced-milk desserts flavored with rose-flower oil or saffron. "Many Indian desserts are based on that," says Rose. "Much like a cajeta, which is a Spanish custard dessert."

D. Jemal Edwards

PASTRY CHEF

BORN: September, 1966, Ankara, Turkey

TRAINING/EXPERIENCE: Mirador and The Cypress Club, Chicago; Elka and Liberté, San Francisco; Montrachet, Nobu, Maxim's, American Park, Tavern on the Green, all in New York

"I have seen people hide things because they're afraid of the chef. But, honestly, you can't be too threatened by a pastry chef with a knife. Pastry chefs have the dullest knives in the kitchen. They cut on any surface—on marble, on steel. They have to."

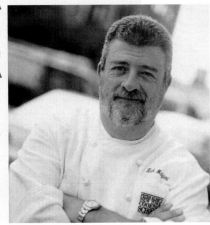

Nick Malgieri

DIRECTOR,
PASTRY PROGRAM,
Peter Kump's New York
Cooking School,
New York, NY

BORN: September 30,
1947, Newark, NJ

TRAINING/EXPERIENCE:
The Culinary Institute of
America, New Haven; ap-
prenticeship, Switzerland;
Hôtel de Paris, The
Sporting Club, both in
Monte Carlo; Reserve de
Beaulieu, Paris; Waldorf-
Astoria, Windows on the
World, New School, New
York Restaurant School,
Total Heaven Baking
Company, all in New
York. Author: *How to
Bake* (HarperCollins,
1995), *Nick Malgieri's
Perfect Pastry* (Macmillan,
1989), *Great Italian
Desserts* (Little, Brown
and Co., 1990), *Chocolate*
(HarperCollins, 1998)

*"A journalist recently re-
marked to me that there are
not a lot of good pastry chefs,
but only good dessert chefs.
This is just putting people
down for doing something
that they are doing well, not
making a cogent statement
about what is going on in this
field. Nowadays, chefs are
concentrating on plated
desserts—this is what is important and what is desired;
customers have come to expect them in good restaurants
and dessert cafes. It may be
true that pastry chefs are not
practicing other parts of the
field that are not in great demand. In the past, chefs were
much more fragmented than
they are today. Someone who
did ices only did ices, and
someone who did ice cream
only did that. It was only
after World War I, when
everything in food started to
become more simplified, that
there was only one pastry
chef who could do all aspects
of pastry and baking."*

Jill Rose lists some ingredients in Chinese and Japanese desserts that she believes should be brought to the American table: red bean paste, mung bean paste, green bean starch, and rice flour starch. Green tea ice cream is not uncommon there, she says. She adds that agar-agar is already gaining wide acceptance here as a gelling agent, over the more common beef-based agents. It is the basis of a particular gelatin dessert in Asia. "We would refer to it as Jell-O but it's denser because it's made with red bean paste. It is sometimes flavored with sweet pumpkin, lime, lemon, mostly artificially flavored. One of my favorite desserts I had in a Malaysian restaurant," Rose continues. "It's a shaved ice dessert but much taller than you think of in America, in a big bowl. It was topped with coconut milk-based sauces—tamarind and other flavors—and it had sweetened corn, sweetened adzuki beans, and a coconut milk broth at the base."

Rose mentions that root vegetables are a component in some Asian petit-four-like pastry items, and as the line between savory and sweet draws thinner, Pat Murakami recalls one memorable dessert she and her husband sampled in Turkey. "It was made from chicken," she says. "The chicken is shredded so fine, it's almost a custard. Eggs were mixed in with a cream and sugar so it was sweet, but every once in a while you would catch a shred, and you would say, oh my God, it's chicken."

"Some of the things I tasted in Japan I enjoyed but I don't think they would go over here," says Jemal Edwards. "Rice paste, bean paste starches that are sweetened. Textures are fairly strange and flavors are to me minimal."

"In Europe, taste is all that matters. They don't give a hoot for height and color and architecture,"

A NEOCLASSIC VIEW OF PLATED DESSERTS

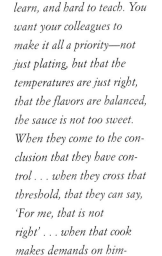

Jill Rose

EXECUTIVE CHEF, Urban Horizons Food Co., Bronx, NY

BORN: July 2, 1963, Salina, KS

TRAINING/EXPERIENCE: The Culinary Institute of America; Aureole, New York; Bread Alone, Boiceville, NY; Lespinasse, New York and Washington, DC

says Michael Hu. "But in America, we are becoming the trendsetters. We are more ready to experiment with fusion-type ingredients, more willing to break the rules. European chefs are not so willing to break the mold.

"It goes back to having a happy shop," Hu adds. "If you give people the freedom to express themselves, they are happy and they do better work in the long run."

THE ELEMENT OF FEAR

Does a happy shop produce higher quality, perhaps more innovative, work? Does a kitchen run on fear hinder creativity? These are not easy questions, but they cut to the very notion of teaching, and how to build an effective kitchen team.

There is not even complete agreement on the widespread stories of tyrannical chefs, tantrums, and utter terror in the kitchens of old. Some say such stories have been exaggerated. Some tell the stories:

Sebastien Canonne remembers a kitchen where he worked in France: "plates flying, everything flying, cooking utensils with the sauces in it. Hot anything. Crazy stuff."

"Commitment is hard to learn, and hard to teach. You want your colleagues to make it all a priority—not just plating, but that the temperatures are just right, that the flavors are balanced, the sauce is not too sweet. When they come to the conclusion that they have control . . . when they cross that threshold, that they can say, 'For me, that is not right' . . . when that cook makes demands on him- or herself, then they are there. It's the confidence to tell the boss, if need be, that something is not right."

Marshall Rosenthal recalls his tyrannical chef. "One time this chef launched a #10 can of tomatoes across the kitchen," says Rosenthal. "It looked like a missile. It left a dent in the refrigerator door. One time I saw a guy get angry, take another guy, and spray him with the steam kettle hose. I've seen people threaten people with knives."

Jemal Edwards saw "a chef get angry that veal bones were thrown into a roasting pan without a certain ingredient. He pulled the roasting pan out at 400 or 500 degrees and threw it across the line."

Keith Jeanminette once worked with a man "that we considered a maniac. He would scream and throw things. He threw handfuls of roasted garlic across the kitchen, and there were many, many obscenities. He had quite a mouth on him, like a drunken sailor. We feared him but we didn't respect him. And I told myself, I will never be like that."

PASTRY CHEF,
Lespinasse, New York

BORN: August 15, 1962,
Philadelphia, PA

TRAINING/EXPERIENCE:
Classes, The Culinary
Institute of America at
Greystone, Brother
Juniper Bakery, Markus
Farbinger, The Notters
and Pascal Janvier;
Odeon, The Ritz-Carlton
Hotel, both in
Philadelphia, PA; Caesar's,
Lake Tahoe, NV

"Americans aren't trained the way they are in Europe, where everyone in the class makes this cookie at this time and they all do it exactly the same way and until they do 100 or 1000 the same way they don't get the next task. Here, it's more a matter of, 'Let's try something else, let's try this flavor combination or that one.' Yes, chefs get bored doing the classics. They forget that there is a challenge to doing it right. When chefs run to do something different, some of the flavors they try sound good, but when you try them you think, why are they doing that? They must be awfully bored."

A resolve to rise above is one thing, but revenge is sweet. Norman Love recalls one small measure of get-back: "It was my first professional kitchen, and I was working the hot side. I was the assistant to the vegetable guy. I had Band Aids all over my fingers, I didn't know anything. All I know is, the guy always yelled at me, in French. Always angry at me. During the expediting of the line, he kept his glass of ice water on the shelf near where my station was, so all night I would drop salt and pepper into his water. And the guy always complained about how salty the water was in Florida."

Lincoln Carson recalls working at a four-star French restaurant, where plates were routinely thrown, and chefs screamed and sent people home daily. "You would try to predict who would get the cigar, as we called it, the proverbial exploding cigar. But I know some of these people, and some of them are better cooks because of it. Whatever doesn't kill you makes you stronger, as they say. It made me better. I can see its place in the world. There are many talented people that are products of such kitchens."

Carson's attitude is evidence that not all chefs agree that a little fear, or a lot of fear, in the kitchen is entirely a bad thing.

Nick Malgieri has experienced an atmosphere of "ultra-perfectionism, where everyone is uptight about making the smallest mistakes." And he sees that in such an atmosphere, people do not perform their best. Then have these stories been exaggerated? From his perspective, yes. "I worked in France and Switzerland and I never encountered anyone who was not good-natured. I think that's a thing of the past. There is a whole generation of people who have gone through this process and have never been abused. We're not the only country that has labor laws."

A fearful atmosphere in the kitchen can have many effects; emotion can lead to bad judgment. "I've seen people get kicked off the line for the day, just to prove a point," says James Foran, pastry chef at Silk's in San Francisco. "Then they put people on the line that are not as qualified, and the situation grows worse."

EXECUTIVE PASTRY CHEF, The Main Street Restaurant Group, Philadelphia, PA

BORN: February 4, 1966, Philadelphia, PA

TRAINING/EXPERIENCE: The Restaurant School of Philadelphia, The Frog Commissary, Apropos, all in Philadelphia, PA

"It was the old school, to motivate by fear," says Todd Johnson. "Their thinking was, 'If I really scream at this guy over a little mistake, he will make damn sure he doesn't make a big mistake.' "

But should a kitchen necessarily be a happy place? "Happy? No," responds Sebastien Canonne. "It should be structured, organized. It must be managed but also weed out the anger. There should be respect, but not fear. You have to be happy to come to work. It can't be cool either, because then you don't push yourself. There should always be a fear of screwing up."

"If you're not tense, are you caring enough about the final product?" agrees Chris Broberg. "If it's that easy, you're denying that there is some learned skill needed. There should be some sense of urgency to meet the guests' needs. And there should be a sense of self-criticism or criticism of the person working with you. You can do better, you can do better."

"A kitchen should be challenging, efficient, and organized," says Jill Rose. "If you can be happy doing all those things, great."

"Love what you do, work hard and the sky's the limit—I've said it before and it's definitely something I believe in. I have four boys and a husband. I'm out the door at four in the morning. It used to be 2:30, and it didn't bother me at all. I've never gotten bored, never burned out. I love working with my hands, and being good at it. Women can have a family and work. Wanting a family shouldn't stop you from pursuing your pastry career. Of course it helps if you have as great a boss as I have."

Jacquy Pfeiffer notes that passion is one of the most important things a mentor can impart to a rookie. But when the training is rigorous, as his was, and strict, bordering on hellish, "it can be difficult to get the passion because sometimes you want to quit. You get beat up too long, and there's no room for passion."

"In my pastry shop, I don't condone that kind of atmosphere, but I will use it if I have to," admits Pat Coston. "I try to be patient. You have to be. I give people a lot of chances. But once you do it right, then it's right from now on. If you have done it right and then you don't, it tells me you're not here in some capacity."

"Were there benefits?" says Keith Jeanminette, recalling his demonic chef. "Maybe in the short term, but you need to decide whether you're going to be a monster or a friend. Some try to be both. I try for a happy medium, to be firm. You can demand people's respect through example, which requires a lot more subconscious attention. You have to monitor yourself."

"I don't think this motivates people," says Todd Johnson. "Certainly you will not be creative. You're going to do things the way he tells you to do things. To venture off the track,

Michael Hu

PASTRY CHEF AND CONSULTANT, New York, NY

BORN: May, 1967, Oahu, HI

TRAINING/EXPERIENCE: Kapalua Hotel Company; Michael's (self-owned), Maui; Chart House Restaurant Company; Zabar's, Ritz-Carlton, Grand Hyatt, Waldorf-Astoria, all in New York

"In the hotel industry, if the product is wrong, then there's something wrong with the management. You see a lot of people spending a lot of time in a hotel, but not accomplishing a whole lot. This business is not just about the end result. It's not just about good food. If you have a great working environment, and you have talented people who work hard and love what they're doing, good food will result, if not now then down the road. Great food is the result of great team effort. There are many variables that try to dissuade you from that, but if you have great people they overcome a lot of that."

and try something new that will potentially result in failure and a tongue lashing? No."

"The day of the executive chef who rants and raves is, I hope, coming to an end," says Jemal Edwards. "It doesn't get anything done faster or better. In fact, it works in the opposite direction. Negative energy produces negative results."

"Take your work seriously, not yourself," advises Bill Hallion, pastry chef at the Renaissance Vinoy Resort in St. Petersburg, Florida. "It's desserts, not war."

BUILDING A TEAM

The first step in building a happy, productive shop is hiring the right people. That much is obvious. But the quality most chefs look for in hiring, especially young people, is not so obvious; it isn't a prestigious degree or acute kitchen skills or a snappy patter. It's attitude. Willingness to learn. Commitment. Passion.

"Seeing a degree from a culinary school is singularly unimpressive," says Todd Johnson. "I wait until I talk to a person and see how he conducts himself in the kitchen. Norman Love is perfect example—he has no formal training, but a great deal of passion."

Passion is not an easy thing to discern in a person, but Michael Hu tries to ferret it out in interviews. "One of the first questions I ask a prospective employee is, where have you eaten? What do you like to cook? What are your passions? What do you read? Who do you admire? Who do you follow? The old way, the person says, 'I really love to cook,' and you say, 'Oh, okay, I'll give you a job.' No more."

"Sometimes people appear to be interested, but it usually takes a couple of weeks for you to be sure whether they're really interested, if it's a forever thing. You can almost feel it," says Norman Love.

"I get a lot of people in my kitchen who have very little experience but a lot of desire," says Keith Jeanminette. "These are people with real interest, real motivation. It's al-

Ann Amernick

PASTRY CHEF AND OWNER, Amernick, Wheaton, MD

BORN: September 15, 1943, Baltimore, MD

TRAINING/EXPERIENCE: Le Pavillon, Palais de Friandises, Place Vendôme, Jean-Louis at the Watergate, The White House, Cashion's, Red Sage, Citronelle, all in Washington, DC. Author: *Special Desserts* (Clarkson Potter, 1992); Co-author: *Soufflés* (Clarkson Potter, 1992)

ways interesting to watch them when they first start." Then the process of learning begins, almost invisibly. "It's amazing. It happens so gradually that you hardly notice it," says Jeanminette. "To see how much they picked up. And I might remind them, 'Look at you, you're a pro.' They kind of stand back. They didn't realize it themselves."

Having measured a newcomer's desire, many chefs then begin to assess physical skills and temperament toward building an effective team.

For newcomers, Jemal Edwards has a word of advice: "You can't show off. You have to wait, listen. It isn't appropriate to come up with your own ideas until you're asked."

"Some people are rough, abrasive; those kind of people I will throw into making large amounts of doughs or sheetcakes," says James Foran. "That's what they enjoy; they're into getting their hands dirty, doing large-scale production. People with some dexterity, some finesse, I like to utilize them with hands-on finish work, more delicate things like garnishes, sugar work, chocolate." Burly or delicate, says Foran, "I like them all to have input and ideas on new desserts, configurations, flavors."

"The older you get, and the more involved you get in the work, the more you realize what you don't know. I learned in kitchens, not in schools, and one thing I've learned is to take criticism in the right way. Somebody can say something negative about your work and, sure, sometimes there's an agenda behind it—you can figure that out. But for the most part you should listen and you should determine if there's something valid in the criticism."

"What I try to do is vary the staff," agrees Jill Rose. "One has strength in one area, another in another area, so that not everyone in my kitchen is necessarily all the same pedigree." One might be strong in banquet production, another in finish work, and so on. "It gives me time to focus on each plate, to detail it," she says.

"Some of the finish people can go down to the bakeshop and do the bulk work," says Stan Ho, "whereas the bulk people would have trouble doing the fine points." Does this mean the "bulk people" are limited in terms of their usefulness, and in terms of future career? Not at all, says Ho. "They are very essential to the operation. Some can step up to become executive pastry chefs." James Foran agrees. "I usually find that's what they like to do," he says of the bulk brigade. "But if they don't enjoy it, I'll teach them what I can. Finesse can be taught to a certain degree. Hand-mind coordination can be taken to a different level of finesse."

Kim O'Flaherty

ASSISTANT PASTRY CHEF, The Four Seasons Hotel, New York, NY

BORN: February, 1967, Billerica, MA

TRAINING/EXPERIENCE: Newbury College, Boston; Sweet Creations, Wakefield, MA; White Barn Inn, Kennebunkport, ME; Ritz-Carlton, San Francisco; Ritz-Carlton, Boston; Essex House Hotel, Waldorf-Astoria, both in New York

"In Europe, the fundamentals are practiced over and over, until you have a very solid base. Only then do you graduate to showpieces. A showpiece is just the display of the completion of your educational achievement. It's a rounding off. A chef in his fifties once said to me that if he could trade in everything he knows for everything he doesn't know, he would do it in a heartbeat. There is that much to learn about cooking, about pastry, about anything."

"I rotate people, let them see the many sides of pastry," says Todd Johnson. "You have to show them there's some incentive other than $9 an hour. And I sometimes will do the less glamorous jobs, like rolling danish, and let my people do the more so-called glamorous jobs, to give them a feeling of accomplishment."

"You have self-motivated people, and you have everyone else," declares Norman Love. "Self-motivated people can reach down and push themselves beyond their limits without the assistance of a superior. Then there are people that constantly need that push."

LEADERSHIP AND ATTITUDE

Teaching effectively, managing with patience, and understanding—it isn't just an obligation to the next generation of chefs, though most chefs in authority do take that obligation seriously. It is also, most agree, the most effective way to run an efficient shop in the long run. And it is no surprise that most chefs list patience as the most important virtue in the teaching process. For Keith Jeanminette, having kids at home has helped him realize the value of patience at work. "In the kitchen I'm afraid I sometimes sound more like a father than a chef," he admits. "But many of the same rules do apply. In the workplace, with kids, even friends, you have to find a way to say it in a patient way so that it is not rejected. You tell yourself, slow down, say it in such a way that it will be accepted."

"A teacher is like a parent," says Nick Malgieri. "You have to be nurturing and strict at the same time. As a teacher, if you pounce on every detail, you will lose your mind eventually. You have to let people feel safe in their triumphs and failings. You have to provide an atmosphere in which they want to continue to learn."

A good teacher, says Jacquy Pfeiffer, is someone "who can pass on the passion, the techniques, the discipline, the knowledge. Pastry is so much about knowledge of ingredients. The rest is not secondary, but we also try to teach our students to be humble and calm at all times. Humble, because there's always somebody better than you, and the food busi-

Heather Ho

PASTRY CHEF, Boulevard, San Francisco, CA

BORN: 1969, Honolulu, HI

TRAINING/EXPERIENCE: The Culinary Institute of America; Aqua, San Francisco; Bouley, Gramercy Tavern, The Screening Room, Clementine, all in New York

ness never stops. Calm, because too many chefs get nervous too quickly in the kitchen."

"Some days you have to be rigid, other days more patient," says Pat Coston of running a kitchen. "The balance is a hard thing to maintain."

"It's a balancing act," agrees Jemal Edwards. "You don't want to insult someone who's coming into the kitchen by assuming they don't know how to prepare something, but you can't take it for granted that they do. You don't want to piss off your entire crew by riding them, but you also want what you want the way you want it—not what they think they know how to produce. You want what you want produced."

"You have to keep a distance, but have people feel comfortable with you," Susan Notter advises the teacher/chef. "Let them know that they can ask questions, that they will not be laughed at. Be compassionate, sensitive, aware of other people's feelings."

"I don't care for extremism. Good, honest food is more appreciated by a diner than something that is cutting edge. The key is balance. If something is balanced in terms of flavors and textures and colors and temperatures, it is more appreciated. In the end, nostalgia seems to sell the best. It's not compromise or selling out to give people what they want."

"My philosophy is that you manage people at their level. You come down to each individual's level," says Michael Hu. "The team is everything. Whether it's an extern, a pastry cook, a senior pastry cook, the sous chef, head baker, pastry chef, or the guy that scoops the ice cream, you have to give of yourself to each and every one of them what they need. I have to be the chameleon. I have to understand what everyone needs. Some people learn by positive reinforcement, other people need a swift kick in the butt sometimes. And that's what I need to assess."

"Talk someone through a procedure," advises Susan Notter. "You cannot assume that people know too much. You have to explain everything."

Obviously, the best way to learn is through hands-on instruction, reinforcement, and practice; this is true of most disciplines. But it applies particularly to pastry because of the ever-expanding role of equipment. As Sebastien Canonne puts it: "A spoon for that, a spoon for the spoon, a bag to put the spoon in, a bag to put the bag in—it's a lot of equipment," he admits. But it is necessary in a competitive environment: "You do have a need for it. All this small equipment makes your life easier. It creates a comfort in working, and when you're comfortable you will work cleaner, work longer. You will be happier, more creative." Still, in the classes he holds at his school, "We never rely too much on equip-

Tom Vaccaro

EXECUTIVE PASTRY CHEF, Trump Plaza Casino Hotel, Atlantic City, NJ

BORN: November 11, 1965, Newark, NJ

TRAINING/EXPERIENCE: The Culinary Institute of America; Hyatt Regency Grand Cypress, Marriott World Center, both in Orlando; Showboat Casino, Atlantic City, NJ; U.S. 1992 Culinary Olympics Team; Waldorf-Astoria Hotel, New York.

"Chefs are craftsmen. You work hard at what you do and you become better. There are phenoms because they're meant to be that way, but 99.9 percent of people work hard to become technically advanced. Proper training in classic technique enables you to be creative and do artistic, technically advanced work."

ment. By working in the old way, you come to appreciate the equipment, what it's about. It doesn't help you as much to learn in the best facilities," he adds. "It's better to learn without a lot of equipment, then down the road you will appreciate the new methods. You have to teach both ways of doing things."

Keith Jeanminette says that he uses a lot of analogies in his kitchen instruction. "One that I use more than others is a golf analogy. The first thing you develop is your swing, then it's just a matter of changing your clubs for height and distance and so on. I teach people that when they're piping rosettes or whatever, develop a swing first. Get consistent with your method. Without consistency you're never going to be able to improve. Once you get the basics down, you can start to elaborate and fine tune it."

Piping is a basic procedure that can make a big difference to a beginner, agrees John Degnan. Taking the time and the mental energy to teach someone can be difficult, he says, but it is a necessary part of the job. "It's monotonous to teach someone how to sit down and stroke and draw," he says, "but if you sit down with them for fifteen minutes, twice a week, have them sit there and practice with an example in front of them, before you know it, after a few weeks pass, they get better."

It is worth the time to teach these fine motor skills, says Degnan, for several reasons. "It can make a good-looking cake look terrible, or it can make a simple cake look elegant," he says. But think of the details involved. "There are techniques to piping that can make your skills far superior to others," says Degnan. "I learned mine from Joe Lanciani, who was phenomenal. Finesse with writing has to do with the flow of the paste coming out of the bag and how hard you touch the bag to the surface. If you're writing on marzipan or chocolate, which is more firm, you have to touch it delicately, just enough; you have to stroke the bag quickly enough so that the paste doesn't clump up. Your hand must go fluidly over the surface without stopping mid-stream. You have to do practice drills until your muscles and your hands know the stroke feel and you don't have to think about it. As soon as you get it, it clicks. When it comes to you, you suddenly have confidence in your decorative work."

Jemal Edwards believes that learning physical cues can mean a lot to a young chef. "Like the way light enters pastry cream when it's finished and the starch is cooked," he

Martin Howard

PASTRY CHEF AND CONSULTANT, New York, NY

BORN: August, 1962, Gouverneur, NY

TRAINING/EXPERIENCE: The Culinary Institute of America; home cake decoration business; La Crémaillière, Bedford, NY; Pier House, Key West, FL; The Hudson River Club, Rainbow!, both in New York

says. "You can say a cake is done in twenty-five minutes, but you have to be able to recognize when it's truly done, to be aware of all the factors—the oven itself as opposed to the one at your last job. Was the oven open and closed many times, was the oven hot or cold when it was put in? Something can be ruined by fooling with it too much—stirring it too much, checking it too much. These are things that can only be learned in a kitchen, through practical experience, not in a lecture hall."

Michael Hu draws on his experience as a sommelier when pondering how to best encourage and educate people in his kitchen. "I was educating myself about wine. And the way to learn about something is to break it all down. In wine it's sugars, tannins, acids, fruit acids, and all that. You need to apply that to food as well. You need to really taste what you're cooking with. Spend a good majority of your time asking yourself, why is this cocoa the best to use, why this fruit purée? My family is into martial arts. The method of teaching there is to rein people in. People want to run before they can walk. Before they master the basics they want to do the fun stuff. My best attribute as a teacher is reining people in, bringing them down, settling them down, having them reassess their priorities to what is most important—what do they need to work on? And, believe me, it's never sugar work or chocolate work or showpieces. It's always cleanliness, efficiency, and flavor. Move outside that recipe, change it a little, spend a little time figuring out how to make it taste better, how to cut back on the sugar, how to intensify the flavors."

"I am combining the homestyle my Mom taught me with the European style that Albert Kumin taught me. What I do now is not exactly classic, but I've done the French classic style; the technique is there. The people who come right out of school into a professional kitchen, they're so cute—they think they know it all, but of course they don't. Whether the schools are not teaching the basic techniques or the people are not getting enough practice, I'm not sure, but many of them refuse to learn more efficient methods. The irony is, I like to teach. One of the guys that's been with me for eight years started as a potwasher."

Although most newcomers want to run (to sugar work, showpieces, etc.) before they can walk (making pastry cream), it is just such a basic that chefs in authority say is most important.

"I still do the basics," says Pat Coston. "Not all the time, but I do make my own ice creams, anglaises, and all the basic doughs every few months. If I don't do it, I'm not in touch with what I'm doing. If it means making brioche every three months just to stay in

Michel Willaume

EXECUTIVE PASTRY CHEF, The Ritz-Carlton Hotel, San Francisco, CA

BORN: June 22, 1966, Nantes, France

TRAINING/EXPERIENCE: apprenticeship, Nantes; Dalloyau, Paris; Matignon (House for the First Minister of France), Paris; Patisserie Jamin, Nantes; The Ritz-Carlton, Barcelona; The Ritz-Carlton, Osaka

"It is very important for pastry chefs to communicate what they know. I always take the time to teach. Not only do the employees like it, but it is hotel policy—every six months we give an evaluation, and we set goals for the employees. 'You are doing fine at such-and-such, but you need to work on this-and-that.' And in the next six months, we work on it together. You are not a great chef alone. You are a great chef with your people. Alone, you make nothing."

touch, to show someone who works for me the most efficient way to do something, I do it. In today's shop that's very important."

"There is not enough time spent in mastering the basics—making a dough, rolling a dough," agrees Norman Love. "If these are not mastered first, you find yourself stumbling. Trial and error becomes the way of doing things."

Taking the time in a busy day to teach the basics, then, may seem like a step backward, but it is a basic way to promote efficiency. Martha Crawford teaches her students to be organized, and to be perfect. That is the message: perfection. Is this, perhaps, a bit too lofty for students? No, says Crawford. "By being perfect, doing normal production, you get quicker, you get cleaner. You are getting to the point of being as efficient as you can be," she says. " 'Work cleaner, work neater,' " she continues, mimicking her technique. " 'Why are you taking so many steps? Why do you spread twenty times when, with this sheetpan, eight will do? Why not count eight times in your head?' " It is a matter of time management, she says. "If you're organized, you will have the time to do more sophisticated things."

Crawford says that her beleaguered students will often protest: "This is the first time I'm making this. Why are you telling me how fast I have to do it?" Even her colleagues advise her to let her students take their time the first time. "But I feel that it is important to project this sense right from the beginning," says Crawford. "The first time you make something, that can become your standard. Next time, you might knock off five minutes, and do something else with that time. But if you never watch the clock . . ."

"I tell my cooks that they have to make their lives easy," says Heather Ho. "In other words, shortcuts, as long as it produces the same end. Put the pastry bag in a cup or glass and fill it that way, rather than on one arm; it frees both hands. Rotate the sheetpan so the

Ewald Notter

OWNER, lead instructor, Notter International School of Confectionery Arts, Gaithersburg, MD

BORN: September, 1955, Baden, Switzerland

TRAINING/EXPERIENCE: apprenticeship, pastry shop, Disler; military service; various seasonal shops and hotels in the mountains; Sprüngli, Zurich, and traveling as instructor; classes in sugar pulling and blowing, Willi Pfund; instructor and co-owner, Pfund School; owner, International School of Confectionery Arts, Zurich

work is always close to you. Every 20 minutes, assess your situation. Clean your work space. It creates waste to stack things or have work."

Nick Malgieri received an important lesson one day watching Albert Kumin doing a pulled sugar basket. An experienced chef with some reputation came in and criticized Kumin's method, much to the shock of Kumin's staff. "An awful lot of different techniques and ways of working have to become personal," says Malgieri. "You can't necessarily always follow other people's rules. You have to know the basics, you have to know the rules, but you have to make it your own, figure it out for yourself. If there's an important principle I want to teach people, it's that before they become 100 percent comfortable with something, they have to make it their own. Maybe you break the rules. Maybe you want to see a boil start when you're making a crème anglaise, as long as you're whipping it a certain way and ready to strain it and it's really cold, it's not going to ruin it. People have their own way of making sure things turn out the way they want them to, and sometimes they contradict each other."

"I don't like too much sugar on a plate. The customer not only can't eat it, he or she must deal with it. A good dessert doesn't need much decoration. Still, you should always have some decorations at the ready. In some venues it's what is expected; in others, they will come in handy for a customer's birthday, for a cake or on a plate. If so, all the work should be fine, delicate. An accent only."

Sometimes, in order to achieve anything in life, you have to break rules. Reimagining the classics for the twenty-first century is a testament to that. In this volume we present conservative reworkings of classic desserts, all of which are accessible to most pastry kitchens. If an entire presentation is not feasible, certainly many of the designs or component recipes will spark some ideas. Like the chefs in this volume, we all must strike a balance—keeping ourselves stimulated while also satisfying the customers. Err on either side—bore the customers or bewilder them—and they will not come back. But if you're uncertain as to which way to lean, remember this: if someone, somewhere, sometime, hadn't been willing to break a rule, to tinker, to push things a bit, we would still be munching flatbread baked in tree bark.

fruit desserts

CHAPTER 1

Roasted Pear with Port-Poached Pears and Vanilla Ice Cream

CHRIS BROBERG

LESPINASSE
NEW YORK, NY

YIELD: *6 servings*

Poached pears are not only overused, in Chris Broberg's estimation, but also, quite often, badly prepared. "Since it is frequently not cored, it's difficult to eat," he says. "It's usually not done enough because the chef wants it to keep its shape. I can see why—it's a very sensual shape. But when someone tries to eat it, it flies across the plate. A good chef always cares that a dessert eats well. This one is deconstructed—it looks like a pear but it's easy to eat." With a roasted pear stuffed with dried fruit, pear soup, pears poached in several ways, and vanilla ice cream, it is like a study in pears—and in temperature contrasts. "This is a good dessert for people who have a problem with dairy," says Broberg. "Just substitute sorbet for the ice cream."

SPECIAL EQUIPMENT: *1½" [3.8 cm] ring mold*

ROASTED PEARS:

6 Anjou pears, peeled, skin reserved

2.5 lb [1.1 kg] granulated sugar

2.1 qt [2 lt] water

1.8 oz [50 g] superfine sugar

1. Preheat the oven to 350°F [175°C].
2. Place the pears in a 6" [15.25 cm] deep roasting pan lined with crinkled foil.
3. Combine the granulated sugar and water. Pour over the pears.
4. Cover the pan and braise for 20 to 30 minutes.
5. Remove the pears and place on a crinkled foil-lined sheet pan. Sprinkle with superfine sugar.
6. Set the oven at 450°F [225°C]. Roast 8 to 12 minutes until pears are caramelized. Let cool.

WHITE PORT-POACHED PEARS:

3 Anjou pears, cut into small rounds

16.9 liq oz [500 ml] white port

7 oz [200 g] granulated sugar

Combine all the ingredients in a saucepan. Bring to a boil. Remove from the heat and cover.

RED PORT-POACHED PEAR:

1 Anjou pear, cut into small dice

8.5 liq oz [250 ml] ruby red port

3.5 oz [100 g] granulated sugar

Combine all the ingredients in a saucepan. Bring to a boil. Remove from the heat and cover.

CARAMEL-POACHED PEARS:

2.2 lb [1 kg] granulated sugar

2.1 qt [2 lt] water

6 Seckel pears, peeled

1.   Cook the sugar in a large, heavy saucepan to a dark caramel. Deglaze the caramel with water; cool.

2.   Add the pears. Bring to a boil, then simmer 10 to 15 minutes or until the pears are soft.

VANILLA ICE CREAM:

2 qt [1.9 lt] milk

2 qt [1.9 lt] heavy cream

28 oz [800 g] granulated sugar, divided

16 vanilla beans, split and scraped

20.8 oz [590 g] egg yolks

1.   Combine the milk, heavy cream, 14 oz [400 g] of the granulated sugar, and vanilla beans in a large saucepan. Bring to a boil.

2.   Temper the yolks with the milk mixture. Return to the heat and cook to 183°F [85°C]. Strain. Cool in an ice bath.

3.   Process in an ice cream machine according to the manufacturer's instructions.

PEAR SOUP:

Reserved pear skins

1 qt [1 lt] water

1.8 oz [50 g] granulated sugar

Lemon juice, to taste

Pinch of salt

Combine the pear skins, water, and sugar in a saucepan. Bring to a boil, then reduce the heat and simmer for 1 hour. Strain. Return to the heat and reduce by half. Adjust the taste with the lemon juice and salt.

DRIED FRUIT STUFFING:

3.9 oz [110 g] dried cranberries

3.9 oz [110 g] angelica, cut into small dice

3.9 oz [110 g] candied orange peel, cut into small dice

1.7 liq oz [50 ml] Grand Marnier

Combine all the ingredients and let stand for at least 1 hour.

CARAMEL CAGE:

1 lb [450 g] fondant patissier*

8 oz [225 g] glucose

*Available from Paris Gourmet Patisfrance 1-800-788-2889

Combine the fondant and glucose in a large saucepan. Cook to the caramel stage. Remove from the heat. Cool in an ice bath until slightly thickened. Drizzle over an oiled small bowl which has been turned upside-down. Let set. Remove the cage from the bowl. Repeat to make a total of 6 cages.

MARZIPAN PEARS:

11 oz [314 g] almond paste

2 Tbs [24 g] Poire William, divided

5.5 oz [156 g] granulated sugar

.4 oz [12 g] glucose

Green, yellow, and brown powdered food coloring, as needed

1. In a mixing bowl, cream the almond paste and 1 Tbs [12 g] of the Poire William.

2. Combine the sugar, glucose, and enough water to make a smooth mixture in a saucepan. Cook to 240°F [116°C]. Pour onto the almond paste and mix until cooled.

3. Mix the food colors separately with some Poire William to dissolve. Form the marzipan into small pear shapes and brush with the food coloring. Let dry. Attach to caramel cages.

ASSEMBLY:

Vanilla ice cream

Confectioners' sugar

1. Place a 1½" [3.8 cm] ring mold on a plate, slightly off-center. Fill ¾" [19 mm] of the mold with the white port-poached pear rounds.

2. Cut a caramel pear in half, keeping the stem intact. Slice one-half of the caramel pear into a fan shape and place it next to the white port pears.

3. Spoon some of the diced red port-poached pears along the inside border of the plate.

4. Preheat the oven to 400°F [205°C]. Remove the core from the roasted pears and stuff the pocket with the dried fruit. Top with the stem portion of the pear half. Sprinkle the pears with confectioners' sugar. Place on a baking sheet and bake just until warm, about 5 minutes. Place one of the warm pears next to the pears on the plate. Serve with a quenelle of vanilla ice cream. Cover the plate with a caramel cage.

Apple Blossom

MARTHA CRAWFORD

JOHNSON & WALES
UNIVERSITY
PROVIDENCE, RI

YIELD: *6 servings*

A subtle visual scheme is at work in this otherwise straight-ahead, classic presentation of sautéed apples, streusel topping, vanilla ice cream, and raspberry sauce in a phyllo cup. "It's like a modern apple strudel, or a rethinking of apple pie. The apple could be served warm or cold." This is a perfect expression of Crawford's attitude toward the classics, which is: "You can't do much more. You can only take them and change them a little. If you look at what people are doing, there is usually one element that is a classic. Baking and pastry is a science. There is a reason why some things work, and some don't."

FRENCH VANILLA CINNAMON ICE CREAM:

16 liq oz [473 ml] whole milk

16 liq oz [473 ml] heavy cream

Pinch of salt

9 oz [255 g] granulated sugar

8 oz [227 g] egg yolks

1 Tbs [14 g] vanilla extract

Ground cinnamon, to taste

1.   Combine the milk, heavy cream, salt, and sugar in a saucepan and bring to a boil.

2.   In a heatproof bowl whisk together the egg yolks, vanilla extract, and cinnamon. Temper the egg yolk mixture into the milk mixture.

3.   Cook the mixture over a double boiler until it coats the back of a wooden spoon. Strain and cool over an ice bath.

4.   Process in an ice cream machine according to the manufacturer's instructions.

PHYLLO CUPS:

10 sheets phyllo dough [11" × 14"/28 cm × 35.5 cm]

8 oz [227 g] unsalted butter, melted

1.   Preheat oven to 350°F [175°C]. Lay the phyllo dough out flat and cover with plastic wrap and a damp towel.

2.   Place a sheet of phyllo dough on a work surface and brush evenly with some of the melted butter. Lay a second phyllo sheet over the butter-coated phyllo sheet. Repeat the process to create 5 layers of phyllo dough.

3.   Cut six 4" [10 cm] squares from the layered phyllo dough. Place each square in a 5 liq oz [148 ml] muffin tin to create individual cups. Bake 12 to 15 minutes, until golden brown.

4.   Repeat the process of layering the phyllo dough. Cut out six 2½" [6.4 cm] squares and place in 2 oz [60 ml] muffin cups.

STREUSEL TOPPING:

6 oz [170 g] unsalted butter

6 oz [170 g] light brown sugar

1 tsp [4 g] ground cinnamon

½ tsp [3 g] salt

12 oz [340 g] bread flour

1.   Preheat oven to 350°F [175°C]. Line a sheet pan with parchment paper.

2.   In a mixer with the paddle attachment, cream together the butter and brown sugar. Blend in the cinnamon and salt. Add the flour and combine until the mixture becomes crumbly.

3.   Spread the mixture evenly on the prepared sheet pan and bake 15 minutes, until golden brown. Allow to fully cool, and break into small pieces.

RASPBERRY SAUCE:

16 oz [454 g] raspberry purée

Kirsch, to taste

3 oz [85 g] granulated sugar

Lemon extract, to taste

Lemon juice, to taste

2 tsp [20 ml] Triquel instant thickener

Place the raspberry purée in a bowl and blend in the kirsch, granulated sugar, lemon extract, and lemon juice, adjusting to taste. Check the consistency of the sauce and add the Triquel thickener as desired.

GREEN APPLE FILLING:

6 Granny Smith apples

4 oz [113 g] unsalted butter

4–6 oz [113–170 g] light brown sugar

1 tsp [1 g] ground cinnamon

2 oz [57 g] raisins

1.   Peel, core, and thinly slice the apples. Melt the butter in a sauté pan and add the brown sugar according to the sweetness of the apples. Stir in the cinnamon. Allow the pan to get hot and add the apples.

2.   Cook the apples over high heat until they begin to soften and turn golden brown. Add the raisins and cook for another minute.

3.   Remove the pan from the heat and let the filling cool.

ASSEMBLY:

Confectioners' sugar

Chopped dried cranberries

Walnuts, chopped and toasted

1.   Create a template using the pattern on page 240. Fill a plastic squeeze bottle with the raspberry sauce.

2.   Place the template on a plate slightly off-center and trace with the raspberry sauce. Create two raspberry sauce "stems" shooting out from the raspberry sauce "leaf." Place a dot of sauce at the end of each "stem."

3.   Fill a large phyllo pastry cup with ⅙ of the apple filling, top with some streusel, and dust with confectioners' sugar. Fill a small phyllo pastry cup with a scoop of French cinnamon vanilla ice cream and sprinkle with chopped dried cranberries and chopped toasted walnuts.

4.   Place each cup at the end of a stem.

Pear Tatin with Vanilla Ice Cream and Caramel Sauce

YIELD: *12 servings*

LINCOLN CARSON
PICASSO
LAS VEGAS, NV

Traditional tarte Tatin is but a faint echo of this pear-starred version by Lincoln Carson. With coconut shortbread replacing the puff pastry and pears in caramel sauce subbing for apples, the dessert is lent presentation, crunch, and flavor with vanilla tuiles. And with vanilla ice cream accompanying the warm tart, there is temperature contrast. "Caramel and pear and ice cream—it is definitely classically based," remarks Carson. "Served hot, it comes together as more than the sum of its parts. It's simple things that work very well together."

SPECIAL EQUIPMENT: *Twelve non-stick aluminum flan molds, 4" [10.2 cm] top diameter × 3⅛" [7.9 cm] bottom diameter × ¾" [1.9 cm] high*

VANILLA ICE CREAM:

16 liq oz [473 ml] heavy cream

27 liq oz [799 ml] half-and-half

9 oz [255 g] granulated sugar

4 vanilla beans, split and scraped

16 oz [454 g] egg yolks

1. In a saucepan, combine the heavy cream, half-and-half, sugar, and vanilla bean seeds and bring to a boil; remove the pan from the heat.

2. In a bowl, whisk the yolks until blended. Temper the yolks with about half of the hot cream mixture and pour the yolk-cream mixture back into the saucepan. Cook over low heat until the mixture reaches the custard stage.

3. Immediately strain the custard into a bowl set over an ice bath and cool completely.

4. Refrigerate until cold or, preferably, overnight.

5. Process the mixture in an ice cream machine according to the manufacturer's instructions.

VANILLA TUILES:

6 oz [170 g] confectioners' sugar, sifted

4.25 oz [120 g] all-purpose flour, sifted

½ vanilla bean, split and scraped

5.25 oz [149 g] egg whites

3 oz [85 g] unsalted butter, melted

1. Combine the sifted sugar and flour with the vanilla bean seeds in a mixer fitted with a paddle attachment. Gradually add the egg whites and beat at medium speed until smooth. Slowly drizzle in the butter and mix until the butter is absorbed and the batter is well blended. Refrigerate for at least one hour.

2. Preheat the oven to 350°F [175°C]. Line a baking sheet with a silicone baking mat. Cut a stencil of a right triangle 8¼" [21 cm] high with a 2" [5.1 cm] base.

3. Place the stencil over the silicone mat and spread a thin layer of vanilla tuile batter through the stencil. Remove the stencil and bake for 6 to 8 minutes or until the tuile is light brown. Bend the tuile over a bowl. Allow to cool completely. Repeat to make 12 tuiles.

COCONUT SHORTBREAD:

7 oz [198 g] cake flour, sifted

8 oz [227 g] unsweetened coconut, shredded

5 oz [142 g] unsalted butter, softened

1.5 oz [43 g] confectioners' sugar

1.5 liq oz [45 ml] water, divided

1. In a bowl, combine the sifted cake flour and coconut.

2. In a mixer fitted with a paddle attachment, beat the butter at medium speed until smooth. Gradually add the confectioners' sugar and continue beating until the mixture is light.

3. Reduce the speed to low and add the dry ingredients; mix until the clumps are the size of peas. Add 1 liq oz [30 ml] of the water and mix until the mixture begins to come together as a dough. Add the remaining .5 liq oz [15 ml] of water if the mixture seems dry, and continue to mix until the dough is formed. Shape the dough into a disk; wrap with plastic wrap and refrigerate for at least one hour.

4. On a work surface that has been lightly dusted with flour, roll the dough out to ⅛″ [.3 cm] thick. Using a 4″ [10.2 cm] round cutter, stamp out 12 rounds of dough. Place them on a parchment-lined baking pan; cover with plastic wrap and chill for at least one hour.

CARAMEL SAUCE:

8 liq oz [237 ml] water, divided

14 oz [397 g] granulated sugar

1. In a heavy saucepan, combine 4 liq oz [118 ml] of the water and the sugar. Cook over medium heat, stirring constantly, until the mixture comes to a boil and the sugar dissolves. Continue to boil the syrup until it almost reaches a medium brown caramel.

2. Remove the pan from the heat and cover the pan [or use a sheet pan as a cover]. Very carefully slide the cover off just enough to create a small opening and slowly pour in the remaining water. Remove the cover and return the pan to the heat. Bring the sauce to a boil, stirring constantly to dissolve any hardened bits of caramel.

3. To check the consistency of the sauce, pour a small amount onto a cold plate. The sauce should be neither too thick nor too runny. Allow the sauce to cool.

PEAR-CARAMEL FILLING:

24 oz [680 g] granulated sugar

4 liq oz [118 ml] water, divided

9 oz [255 g] unsalted butter, softened

1½ vanilla beans, split and scraped

3 liq oz [89 ml] Poire William

30 lightly poached, peeled, halved, and cored baby Seckel pears

1. Place the sugar in a large heavy-bottomed saucepan. Use a metal spoon to mix in as much of the water as is needed so that the mixture is the consistency of wet sand. Cook the mixture over medium-high heat until the sugar begins to melt and caramelize around the edges. At this point, reduce the heat and stir the melting sugar so that it caramelizes evenly. Allow the syrup to reach a medium brown caramel. If any lumps of sugar remain, reduce the heat to its lowest setting and stir constantly until the sugar is completely melted.

2. Remove the pan from the heat and add in the butter, stirring gently until completely incorporated. Add the vanilla bean seeds and then carefully add the Poire William.

3. Arrange 5 Seckel pear halves in each of the flan pans, cut side down. Spoon enough melted caramel filling in the spaces between the pear halves to come almost to the top of the pan.

ASSEMBLY:

Caramel spiral decorations

Mint sprigs

1. Preheat the oven to 350°F [175°C].

2. Top a pear-caramel filled pan with a round of coconut shortbread. Bake for 25 to 30 minutes or until the shortbread is light brown. Let rest for 5 minutes.

3. Invert the warm pear Tatin onto the center of a dessert plate. Drizzle caramel sauce around the tart. Top the pears with a scoop of vanilla ice cream.

4. Arrange a vanilla tuile, a caramel spiral, and a mint sprig on the tart.

Caramelized Apple Phyllo Crisp

YIELD: *8 servings*

JAMES FORAN

SILK'S
SAN FRANCISCO, CA

James Foran presents "a different version of a crisp." Sheets of phyllo are baked with honey, butter, and finely ground hazelnuts. And then comes a torrent of what Foran calls "big flavors:" the apples are sautéed in Calvados, the ice cream is flavored with cassina, an Indian cinnamon that is, says Foran, very fruity and strong. The red wine cherry sauce features a dry, medium-body Merlot with cinnamon, chestnut honey, and orange zest. The dramatic garnish is a matter of placing apple chips in descending order and bonding them with powdered sugar in the oven.

SPECIAL EQUIPMENT: *Eight stainless steel ring molds, 3" [7.6 cm] diameter*

CRISP:

1.9 oz [54 g] light brown sugar

1.75 oz [50 g] granulated sugar

3.7 oz [105 g] all-purpose flour

.75 oz [21 g] quick-cooking oats

1.25 oz [35 g] hazelnuts, toasted and skinned

¼ tsp [2 g] salt

4 oz [113 g] unsalted butter, cold and cubed

1.   Preheat oven to 325°F [165°C]. In a food processor combine the brown sugar, granulated sugar, flour, oats, hazelnuts, and salt. Add the butter and pulse until the mixture has reached a crumbly texture.

2.   Spread the mixture evenly onto a half sheet pan and bake for 10 to 15 minutes or until it is light brown. Cool completely, then break it into large pieces.

CARAMELIZED APPLES:

8 tart apples, large and firm

8.75 oz [248 g] granulated sugar

1 vanilla bean, split and scraped

1 lemon, juiced

¼ tsp [2 g] salt

3 oz [85 g] unsalted butter

4 liq oz [118 ml] Calvados

1.   Peel the apples and cut them into ½" [13 mm] thick slices. Toss the apples with the sugar, vanilla, lemon juice, and salt.

2.   In a large sauté pan, melt the butter over medium-high heat. Add the apple mixture and sauté until the apples are soft and evenly caramelized, turning as infrequently as possible so as to keep the apples intact. Remove the pan from the heat and carefully deglaze it with the Calvados.

PHYLLO SHELLS:

3 sheets phyllo dough

2 oz [57 g] unsalted butter, melted

1.5 oz [43 g] honey

1 oz [28 g] hazelnuts, toasted and finely ground

¼ tsp [2 g] salt

1.   Preheat oven to 350°F [175°C]. Brush one sheet of phyllo with butter and drizzle half of the honey over it. Sprinkle with half of the hazelnuts and salt. Place another sheet of phyllo on top, brush it with butter, and repeat the process with the remaining honey, hazelnuts, and salt. Top with the third sheet of phyllo. Cover the dough with a clean, dry cloth and flatten it with a rolling pin.

2.   Cut the dough crosswise into ¾″ [19 mm] strips. Wrap each strip around a buttered ring mold and fasten the end with a drop of water. Bake seam side down for 8 to 12 minutes or until light brown. Remove the rings immediately and cool.

RED WINE-DRIED CHERRY SAUCE:

10 liq oz [296 ml] Merlot wine

1 strip orange zest

2 Tbs [30 ml] orange juice

¼ cinnamon stick

1.3 oz [37 g] granulated sugar

1 Tbs [21 g] chestnut honey

½ vanilla bean, scraped

1.75 oz [50 g] dried cherries

1.   In a saucepan combine all the ingredients except the cherries and reduce the mixture over low heat until syrupy, about one hour.

2.   Strain the syrup and return it to the pan. Add the cherries and heat over a low flame for a few more minutes or just until the cherries are soft. Remove the pan from the heat and cool.

INDIAN CINNAMON ICE CREAM:

8 liq oz [237 ml] milk

8 liq oz [237 ml] heavy cream

2 oz [57 g] cassina [Indian cinnamon]

2.6 oz [74 g] egg yolks

3.5 oz [99 g] granulated sugar

¼ tsp [1 g] vanilla extract

Pinch of salt

1. In a saucepan combine the milk, cream, and cassina and bring to a boil. Remove the pan from the heat, cover it, and let it steep for 30 minutes.

2. Strain the milk mixture to remove the cassina, and return it to a boil. Whisk together the egg yolks and sugar and temper them into the milk mixture. Cook gently, stirring, until the mixture coats the back of a wooden spoon. Add the vanilla and salt and cool completely over an ice bath.

3. Process in an ice cream machine according to the manufacturer's instructions.

APPLE GARNISH:

2 large firm apples

1.5 oz [43 g] confectioners' sugar

1. Preheat a convection oven to 200°F [95°C]. Slice the apples to about the thickness of a dime and cut a hole from the center of each slice.

2. Dust a silicone baking mat with half of the confectioners' sugar. Arrange the apples in 8 rows of 5 slices of descending size, with adjacent slices overlapping. Dust the tops of the apples with the remaining sugar and bake for 30 to 40 minutes or until the apples are dry.

ASSEMBLY:

1. Drizzle some of the red wine-dried cherry sauce on each dessert plate. Place a phyllo shell in the center. Fill the shell about three-quarters of the way with caramelized apples, packing them in tightly. Fill the shell to the top with crisp.

2. Top the crisp with a quenelle of Indian cinnamon ice cream and an apple garnish.

Quince and Apple Dome

YIELD: *12 servings*

MICHAEL HU

NEW YORK, NY

"This is a version of a tarte Tatin," says Michael Hu. "The downfall of tarte Tatin is that if you don't do it à la minute, right out of the oven onto the plate, the puff pastry starts to get soggy. And the key to tarte Tatin is that each ingredient has its own identity but it harmonizes with the others." Here, the puff pastry is fashioned into thin discs, which serve as a base for poached red, green, and yellow apples, quince poached in a Sauterne and then caramelized, and dried fruits. Packed into a demisphere and unmolded, it is served with caramelized hazelnuts, caramel apple cider sauce, and zucchini flowers, which are sprayed with sugar syrup and dried in a low oven. "It's labor-intensive but it's worth it," says Hu.

SPECIAL EQUIPMENT: *Twelve 4 oz [118 ml] demisphere molds*

PUFF PASTRY DISCS:

3 oz [85 g] cocoa paste, melted

3 oz [85 g] almond paste

1 sheet frozen puff pastry, thawed

Confectioners' sugar

1. Combine the cocoa paste and almond paste in a mixing bowl.

2. Spread a thin layer of the mixture on the puff pastry sheet. Roll up lengthwise into a log, 2" to 3" [5 cm to 7.6 cm] in diameter. Freeze until firm, about 1 hour.

3. Preheat the oven to 400°F [205°C]. Slice the log into ½" [1.3 cm] slices. Sprinkle with confectioners' sugar and roll out the slices as thinly as possible, 4" to 5" [10 cm to 12.7 cm] in diameter.

4. Bake the discs in between parchment paper on a sheet pan with several sheet pans on top until golden brown, about 20 minutes.

5. Cut the discs while still warm into 4" [10 cm] circles. With a 1" [2.5 cm] circle, cut a round out of each that is slightly off-center.

STREUSEL TOPPING:

4 oz [113 g] almond paste

4 oz [113 g] brown sugar

4 oz [113 g] granulated sugar

3 oz [85 g] muesli

9.5 oz [269 g] unsalted butter, divided

11 oz [312 g] bread flour

2 tsp [8 g] cinnamon

½ tsp [2 g] salt

1. In a mixer with the paddle attachment, cream the almond paste, both sugars, and the muesli.

2. Add 4 oz [113 g] of the butter. Add the dry ingredients.

3. Melt the remaining 5.5 oz [156 g] butter. Add it to the almond paste mixture.

4. Refrigerate the dough for 2 hours or overnight.

5. Preheat the oven to 350°F [175°C]. Push the dough through a cooling rack. Bake on a parchment-lined half sheet pan until the outside is crunchy but the inside is still soft, about 15 to 20 minutes. Let cool.

POACHED QUINCE:

1 qt [946 ml] water

2 lb [907 g] granulated sugar

8 liq oz [227 ml] Sauterne wine

1 vanilla bean, split and scraped

2 tsp [8 g] anise seed

3 large quince, peeled and cored

1. Combine the water, sugar, Sauterne, vanilla bean, and anise in a saucepan. Bring to a boil.

2. Add the quince and simmer until a skewer will go through the center of the fruit. Remove the quince and place it in an ice bath. Reserve the quince in the poaching liquid.

POACHED APPLE SLICES:

1 red apple

1 green apple

1 yellow apple

1.5 qt [1.4 lt] reserved quince poaching liquid

1. Slice the apples into thin slices using a mandoline.

2. In a saucepan bring the poaching liquid to a boil and pour it over the apple slices. Allow to cool.

SAUTÉED DRIED FRUITS:

3.5 oz [99 g] dried strawberries, cut into small dice

3.5 oz [99 g] dried cherries, cut into small dice

3.5 oz [99 g] dried apricots, cut into small dice

3.5 oz [99 g] dried figs, cut into small dice

8 liq oz [237 ml] Calvados or apple brandy

2 Granny Smith apples, peeled, cored, and cut into small dice

6 oz [170 g] unsalted butter

1. In the mixing bowl combine the dried fruits and Calvados. Let the fruits soak for 1 hour. Strain.

2. Sauté the dried fruits and half of the diced apples in the butter. Cook so that the apples remain firm.

3. Reserve the remaining diced apples.

SAUTÉED QUINCE:

3 oz [85 g] granulated sugar

3 oz [85 g] unsalted butter

3 poached quince, cut into 16 wedges each

4 oz [113 g] Calvados

In a saucepan caramelize the sugar. Stir in the butter. Add the quince and cook until tender and golden brown. Stir in the Calvados.

CARAMELIZED HAZELNUTS:

8 oz [227 g] granulated sugar

16 whole hazelnuts, toasted

1. In a saucepan caramelize the sugar.
2. Attach the bamboo skewers to the hazelnuts using a drill-like motion. Dip the hazelnuts into the caramel. Allow the caramel to drip off of the nuts. Reserve 1 Tbs [14 g] of the caramel.

CARAMEL APPLE CIDER SAUCE:

1 Tbs [14 g] reserved caramel

2 Tbs [28 g] unsalted butter

8 liq oz [237 ml] apple cider

3 Tbs reserved quince poaching liquid

1. In a saucepan heat the caramel.
2. Stir in the butter, cider, and poaching liquid. Bring the mixture to a boil and simmer until it has thickened.

ASSEMBLY:

Quince poaching liquid

Puff pastry discs

Caramelized hazelnuts

Caramel apple cider sauce

1. Line twelve 4 oz [118 ml] demisphere molds with apple slices.
2. Place 4 wedges of sautéed quince on top.
3. Combine the dried fruit with the remaining diced apples and 7 oz [198 g] of the streusel. Pack the mixture into the molds on top of the fruit.
4. Pour some of the poaching liquid on top of the fruit.
5. Cut out a small cardboard circle and use it to unmold each sphere.
6. Place each demisphere on a plate. Garnish with a puff pastry disc, caramelized hazelnut, and some caramel apple cider sauce.

Citrus-Laced Strawberry Crêpes with Poppy Seed Ice Cream

KEITH JEANMINETTE

MASA'S
SAN FRANCISCO, CA

Crêpes flavored with citrus support a mixed grill of mango and strawberry coulis, mango sorbet, poppy seed ice cream, fresh strawberries, and a citrus-kissed sauce. "I love extremely moist and light desserts with a minimum of sugar," says Keith Jeanminette. "I like to make my desserts so moist that they just about quench your thirst."

CRÊPES:

4.25 oz [120 g] all-purpose flour

1.5 Tbs [18 g] granulated sugar

1 Tbs [6 g] finely grated orange zest

Pinch of salt

6 liq oz [177 ml] nonfat or low-fat milk

3.5 oz [99 g] eggs

.65 oz [18 g] egg yolks

4 liq oz [118 ml] water

4 liq oz [118 ml] orange juice

1 tsp [4 g] vanilla extract

2 oz [57 g] unsalted butter, melted

1. In a mixing bowl combine the flour, sugar, orange zest, and salt. Whisk in about two-thirds of the milk to make a thick batter, then whisk in the remaining milk. Add the eggs and egg yolks and whisk thoroughly. Mix in the water, orange juice, and vanilla extract. If the batter is too thick, add a little more water.

2. Heat a crêpe pan or a small skillet. Lightly brush the pan with melted butter. Pour approximately 1 liq oz [30 ml] of crêpe batter into the center of the pan and tilt the pan until the batter coats the entire surface. Cook just until the edges of the crêpe turn golden. Flip the crêpe and cook the reverse side for about 10 seconds, then remove the crêpe from the pan. Repeat the process with the remaining batter.

POPPY SEED ICE CREAM:

1 pint [473 ml] half-and-half

.9 oz [26 g] poppy seeds

1 vanilla bean, split and scraped

5.25 oz [149 g] granulated sugar, divided

6.5 oz [184 g] egg yolks

1 pt [473 ml] heavy cream

4.2 oz [119 g] sour cream

1.   In a saucepan combine the half-and-half, poppy seeds, vanilla bean, and 3.5 oz [99 g] of the sugar and bring it to a simmer over medium heat. In a bowl whisk together the egg yolks and the remaining 1.75 oz [50 g] of sugar. Temper in the hot liquid. Reduce the heat to low and cook, stirring, until the mixture reaches 160°F [71°C]. Pour the mixture into a clean bowl and chill over an ice bath.

2.   Remove the vanilla bean and mix in the heavy cream and sour cream. Process in an ice cream machine according to the manufacturer's instructions.

MANGO SORBET:

7 oz [198 g] granulated sugar

8 liq oz [237 ml] water

2 drops lemon juice

4 mangoes, peeled and cut into small pieces

5 limes, juiced

1.   In a saucepan combine the sugar, water, and lemon juice. Bring the mixture to a boil. Remove the pan from the heat and let the syrup cool completely.

2.   Purée the mango pieces in a blender. Add the lime juice and 2 liq oz [59 ml] of the syrup. Taste the mixture and, if necessary, add up to 1 liq oz [30 ml] of additional syrup. Process in an ice cream machine according to the manufacturer's instructions.

CRÊPE SAUCE:

14 oz [397 g] granulated sugar

2 liq oz [59 ml] water

6 liq oz [177 ml] lemon juice

6 liq oz [177 ml] orange juice

1 vanilla bean, split and scraped

1 cinnamon stick, lightly toasted

2 oranges

1.   In a saucepan combine the sugar and water and cook until it becomes a pale amber-colored syrup. Slowly add the lemon juice and orange juice. Add the vanilla bean and cinnamon stick. Bring the syrup to a simmer just until all the hardened sugar has dissolved, then remove it from the heat.

2.   Wash the oranges in very hot water to remove any pesticides, residue, and wax. Zest the oranges over the pot using a zesting stripper so that the zest and orange oil fall into the pot. Remove the vanilla bean and cinnamon stick.

ASSEMBLY:

Unsalted butter

Fresh strawberries, thinly sliced

Mango coulis

Strawberry coulis

Caramel-dipped almond slices

Mint sprigs

1. For each serving being assembled, warm 2 Tbs [30 ml] of crêpe sauce and whisk in 1 Tbs [14 g] of butter.

2. Place two crêpes in the center of each dessert plate. Cover the crêpes with circles of thinly sliced strawberries. Drizzle the strawberries and crêpes with the sauce. Place a scoop of poppy seed ice cream in the center of the crepes. Top the ice cream with a quenelle of mango sorbet.

3. Decorate the plate with dots of mango coulis, and make a small dot of strawberry coulis in the center of each. Garnish with caramel-dipped almond slices and mint sprigs.

Trio of Apples

YIELD: *12 servings*

JILL ROSE

URBAN HORIZONS
FOOD CO.
BRONX, NY

Granny Smith and Braeburn are the duo from which is spun the trio of refashioned classics—apple tarte Tatin [employing cardamom dough], confit of apple, and apple sauce [frozen]. Benign apple flavor, its sweetness cut with lemon juice, plays beautifully against the cranberry compote, the Kahlua-kissed chocolate sauce, and the cardamom. Calvados sabayon, brisk apple cider granité, cranberry and Calvados anglaise, fresh apples, and apples in a citric syrup finish the plate.

SPECIAL EQUIPMENT: *Twelve 2¼″ [5.7 cm] square ring molds*

CARDAMOM DOUGH:

18 oz [510 g] unsalted butter

13.5 oz [383 g] granulated sugar

1.8 oz [50 g] eggs

1 vanilla bean, split and scraped

1.5 lb [680 g] pastry flour

¼ tsp [2 g] salt

¼ tsp [.5 g] ground cardamom

In mixing bowl cream together the butter and sugar. Add the eggs and vanilla bean. Add the remaining ingredients and mix until combined. Refrigerate until firm, about ½ hour.

APPLE TARTE TATIN:

20 Granny Smith apples, peeled, cored, and cut into ¼″ [.63 cm] slices

3.9 oz [110 g] unsalted butter

7 oz [200 g] granulated sugar

1. Preheat oven to 350°F [175°C]. Butter and sugar twelve 2¼″ [5.7 cm] square ring molds and place on a silicone baking mat-lined sheet pan.

2. In a saucepan, sauté the apples in the butter and sugar. Drain off the liquid.

3. Place the apples in the prepared molds. Bake for 45 minutes, or until caramelized.

4. Roll out the cardamom dough and cut twelve 2½″ [6.3 cm] squares. Dock the dough and place it on top of the apples. Bake until browned, about 20 minutes. Invert the tartes while still warm.

APPLE SAUCE:

6 Braeburn apples, peeled, cored, and chopped

6 Granny Smith apples, peeled, cored, and chopped

3 qt [2.8 lt] water

7 oz [200 g] granulated sugar

3 cinnamon sticks

Lemon juice, to taste

1. In a large saucepan, combine all the ingredients except the lemon juice and bring to a boil.

2. Simmer, covered, until the liquid is reduced. Add the lemon juice. Spread the mixture on a parchment-lined sheet pan. Place in the freezer until firm, about 1 hour.

3. Cut out twelve 2″ [5 cm] rounds.

APPLE CONFIT:

15 Braeburn apples, round sides sliced off

14 oz [397 g] granulated sugar

1. Preheat oven to 350°F [175°C].

2. Toss the apple slices with the sugar. Bake, uncovered, on a double-perforated pan for 20 minutes. Cover and bake for 15 to 20 minutes. Reserve the liquid.

CRANBERRY COMPOTE:

3.5 oz [100 g] cranberries

3.5 oz [100 g] granulated sugar

1 vanilla bean, split and scraped

In a saucepan, combine the ingredients, cover with water, and bring to a boil. Simmer until the mixture becomes syrupy. Drain the cranberries, reserving the liquid.

APPLE CIDER GRANITÉ:

1 gal [3.8 lts] apple cider

17.7 oz [500 g] light corn syrup

3.5 oz [100 g] lemon juice

14 oz [400 g] Calvados

2 cinnamon sticks

1. In a saucepan, combine all the ingredients and bring to a boil. Simmer and reduce by half.

2. Pour into a hotel pan and freeze, scraping occasionally until set.

CALVADOS SABAYON:

11.7 oz [332 g] egg yolks

2.5 oz [70 g] granulated sugar

1.8 oz [50 g] Calvados

2 Tbs [25 ml] lemon juice

In a mixing bowl, whisk all the ingredients over a water bath until thickened. Refrigerate until ready to serve.

NOUGATINE:

8.8 oz [250 g] unsalted butter

5.3 oz [150 g] glucose

3.5 oz [100 g] milk

10.6 oz [300 g] granulated sugar

.2 oz [5 g] pectin

1.8 oz [50 g] cocoa bean nibs

1. Preheat oven to 350°F [175°C]. Line a sheet pan with a silicone baking mat.

2. In a saucepan, combine the butter, glucose, and milk. Heat to 115°F [47°C].

3. Add the sugar and pectin. Cook to 243°F [117°C].

4. Spread onto the prepared pan. Roll out very thinly. Sprinkle with cocoa bean nibs. Bake just until caramelized.

CALVADOS ANGLAISE:

8.5 liq oz [250 ml] milk

8.5 liq oz [250 ml] heavy cream

3.5 oz [100 g] granulated sugar, divided

5.25 oz [149 g] eggs

1.95 oz [55 g] egg yolks

1.8 oz [50 g] Calvados

1 tsp [4 g] vanilla extract

1. In a saucepan, bring the milk, heavy cream, and 1.75 oz [50 g] of the sugar to a boil.

2. In a separate bowl, combine the eggs, yolks, and remaining 1.75 oz [50 g] of the sugar. Temper and add to milk mixture. Add the Calvados and vanilla extract. Cook to 185°F [85°C], stirring constantly. Strain. Cool over an ice bath.

APPLES IN CITRIC SYRUP:

3.4 liq oz [100 ml] lemon juice

1.7 liq oz [50 ml] water

1.8 oz [50 g] granulated sugar

1 Granny Smith apple, cored and thinly sliced

In a saucepan, bring the lemon juice, water, and sugar to a boil. Cool. Add the apple slices to the syrup.

PASTRY TRIANGLES:

2 phyllo sheets or Yufka pastry dough

2 liq oz [59 ml] simple syrup

1.   Preheat oven to 350°F [175°C]. Line a sheet pan with greased crinkled foil.

2.   Brush 2 layered sheets of pastry with syrup. Cut into 5″ × 3″ [12.7 cm x 7.6 cm] triangles. Place on the prepared pan. Bake until browned, about 10 minutes.

CHOCOLATE SAUCE:

4.4 oz [125 g] bittersweet chocolate, melted

1.4 oz [40 g] clabber cream

1.4 oz [40 g] unsalted butter, melted

.2 oz [5 g] coffee paste

.7 oz [20 g] brandy

.7 oz [20 g] Kahlua

.5 oz [15 g] corn syrup

In a saucepan, combine all the ingredients and heat until smooth. Strain.

ASSEMBLY:

1 Granny Smith apple, julienned and tossed with apple jus

1.   Cut the apple tarte in half. Place one half on a plate with a pastry triangle against the cut side.

2.   Place an apple sauce disc next to the tarte and wrap apple slices around three-quarters of the disc. Top with sabayon, granité, and some julienned apple.

3.   Place some julienned apple on the plate. Top with apple confit and cranberry compote. Drizzle with cranberry jus and Calvados anglaise.

Cassis-Poached Pear with Pistachio Ice Cream and Lavender Crystallized Sugar

YIELD: *12 servings*

SEBASTIEN CANONNE

THE FRENCH PASTRY SCHOOL
CHICAGO, IL

A depth of tantalizing flavors and spectacular presentation hoist the familiar poached pear into another realm. Poached in a cassis-red wine sauce also flavored with rosemary, thyme, black peppercorns, and fruit, the pear is accompanied by lavender-flavored rock sugar shards, pistachio ice cream, sauce from the poaching liquid, pastillage coral, and a spun sugar nest.

CASSIS-POACHED PEARS:

48 liq oz [1 lt, 420 ml] red wine

1 bay leaf

1 sprig fresh rosemary

1 sprig fresh thyme

6 black peppercorns

1 lb [454 g] red currants [individually quick-frozen]

4.4 oz [125 g] raspberries [individually quick-frozen]

4.4 oz [125 g] blackberries [individually quick-frozen]

4.4 oz [125 g] blueberries [individually quick-frozen]

9 oz [255 g] sucrose

12 Florelle pears

1. In a large saucepan, combine all the ingredients except the pears. Bring to a boil; add the pears. Cook the pears in the simmering syrup until tender.

2. Leave the pears in the poaching liquid, refrigerated, for at least 2 days.

CRYSTALLIZED SUGAR:

1 pt [473 ml] water

3 lb [1.36 kg] granulated sugar

Lavender essence, as needed

Lavender flowers, as needed

1. Boil the water and sugar to 198°F [92°C]. Pour the syrup into a very clean container.

2. Sprinkle some sugar crystals [about 2 oz/57 g], lavender essence, and flowers on top of the syrup. Allow the container to stand undisturbed for 24 to 72 hours to promote crystal formation.

PISTACHIO ICE CREAM:

4 oz [113 g] granulated sugar, divided

1.4 oz [40 g] trimoline

22 liq oz [650 ml] whole milk

1.3 oz [37 g] nonfat milk powder

2.4 oz [68 g] unsalted butter [preferably 82% fat]

1.2 oz [34 g] pistachio paste

1.2 oz [34 g] pistachio purée

1 oz [28 g] egg yolks

1¼ tsp [5 g] ice cream stabilizer

1¼ tsp [5 g] kirsch

1. Combine half the sugar with the trimoline by rubbing together. Combine the whole milk and milk powder in a saucepan and heat to 77°F [25°C]. Add the trimoline-sugar mixture to the warm milk.

2. Continue heating and stirring the mixture. Add the butter at 95°F [35°C]. Add the pistachio paste and pistachio purée at 98.5°F [37°C]. Add the egg yolks at 104°F [40°C].

3. Rub together the remaining sugar with the ice cream stabilizer and add to the mixture when it reaches 113°F [45°C]. Continue stirring the mixture, heat to 185°F [85°C], and cook for another 2 minutes.

4. Cool the mixture over an ice bath, whisking occasionally to ensure emulsification. Whisk in the kirsch. Allow the mixture to mature for 12 hours in the refrigerator.

5. Process in an ice cream machine according to the manufacturer's instructions.

SUGAR NESTS:

32 oz [907 g] isomalt

8 liq oz [237 g] water

Pinch of cream of tartar

Food coloring, as needed

1. Mix together the isomalt, water, and cream of tartar in a heavy saucepan. Heat to between 300°F and 310°F [150°C to 155°C] over high heat and add the food coloring.

2. Continue to cook the mixture to 329°F [165°C]. Immediately remove the pan from the heat and plunge the bottom of the pan in cold water to stop the cooking process. Remove the pan from the water and allow the syrup to stand for a few minutes to thicken slightly.

3. Spread silicone baking mats over a work surface. Dip a cut-off whisk in the syrup and flick it back and forth over the baking mats to create spun sugar. Form the spun sugar into "nests."

4. Place the sugar "nests" into an airtight container with a small cup of limestone.

fruit desserts

CASSIS-RED WINE SAUCE:

Reserved poaching liquid, as needed

2 oz [57 g] unsalted butter [preferably 82% butterfat]

1.   Strain the poaching liquid into a saucepan and reduce until the mixture coats the back of a spoon.

2.   Add the butter in small amounts, stirring the liquid gently with a wooden spoon until the butter is completely combined. Serve immediately.

ASSEMBLY:

Black or red currants, as needed

1.   Drizzle each plate with a small amount of cassis-red wine sauce. Place a sugar nest in the center of each plate. Slice the pears in half and remove the cores. Make horizontal slices in half of the pear halves.

2.   Place one horizontally sliced pear half and one whole pear half in each nest. Place a quenelle of pistachio ice cream next to the pear halves and top with crystallized sugar. Garnish the plates with a few black or red currants.

Pinot Gris-Saffron-Poached Pears with Vanilla Bean Panna Cotta

MARSHALL ROSENTHAL

THE RENO HILTON
RENO, NV

Key lime juice, Pinot Gris, and saffron punch up the poaching liquid in this exotic and flavorful neoclassic, while oven-roasted sundried cranberries poached in Tawny port add even more tang and zest. The saffron adds not only pungency but an intriguing color as well. "This is one of the desserts I made for the Culinary Olympics in Germany in 1996," notes Rosenthal. "The judges seemed pleased."

SPECIAL EQUIPMENT: *Three 3¼" [8.25 cm] savarin molds*

POACHED PEARS:

5 Bartlett pears

33.8 liq oz [1 lt] Pinot Gris wine

8 liq oz [237 ml] Key lime juice

10 saffron stamens

1 lb, 4 oz [567 g] granulated sugar

1. Carefully peel the pears, cut them in half, and remove the cores using a melon baller. De-vein and remove the stem. Level the bottom [not the cut side] of the pear halves so they will sit level on the plate. Reserve the pears in a bowl of lemon water.

2. Combine the wine, Key lime juice, saffron stamens, and sugar. Bring to a boil. Reduce to a simmer and add the pears. Poach for 20 to 30 minutes, until fork tender.

3. Keep the pears in the poaching liquid, refrigerated for 3 days before serving.

PANNA COTTA CREAM:

1¾ tsp [4 g] powdered gelatin

4 oz [113 g] whole milk

7 oz [198 g] heavy cream

2 oz [57 g] granulated sugar

¼ tsp lemon zest

Pinch of ground cinnamon

1 Bourbon vanilla bean, split and scraped

1. Bloom the gelatin in the milk. Lightly coat three 3¼" [8.25 cm] savarin molds with non-stick spray.

2. Combine the heavy cream, sugar, lemon zest, and cinnamon in a saucepan. Scrape the vanilla bean seeds into the mixture. Bring to a boil over medium-high heat. Reduce the heat and cook for 5 minutes, stirring often.

3. Gradually stir the gelatin-milk mixture into the cream mixture. Stir the mixture until completely combined. Do not bring to a boil.

4. Pour the mixture into a bowl and place in an ice bath. Stir continuously until the mixture begins to cool.

5. Fill the prepared savarin molds to the top with the mixture. Refrigerate for about 3 hours, until set.

STEWED SPICED CRANBERRIES:

10 oz [283 g] dried cranberries

8 oz [227 g] Tawny port

4 oz [113 g] spring water

½ tsp [1 g] orange zest

¼ tsp [.5 g] grated nutmeg

1 cinnamon stick

Combine all of the ingredients in a saucepan and bring to a boil. Reduce the heat and simmer for approximately 40 minutes, until the mixture begins to thicken. Remove from the heat and chill completely.

HIPPEN LEAVES:

10 oz [283 g] almond paste

3.15 oz [89 g] large egg whites

1 oz [28 g] high gluten flour

1 tsp [7 g] salt

¼ tsp [.5 g] allspice

¼ liq oz [7 ml] orange juice

1.   In a mixer, using a paddle attachment, begin mixing the almond paste and gradually add the egg whites. Blend in the remaining ingredients and mix well. Cover and refrigerate for 1 hour.

2.   Preheat oven to 350°F [175°C]. Lightly grease and flour the back of a sheet pan. Prepare a leaf template. Stencil the batter using the leaf template and bake until golden brown.

3.   Remove the leaves while still hot, and bend to give "lifelike" shape.

ASSEMBLY:

Honeydew melon balls

1.   Place a pear half in the center of a plate. Unmold a panna cotta and cut in half. Fit the semicircle of panna cotta around the rounded back of the pear. Slice a pear half into 2 pieces and fan one of the quarters on one side of the plated pear. Halve a melon ball and place it off the side of the fanned pear.

2.   Place a hippen leaf behind the standing pear, in the panna cotta. Strain the cranberries and place a few of the berries on the plate. Garnish the plate with the cranberry sauce.

Pineapple Surprise

YIELD: *10 servings*

JACQUY PFEIFFER

THE FRENCH PASTRY
SCHOOL
CHICAGO, IL

*"In Europe they have desserts
that they call this-or-that surprise," says Jacquy Pfeiffer.
"It is usually pineapple filled
with sorbet and with
meringue on top. Instead, I
have caramelized the pineapple with some vanilla beans
to cut some of the acidity. We
put a coconut sorbet on top
and a pineapple chip. I like
to cut the pineapple lengthwise—it gives you a different
look."*

PINEAPPLE CHIPS:

24 oz [675 g] granulated sugar

17 liq oz [500 ml] water

1 unripe pineapple, peeled, thinly sliced lengthwise, 1½" [3.8 cm] widthwise

1. Preheat oven to 200°F [95°C].

2. In a saucepan, combine the sugar and water and bring to a boil. Keep the syrup hot.

3. Pour the hot syrup over the pineapple slices and cover with plastic wrap. Let stand for 3 hours.

4. Drain the slices. Spread on a silicone baking mat-lined sheet pan and bake until dry, about 1 hour. Let cool. Store in an airtight container.

ROASTED PINEAPPLE:

1 large pineapple, peeled

2.1 oz [60 g] unsalted butter

2.1 oz [60 g] brown sugar

1½ Tahitian vanilla beans, split and scraped

Cornstarch, as needed

1. Preheat oven to 400°F [205°C].

2. Place the pineapple, butter, sugar, and vanilla beans in a deep sauté pan.

3. Roast the pineapple until a golden brown color, about 15 to 20 minutes. Add water as needed. Baste with juice from the pan.

4. Remove the pineapple. Thicken the juice with cornstarch. Strain. Keep the pineapple warm.

COCONUT SORBET:

24.5 liq oz [724 ml] water

12 oz [340 g] granulated sugar

2.4 oz [68 g] dextrose

4 oz [113 g] powdered glucose

.2 oz [7 g] ice cream stabilizer

.1 oz [4 g] sorbet stabilizer

2.2 lb [1 kg] coconut purée

Heat the water in a saucepan. Add the dry ingredients, stirring quickly. Cover and cook to 185°F [85°C]. Cool in an ice bath. Let stand for 3 hours. Fold in the purée and mix with a handheld blender. Process in an ice cream machine according to the manufacturer's instructions.

ASSEMBLY:

Vanilla beans

Place a slice of roasted pineapple on a warm plate. Top with a quenelle of sorbet, a pineapple chip, and a vanilla bean. Serve with the roasted pineapple juice.

Tropical Fruit Glaze

YIELD: *4 servings*

THOMAS WORHACH

FOUR SEASONS HOTEL
AND RESORT
PALM BEACH, FL

Shimmering gelatin sheaths a marbelized chocolate wrap, which encloses a coconut cream and chiffon cake center, with diced tropical fruits and coulis to finish the plate. Worhach has served this as a passion fruit gelatin for extra flavor dimension, but it is painstaking to achieve: "What's hard about making it is to get it so that it's still pliable," he says. "You don't want it too rubbery, so you have to measure exactly." Adorning his plate is a ginger flower, the petals of which do carry a ginger flavor, and cactus pear, mango, kiwi, and crème fraîche sauces. "This is a very light dessert," says Worhach, "and rather than serving whipped cream on top, we've placed the cream portion in the middle."

SPECIAL EQUIPMENT: *Four 5 oz [148ml] [2½" [6.3 cm] high] timbale molds*

RUM-SOAKED CHIFFON CAKE:

9 oz [255 g] cake flour

3¾ tsp [18 g] baking powder

½ Tbs [10 g] salt

3.9 oz [111 g] egg yolks

5 liq oz [148 ml] vegetable oil

11 oz [312 g] granulated sugar

½ Tbs [6 g] vanilla extract

½ tsp [2 g] lemon extract

6 liq oz [177 ml] water

9 oz [255 g] egg whites

¾ tsp [2 g] cream of tartar

4 oz [113 g] rum-flavored simple syrup

1. Preheat the oven to 350°F [175°C]. Spray a half sheet pan with nonstick cooking spray and line it with parchment paper.

2. Sift together the flour, baking powder, and salt; set aside.

3. In a mixer with the whisk attachment, beat together the yolks, oil, sugar, and vanilla and lemon extracts at high speed for 5 minutes, or until pale and doubled in volume. Add the water and beat 2 minutes longer. Gently fold in the dry ingredients in 3 additions.

4. Beat the egg whites and cream of tartar until stiff, but not dry. Fold the whites into the batter. Spread the batter into the prepared pans and bake 10 to 15 minutes, until golden. Unmold and cool the cake.

5. Cut out four 1¼" [4.4 cm] circles from the cake and soak them with the rum-flavored simple syrup.

COCONUT CREAM:

.6 oz [18 g] large-flake shredded coconut

1 oz [28 g] white chocolate

3 oz [113 g] pastry cream

3 oz [113 g] cream of coconut, such as Coco Lopez

8 oz [227 g] heavy cream, whipped

1. Toast the coconut. Melt the white chocolate and quickly stir into the pastry cream.

2. Blend the cream of coconut with the white chocolate mixture.

3. Gently fold the coconut and whipped cream into the mixture. Measure the diameter of the openings of the 5 oz timbale molds. Pipe the mixture into four rounds that are the same size as the openings of the molds and refrigerate until set.

4. Place one of the coconut cream discs on each of the four 1¾" [4.4 cm] diameter cake circles.

ASSEMBLE THE WHITE CHOCOLATE WRAP:

2 oz [57 g] yellow chocolate, tempered

2 oz [57 g] orange chocolate, tempered

8 oz [170 g] white chocolate, tempered

One 3 oz [85 g] package Tropical Fruit Jell-O

1. Cut a sheet of acetate into four 3" × 6" [7.6 cm × 15.24 cm] strips. Pour the yellow and orange chocolates into parchment cones. Randomly pipe the 2 chocolates on each acetate strip. Allow the chocolate to partially set. Spread a thin layer of white chocolate over the yellow and orange design on each strip.

2. When the chocolate is almost set, wrap 1 strip around each chiffon-coconut cream disc. Refrigerate until the chocolate is completely set.

3. Carefully peel the acetate from the chocolate wrap. Place each cylinder upside-down in a 2½" [6.3 cm] high, 5 oz [148 ml] timbale mold.

4. Dissolve the gelatin and allow to cool. Fill each timbale with the gelatin and refrigerate until set.

5. Carefully unmold by running each timbale under warm water.

ASSEMBLY:

4 oz [113 g] mango, peeled and cut into medium dice

4 oz [113 g] papaya, peeled and cut into medium dice

4 oz [113 g] kiwi, peeled and cut into medium dice

4 oz [113 g] pineapple, peeled and cut into medium dice

Rasberries

Assorted tropical fruit coulis

1. Toss all the diced fruits together and reserve.

2. Place a chocolate-wrapped dessert onto a dessert plate, slightly off-center. Fill the remainder of each cylinder with the melange of chopped tropical fruits. Garnish the plate with a few halved raspberries and an assortment of tropical fruit coulis.

Delice de Saveurs Exotique Glacé

YIELD: *10 servings*

MICHEL WILLAUME

THE RITZ-CARLTON HOTEL
SAN FRANCISCO, CA

Tropical flavors burst from every sauce, tuile, sorbet, and parfait on this vibrant plate. Mango sorbet encloses a core of frozen coconut vanilla parfait and pineapple juice, with exotic [mango, passion fruit, lemon, and banana] sauce, vanilla juice, exotic [orange and mango] tuiles, and a spicy Kalamansi jelly to round out the dizzying flavor experience.

SPECIAL EQUIPMENT: *Ten demisphere molds, 1½" [3.8 cm] diameter; ten demisphere molds, 3" [7.6 cm] diameter*

BISCUIT MOELLEUX PINEAPPLE COCONUT:

9.6 oz [272 g] egg whites, divided

4.2 oz [119 g] granulated sugar

3.7 oz [105 g] almond flour

3.7 oz [105 g] confectioners' sugar

1.8 oz [51 g] all-purpose flour

.7 liq oz [21 ml] heavy cream

1.8 oz [51 g] fresh pineapple, finely chopped

2.1 oz [60 g] fresh coconut, grated and toasted

1.   Preheat oven to 425°F [220°C]. In a mixer whip 7 oz [198 g] of the egg whites to soft peaks while slowly adding the granulated sugar. Sift together the almond flour, confectioners' sugar, and all-purpose flour and gently fold the mixture into the whipped egg whites. Fold in the heavy cream and the remaining 2.6 oz [74 g] of the egg whites.

2.   Spread the batter evenly onto a half sheet pan lined with a silicone baking mat. Sprinkle the pineapple and coconut over the cake. Bake for 7 to 9 minutes or until it springs back when gently pressed with a finger. Cool completely.

COCONUT VANILLA PARFAIT:

6 liq oz [177 ml] coconut purée [10% sugar]

6 oz [170 g] fresh coconut, grated

4 vanilla beans

4.2 oz [119 g] granulated sugar

4.4 oz [125 g] egg yolks

1.1 oz [31 g] invert sugar

12 liq oz [355 ml] heavy cream, whipped to soft peaks

1.   In a saucepan, combine the coconut purée, grated coconut, and vanilla beans, and heat until the vanilla beans puff. Remove the pan from the heat and scrape the seeds from the vanilla beans into the coconut mixture. Cover with plastic wrap and steep for 30 minutes.

2.   Add the sugar and egg yolks to the saucepan and cook gently, stirring, until the mixture reaches 185°F [85°C]. Strain it through a chinois into a mixer bowl and whip until cool.

3.   Add the invert sugar and gently fold in the whipped cream. Fill 1½" [3.8 cm] diameter demisphere molds with the parfait and freeze until set.

MANGO SORBET:

9.6 liq oz [284 ml] water

5 oz [142 g] granulated sugar, divided

2.3 oz [65 g] atomized glucose

1.1 oz [31 g] stabilizer

27 oz [765 g] mango purée [10% sugar]

1.   In a saucepan, combine the water, 3.5 oz [99 g] of the sugar, and the glucose, and bring to a boil. Remove the pan from the heat and add the stabilizer mixed with the remaining 1.5 oz [43 g] of the sugar. Heat the mixture to 185°F [85°C], then cool over an ice bath. Refrigerate for at least 3 hours.

2.   Combine the syrup with the mango purée and strain through a chinois. Process in an ice cream machine according to the manufacturer's instructions.

KALAMANSI JELLY:

10 liq oz [296 ml] water

10.5 oz [298 g] granulated sugar

3 dried red peppers

10.5 oz [298 g] Kalamansi lemon purée

.44 oz [12.5 g] gelatin sheets, bloomed

1.   In a saucepan, combine the water, sugar, and red peppers, and heat just until all of the sugar has dissolved. Add the Kalamansi lemon purée and the gelatin.

2.   Strain the mixture through a chinois and pour it onto a half sheet pan. Chill until set.

EXOTIC TUILES:

14.1 oz [400 g] granulated sugar

3.5 oz [99 g] all-purpose flour

2.1 liq oz [62 g] orange juice

3 oz [85 g] mango purée

5 oz [142 g] unsalted butter, melted

1. Preheat oven to 375°F [190°C]. Place a sheet pan in the oven to warm. In a mixer with the paddle attachment, combine the sugar and flour. Add the orange juice and mango purée. Mix in the melted butter.

2. Spread a thin coat of the batter through a triangle-shaped stencil onto a silicone baking mat. Transfer the mat onto the warm sheet pan and return it to the oven. Bake for 4 to 5 minutes or until the edges turn golden. As soon as the tuiles have begun to set, flip them over onto a cool surface. Let set completely.

EXOTIC SAUCE:

16 liq oz [473 ml] exotic purée [mango, passion fruit, lemon, and banana] [10% sugar]

½ tsp [3 g] pectin

.9 oz [26 g] granulated sugar

2.7 g [77 g] invert sugar

1. In a saucepan heat the exotic purée to 113°F [45°C]. Add the pectin mixed with the granulated sugar.

2. Bring the purée to a boil, then remove it from the heat and add the invert sugar. Cool over an ice bath.

VANILLA JUICE:

16 liq oz [473 ml] water

½ lemon, zested

½ orange, zested

6 vanilla beans

7 oz [198 g] granulated sugar

1 Tbs [14 g] pectin

1 Tbs [16 g] lemon juice

1. In a saucepan combine the water, lemon zest, orange zest, and vanilla beans, and heat to 113°F [45°C]. Add the sugar and pectin and bring the mixture to a boil for 3 minutes, then remove the pan from the heat. Add the lemon juice and steep for 30 minutes.

2. Strain the juice through a chinois and refrigerate.

PINEAPPLE COULIS:

12 liq oz [355 ml] fresh pineapple purée

1.1 oz [31 g] invert sugar

Mix together the pineapple purée and invert sugar.

Pulled sugar leaves and stems

1.   Fill 3″ [7.6 cm] diameter demisphere molds about two-thirds of the way with mango sorbet, packing it tightly to make sure there are no air bubbles. Scoop out a 1½″ [3.8 cm] ball from the center. Pour a small amount of pineapple coulis into the hole, then fill it with a demisphere of frozen coconut vanilla parfait. Fill the mold almost all the way with mango sorbet, then top it with a 3″ [7.6 cm] circle of biscuit. Freeze until set.

2.   Place a bombe in the center of each dessert plate. Carefully attach a tuile and a pulled sugar stem and leaf to the bombe. Decorate the plate with exotic sauce, vanilla juice, and small cubes of Kalamansi jelly.

spoon desserts

CHAPTER 2

Butterscotch Rice Pudding with Huckleberries and White Chocolate Ice Cream

YIELD: *14 servings*

CHRIS BROBERG

LESPINASSE
NEW YORK, NY

"Rice pudding is everyone's baby food, basically, but adults love it," says Chris Broberg. "We've played with it. Inside are whole almonds, pistachios, and raisins." Accompanying the rice pudding are the contrasting and reinforcing flavor elements of a huckleberry compote, white chocolate ice cream and mousse, butterscotch sauce, and a honey tuile. "Huckleberries are tart and white chocolate is sweet. With a side-by-side presentation, we're placing two things you wouldn't expect together. We call attention to that. The almonds are cooked with the milk, and they become soft, which gives them a texture you wouldn't expect as well."

SPECIAL EQUIPMENT: *Twelve 2¼" [7 cm] diameter × 1¼" [3.2 cm] high individual cake molds; ice cream machine; silicone baking mat*

RICE PUDDING:

4.2 oz [120 g] white rice

16.9 liq oz [500 ml] milk

2.8 oz [80 g] brown sugar

4.2 oz [119 g] eggs

1 Tbs [12 g] vanilla extract

.7 oz [20 g] dark raisins

1 oz [30 g] almonds, toasted

.7 oz [20 g] pistachios

1 lb [450 g] granulated sugar

1. Preheat the oven to 325°F [165°C]. Combine the rice with enough water to cover, and boil for 20 minutes. Drain.

2. Scald the milk in a saucepan. Add the rice and simmer covered for 15 minutes.

3. Combine the brown sugar, eggs, vanilla extract, raisins, toasted almonds, and pistachios. Temper with the hot rice mixture. Remove from the heat.

4. Caramelize the granulated sugar in a saucepan. Pour into twelve 2¼" [7 cm] diameter × 1¼" [3.2 cm] high individual cake molds. Pour 4 oz [115 g] of rice pudding on top. Bake in a water bath for about 15 minutes.

WHITE CHOCOLATE ICE CREAM:

12.8 liq oz [379 ml] milk

12.8 liq oz [379 ml] heavy cream

5.6 oz [160 g] granulated sugar, divided

1.3 oz [36 g] egg yolks

10.6 oz [300 g] white chocolate, chopped

1. Combine the milk, cream, and 2.8 oz [80 g] of the granulated sugar in a saucepan.

2. Combine the egg yolks and the remaining 2.8 oz [80 g] of granulated sugar. Temper with the milk mixture. Return to the heat and cook to 183°F [85°C]. Strain. Add the white chocolate and stir until melted. Cool over an ice bath. Process in ice cream machine according to the manufacturer's instructions.

HUCKLEBERRY COMPOTE:

14 oz [400 g] huckleberries

3.2 oz [90 g] granulated sugar

3.4 liq oz [100 ml] water

Combine all the ingredients in a saucepan. Simmer until thickened.

WHITE CHOCOLATE MOUSSE:

12.7 oz [360 g] white chocolate, chopped

1 oz [28 g] unsalted butter

20.3 liq oz [600 ml] heavy cream, divided

1.3 oz [36 g] egg yolks

.35 oz [10 g] gelatin sheets, bloomed and melted

1.   Combine the white chocolate, butter, and 3.4 liq oz [100 ml] of the heavy cream over a water bath.

2.   In a mixing bowl, whip the remaining 16.9 liq oz [500 ml] of heavy cream to soft peaks.

3.   Combine the yolks and melted gelatin. Add to the chocolate mixture. Fold in the whipped cream. Chill.

BUTTERSCOTCH SAUCE:

2.3 oz [64 g] corn syrup

3 oz [86 g] brown sugar

.6 oz [17 g] unsalted butter

¼ tsp [2 g] salt

1.6 liq oz [48 ml] half-and-half

Combine the corn syrup, brown sugar, butter, and salt in a saucepan. Bring to a boil and cook for 5 minutes. Add the half-and-half. Strain.

HONEY TUILE:

.4 oz [11 g] unsalted butter

1.6 oz [44 g] confectioners' sugar

1.6 oz [44 g] honey

.4 oz [12 g] egg whites

2 oz [56 g] all-purpose flour

.13 liq oz [4 ml] hot water

1. Preheat oven to 325°F [165°C].

2. In mixing bowl, cream together the butter and sugar. Add the remaining ingredients, scraping down the sides after each addition.

3. Spread the batter over a 4″ [10 cm] 7-petal stencil onto a silicone baking mat-lined sheet pan. Bake until lightly browned, 6 to 8 minutes. Press the tuile into a tea strainer to form a cup. Repeat with the remaining batter.

SPUN SUGAR:

3.5 oz [100 g] fondant patissier

1.8 oz [50 g] glucose

Red and yellow powdered vegetable dye, as needed

Combine the fondant patissier and glucose in a saucepan and cook to a light caramel. Add the red and yellow powdered vegetable dyes to create an orange color. Remove from the heat and cool until thickened. Spin over oiled rods.

ASSEMBLY:

Spoon some butterscotch sauce onto a plate. Place a rice pudding on top of the sauce. Top with a flower tuile. Pipe a rosette of mousse in the tuile. Place the spun sugar in a tea strainer. Top with a quenelle of white chocolate ice cream and huckleberry compote.

Milk Chocolate and Banana Mousse Box with Amaretto Ice Cream and Caramelized Bananas

YIELD: *16 servings*

PAT COSTON

MERCER KITCHEN
NEW YORK, NY

Inside the deceptively simple box are nine layers—four layers of B&B-soaked devil's food cake, two layers of milk chocolate ganache, one layer of banana mousse, and two layers of milk chocolate squares, "for textural difference," says Coston. "The fork goes through it very easily, then you hit the milk chocolate disks submerged in banana mousse." A milk chocolate triangle, caramelized bananas, chocolate tuiles, and milk and dark chocolate sauces finish the plate.

SPECIAL EQUIPMENT: *Sixteen square metal molds, 2" × 2" × 2½" [5 × 5 × 6.3 cm]; sixteen round cylinders, 1½" × 1" [3.8 × 2.5 cm]; Wagner airless paint sprayer; acetate sheets*

DEVIL'S FOOD CAKE:

3.5 oz [99 g] eggs

1.3 oz [37 g] egg yolks

2 oz [57 g] unsalted butter, melted

8 liq oz [237 ml] brewed coffee

8 liq oz [237 ml] buttermilk

1 tsp [4 g] vanilla extract

14 oz [397 g] granulated sugar

7.5 oz [213 g] all-purpose flour

3.3 oz [95 g] cocoa powder

2 tsp [10 g] baking soda

1 tsp [5 g] baking powder

¼ tsp [2 g] salt

1. Preheat oven to 350°F [175°C]. Line 2 half sheet pans with greased parchment paper.

2. In a mixing bowl, whisk together the eggs, yolks, and butter. Add the remaining liquid ingredients.

3. In a separate mixing bowl combine the dry ingredients. Add to the liquid ingredients.

4. Pour into the prepared pans. Bake until the cake springs back when touched, about 10 minutes.

SYRUP:

14 oz [397 g] granulated sugar

4 liq oz [118 ml] B&B liqueur

12 liq oz [355 ml] water

Combine all the ingredients in a saucepan and bring to a boil. Let cool.

MILK CHOCOLATE AND AMARETTO ICE CREAM:

32 liq oz [237 ml] heavy cream

16 liq oz [473 ml] milk

6 oz [170 g] granulated sugar

4 liq oz [118 ml] amaretto liqueur

9.8 oz [278 g] egg yolks

5.3 oz [150 g] milk chocolate

1. Line a half sheet pan and the 16 round cylinders with parchment paper.

2. In a saucepan bring the cream, milk, and sugar to a boil.

3. Combine the amaretto and yolks. Whisk some of the hot cream mixture into the yolks and return this mixture to the saucepan. Cook until the temperature reaches 185°F [85°C]. Remove from the heat and add the milk chocolate. Stir until the chocolate is melted. Strain through a fine-mesh sieve. Cool the mixture over an ice bath. Process in an ice cream machine according to the manufacturer's instructions. While the ice cream is still soft, pipe into the cylinders. Level off the top and freeze for at least 2 hours or overnight.

MILK CHOCOLATE SAUCE:

16 liq oz [473 ml] heavy cream

8 oz [227 g] milk chocolate

In a saucepan, bring the cream to a boil. Pour over the chocolate and stir until blended. Let cool.

DARK CHOCOLATE SAUCE:

8 liq oz [237 ml] heavy cream

3.5 oz [99 g] granulated sugar

2 oz [57 g] unsalted butter

4 oz [113 g] bittersweet chocolate, chopped

In a saucepan, bring the cream, sugar, and butter to a boil. Pour over the chocolate and stir until the chocolate is completely melted. Let cool.

BANANA MOUSSE:

11.8 oz [335 g] banana purée

1.8 oz [50 g] granulated sugar

2 Tbs [25 g] lemon juice

.17 oz [5 g] gelatin sheets, bloomed and drained

4 liq oz [118 ml] heavy cream, whipped to soft peaks

1. Combine the banana purée, sugar, and lemon juice. Strain through a fine-mesh sieve.

2. Dissolve the gelatin over low heat and add to the purée mixture.

3. Fold in the whipped cream.

MILK CHOCOLATE GANACHE:

8 liq oz [237 ml] heavy cream
8 oz [227 g] milk chocolate

In a saucepan, bring the heavy cream to a boil. Pour over the milk chocolate and stir until blended.

MILK CHOCOLATE SQUARES:

12 oz [340 g] tempered milk chocolate

1. Spread the chocolate in thin layers on acetate sheets.

2. Cut thirty-two 1½″ [3.8 cm] squares while chocolate is still slightly soft. Refrigerate.

ASSEMBLY:

Caramelized bananas
White and dark chocolate cigarettes
Chocolate triangles
Tuiles
Sugar rods

1. Brush the cake with syrup.

2. Cut sixty-four 2″ [5 cm] squares and sixteen 1½″ [3.8 cm] rounds from the cake.

3. Line a half sheet pan with parchment paper and sixteen 2″ [5 cm] square molds.

4. Layer each mold with a square cake layer, ⅜″ [9.5 mm] layer of ganache, a second cake layer, ¾″ [19 mm] layer of banana mousse, a milk chocolate square pressed into the mousse touching the cake, another chocolate square, a third cake layer, a layer of ganache, and a fourth cake layer.

5. Weigh down the top of the molds with a piece of parchment paper and a sheet pan and refrigerate overnight.

6. Place the boxes in the freezer for 1 to 2 hours. Unmold and place in the freezer for 15 minutes.

7. Pour spraying chocolate into the Wagner paint sprayer and spray the boxes until covered.

8. Place sixteen 1½″ [3.8 cm] rounds of cake in the freezer. Unmold the ice cream cylinders and place on the cake. Return to the freezer.

9. Place the painted box on the plate with an ice cream cylinder. Garnish with milk and dark chocolate sauces, caramelized bananas, cigarettes, chocolate triangles, tuiles, and sugar rods.

Dark Chocolate and Macadamia Mousse Timbale

YIELD: *8 servings*

PAT COSTON

MERCER KITCHEN
NEW YORK, NY

"Rarely do you see macadamia nut taken to this extent," says Pat Coston with characteristic understatement. "I wanted to utilize it in its whole form, and then purée it, making paste and using the oil." The result of this experiment: Under a chocolate glaze are layers of macadamia chocolate cake, macadamia brûlée, and macadamia mousse, with macadamia praline and macadamia anglaise as accompaniments. "This was one of our best sellers at the Cypress Club," says Coston. "It's not as heavy as it looks; the macadamia brûlée cuts the richness of the mousse, and the mousse is not that heavy—we lightened it with whipped cream and crème fraîche."

SPECIAL EQUIPMENT: *Eight 2" × 3" × 2" [5 cm × 7.6 cm × 5 cm] elliptical molds; eight 2" × 10" [5 cm × 25 cm] acetate sheets*

MACADAMIA CRÈME BRÛLÉE:

8 liq oz [237 ml] heavy cream

8 liq oz [237 ml] milk

2.5 oz [71 g] granulated sugar

2 oz [57 g] macadamia paste

3.25 oz [92 g] egg yolks

.17 oz [5 g] gelatin sheets, softened and drained

1. Preheat oven to 250°F [121°C].

2. In a saucepan, bring the cream, milk, sugar, and macadamia paste to a boil. Remove from heat and cool in an ice bath.

3. Add the egg yolks. Strain. Pour the brûlée mixture into a half sheet hotel pan and cover with foil.

4. Place the pan in a larger pan and fill with water to the same level as the brûlée. Bake until set, about 1½ hours.

5. Refrigerate overnight.

6. Add the gelatin; set aside.

MACADAMIA CHOCOLATE CAKE:

4 oz [113 g] unsalted butter

8.5 oz [241 g] granulated sugar

4 oz [113 g] macadamia paste, divided

3.5 oz [99 g] eggs

6.3 oz [177 g] cake flour

2 oz [57 g] cocoa powder

1¼ tsp [8 g] salt

1 tsp [5 g] baking soda

1 tsp [5 g] baking powder

8 liq oz [237 ml] water

2 liq oz [59 ml] simple syrup

1. Preheat oven to 350°F [175°C]. Line a half sheet pan with greased parchment paper.

2. In a mixing bowl, cream the butter, sugar, and 2 oz [57 g] of the macadamia paste. Gradually beat in the eggs.

3. Sift together the dry ingredients and add to the egg mixture. Add the water.

4. Spread the mixture into the prepared pan. Bake 10 to 12 minutes.

6. While the cake is still hot, brush with the remaining 2 oz [56 g] of macadamia paste and simple syrup. Let cool.

7. Cut into sixteen 2″ × 3″ × 2″ [5 cm × 7.6 cm × 5 cm] elliptical pieces.

MACADAMIA CHOCOLATE MOUSSE:

6 oz [170 g] macadamia paste

2 oz [57 g] bittersweet chocolate

1.3 liq oz [37 ml] milk

1 oz [28 g] unsalted butter

2 oz [55 g] egg yolks

4 oz [113 g] granulated sugar

6 liq oz [177 ml] heavy cream, whipped to soft peaks

4 oz [113 g] crème fraîche

2.5 oz [71 g] dry cake crumbs

1. In a saucepan, heat the macadamia paste, chocolate, milk, and butter until warm.

2. In a mixing bowl, whip the yolks and sugar to the ribbon stage. Temper in the chocolate mixture.

3. Fold in the whipped cream, crème fraîche, and cake crumbs.

PRALINE:

1 oz [28 g] macadamia paste, melted

1.8 oz [50 g] bittersweet chocolate, melted

2.6 oz [75 g] toasted macadamia nuts, ground

1. Combine the macadamia paste and chocolate. Add the nuts. Spread onto a parchment-lined sheet pan about ⅛″ [3 mm] thick. Refrigerate.

2. Cut out eight 2″ × 3″ × 2″ [5 cm × 7.6 cm × 5 cm] elliptical shapes. Place in the freezer until ready to assemble.

CHOCOLATE GLAZE:

2.8 oz [78 g] bittersweet chocolate, chopped

.8 oz [21 g] cocoa butter, chopped

2 liq oz [59 ml] milk

1.5 liq oz [44 ml] water

1 oz [28 g] granulated sugar

1 oz [28 g] unsalted butter

1.   In a mixing bowl combine the chocolate and cocoa butter.

2.   In a saucepan bring the milk, water, sugar, and butter to a boil. Pour over the chocolate mixture and mix until blended. Strain.

ASSEMBLY:

Tempered chocolate

Chocolate cigarettes

Piped sugar strands

Tuile shapes

Chocolate sauce

Macadamia anglaise

1.   Place eight 2″ × 3″ × 2″ [5 cm × 7.6 cm × 5 cm] elliptical molds on a half sheet pan.

2.   Place a layer of cake in the bottom of each mold followed by a layer of mousse, a layer of praline, a layer of brûlée [equal in thickness to the mousse layer], and a layer of cake. Lightly press down on the layers. Refrigerate until firm or overnight.

3.   Remove the timbales from the molds and pour chocolate glaze on top.

4.   Spread an even layer of tempered chocolate over the acetate sheets and let set.

5.   While still pliable, wrap the strips around the timbales. Refrigerate until set. Remove the acetate. Garnish with chocolate cigarettes, piped sugar strands, and tuile shapes. Serve with chocolate sauce and macadamia anglaise.

Tropical Rice Pudding

YIELD: *6 servings*

BILL HALLION

THE RENAISSANCE
VINOY RESORT
ST. PETERSBURG, FL

Tropical fruits add flavor, texture, and exotica to this blank-slate childhood favorite. The accompanying kumquats are cooked in grenadine, for flavor as well as intriguing color. Chocolate work, a sugar thread, and sprayed cocoa powder beautify the plate. "A clear liqueur, like crème de cocoa, helps the cocoa powder to dry quickly on the plate," says Bill Hallion.

CHOCOLATE GARNISH:

Bittersweet chocolate, tempered, as needed

White chocolate, tempered, as needed

1. Pipe a freeform outline of a design on a piece of acetate with the tempered dark chocolate. Allow to set completely.

2. Fill in the dark chocolate outline with the tempered white chocolate. Allow to set completely.

RICE PUDDING:

1.5 qt [1.4 lt] whole milk

7 oz [198 g] long grain white rice

7 oz [198 g] granulated sugar

6 oz [170 g] tropical fruits, dried, finely diced

1 tsp [2 g] ground cinnamon

Pinch of salt

4 oz [113 g] unsalted butter, room temperature

7 oz [198 g] eggs

4.5 oz [128 g] egg yolks

2 Tbs orange compound

1. Combine the milk and rice in a saucepan and bring to a boil over medium heat. Reduce the heat to low and cook the rice for 1 hour.

2. Stir the sugar, dried tropical fruits, cinnamon, and salt into the rice. Continue to cook for another 30 minutes. Remove the pan from the heat. Preheat oven to 325°F [165°C]. Grease a half sheet pan with 1 oz [28 g] of the butter.

3. In a mixer, using the whisk attachment, beat the eggs and egg yolks until thick. Blend the beaten eggs, orange compound, and the remaining butter into the rice mixture.

4. Evenly spread the mixture onto the prepared pan. Bake in a water bath for 35 minutes.

GRENADINE KUMQUATS:

10 kumquats

7.8 oz [221 g] grenadine syrup

Slice the kumquats and cook in a saucepan with the grenadine syrup until the liquids reduce to a syrup. Remove the kumquats and allow to cool completely.

ROSE WATER ORANGE SAUCE:

8 liq oz [237 ml] orange juice

2 liq oz [59 ml] simple syrup

Rose water, as needed

Combine the orange juice and simple syrup in a saucepan and cook over medium heat until it thickens to a sauce-like consistency. Blend in the rose water to taste.

ASSEMBLY:

1 oz [28 g] cocoa powder

Clear liquor, such as vodka, as needed

1.   Combine the cocoa powder with enough clear liquor to make a sprayable consistency.

2.   Create a template for a plate design that mimics the design of the chocolate garnish. Place the template on the plate and lightly stencil the cocoa mixture with an airbrush.

3.   Line a 2¾″ [7 cm] diameter × 2⅓″ [5.8 cm] high cylinder mold with plastic wrap. Fill the mold with rice pudding. Remove the mold and place the pudding on the plate with a few kumquats and some rose water orange sauce. Place a chocolate garnish on top of the pudding.

Raspberry Bavarian

YIELD: *12 servings*

JOHN HUI

CAESAR'S PALACE
CASINO HOTEL
LAS VEGAS, NV

"This is a classic Bavarian, not lightened at all," says John Hui. "Of course, it is served more in the modern manner. In the old days, it would have been formed in a Jell-O mold and presented to the table for portioning." Raspberry is one of Hui's favorite dessert flavors, and it is the clear star of this dessert—in the Bavarian, in the coulis that accompanies it, and as a fresh garnish. Chopped pistachios add a faint crunch, and the tempered chocolate band is a chewy element in an otherwise smooth dessert that is, says Hui, "very refreshing for the summer."

SPECIAL EQUIPMENT: *Twelve ring molds, 3" [7.6 cm] diameter × 1½" [3.8 cm] high*

BAVARIAN:

5 liq oz [148 ml] milk

4 oz [113 g] egg yolks

2.5 oz [71 g] granulated sugar

.35 oz [10 g] gelatin, bloomed

7.5 oz [213 g] raspberry purée

20 liq oz [591 ml] heavy cream, whipped to soft peaks

1. In a saucepan, bring the milk to a boil. Whisk together the egg yolks and sugar and temper into the hot milk. Cook gently, stirring, until the mixture coats the back of a wooden spoon. Remove the pan from the heat. Add the gelatin and stir until it dissolves. Transfer the custard to a bowl and chill over an ice bath, whisking until it cools.

2. Fold the custard and the raspberry purée into the whipped cream. Fill the ring molds and chill to set.

RASPBERRY SAUCE:

1 oz [28 g] Clear Gel starch

10 liq oz [296 ml] water, divided

1 lb [454 g] granulated sugar

1 lb [454 g] raspberry purée

1. Dilute the Clear Gel in 2 liq oz [59 ml] of cold water. In a large saucepan, boil the remaining 8 liq oz [237 ml] of water. Whisk in the Clear Gel mixture and cook until thickened. Remove the pan from the heat. Add the sugar and stir until it dissolves. Mix in the raspberry purée.

2. Strain through a chinois and cool.

PASSION FRUIT SAUCE:

Follow the above recipe for Raspberry Sauce, substituting passion fruit purée for the raspberry purée.

WHITE CHOCOLATE SAUCE:

1 lb [454 g] white chocolate, finely chopped

1 pt [473 ml] heavy cream

1.   Place the chocolate in a large bowl. In a saucepan, bring the cream to a boil. Pour the hot cream over the chopped chocolate.

2.   Whisk until the chocolate is completely melted and smooth.

ASSEMBLY:

Raspberry Soft Gel

Gold-flecked transfer sheets

Tempered white chocolate

Tempered dark chocolate

Crème chantilly

Fresh raspberries

Chocolate curls

Chopped pistachios

1.   Spread a thin layer of raspberry Soft Gel on top of the Bavarians and unmold them.

2.   Cut the transfer sheets into 9¾" [24.8 cm] × 1¼" [3.2 cm] strips and pipe a design on them with tempered white and dark chocolates. Immediately wrap the strips around the Bavarians. When the chocolate has set, remove the plastic.

3.   Pipe the white chocolate sauce onto the dessert plates and allow it to set. Add the passion fruit sauce and raspberry sauce. Place a Bavarian in the center of each plate. Garnish with crème chantilly, fresh raspberries, chocolate curls, and chopped pistachios.

Maple Panna Cotta with Cranberry Coulis and Orange Sauce

YIELD: *14 servings*

DANIEL JASSO

WESTERN CULINARY
INSTITUTE
PORTLAND, OR

Nutty and fruity notes har-monize in Daniel Jasso's ren-dition of the classic Italian dessert, which has undergone a renaissance on American menus. Traditionally served in ramekins, this lightly ge-latinized cream is placed in teardrop molds for a sleek presentation. Accompanied with cranberry coulis, orange sauce, candied dried fig, and handpainted pulled-sugar tiger lily, the effect is, says Jasso, "still very simple."

SPECIAL EQUIPMENT: *Fourteen teardrop ring molds, 3½" [8.9 cm] long × 1⅛" [2.8 cm] high*

MAPLE PANNA COTTA:

12 liq oz [355 ml] heavy cream

16 liq oz [473 ml] maple syrup

20 liq oz [591 ml] milk

2 tsp [8 g] vanilla extract

1 oz [28 g] gelatin sheets, softened in cold water

1. Place the 14 teardrop ring molds on a sheet pan.

2. Combine the cream, maple syrup, milk, and vanilla extract in a large saucepan and cook over medium-low heat until the sugar is dissolved. Raise the heat and bring the mixture to a simmer; do not let boil. Remove the pan from the heat.

3. Drain the gelatin and whisk it into the hot cream mixture; strain the mixture into a stainless steel bowl, set over an ice bath, and stir until thickened but not set.

4. Fill the prepared molds with the maple panna cotta and refrigerate overnight.

CRANBERRY COULIS:

20 liq oz [591 ml] water

8 oz [227 g] granulated sugar

12 oz [340 g] fresh cranberries

1. In a large nonreactive saucepan, combine the water, sugar, and cranberries and bring the mixture to a boil; reduce the heat and simmer, stirring occasionally, for 10 minutes.

2. Purée the cranberry mixture in a food processor fitted with a metal blade. Pass the purée through a fine chinois into a clean saucepan.

3. Return the saucepan to the heat and bring the purée to a boil; skim off the foam; remove the pan from the heat and let the mixture cool.

4. Refrigerate the cranberry coulis until cold.

ORANGE SAUCE:

2.5 Tbs [19 g] cornstarch

20 liq oz [591 ml] fresh orange juice, strained, divided

4 oz [113 g] granulated sugar

1 Tbs [15 ml] fresh lemon juice

1.   In a small bowl, dissolve the cornstarch in 3 liq oz [89 ml] of the orange juice; set aside.

2.   Combine the remaining orange juice, the sugar, and the lemon juice in a large, nonreactive saucepan and cook over medium heat until the sugar is dissolved.

3.   Whisk in the dissolved cornstarch mixture and bring to a boil. Lower the heat and continue to cook for 1 minute, stirring constantly. Remove the pan from the heat and let the mixture cool.

4.   Refrigerate the orange sauce until cold.

CANDIED DRIED FIGS:

7 dried figs, cut in half vertically

16 liq oz [473 ml] water

32 oz [907 g] granulated sugar

7 oz [198 g] glucose

1.   Have ready 14 bamboo skewers and a pan of cold water to cool the bottom of the saucepan in which the syrup will be cooked. Place a few sheets of parchment paper on the floor, in front of a work surface, to catch excess dripping syrup. Place a strip of wood, such as a ruler, at the edge of the work surface, securing it by placing heavy weights at each end of the wood strip.

2.   Insert a bamboo skewer into the flat side of each fig half, penetrating about halfway through the dried fruit. Place the water, sugar, and glucose in a large heavy-bottomed saucepan and cook the syrup until golden brown. Immediately place the bottom of the saucepan in the pan of cold water. Let the caramel cool until thickened, but still liquid.

3.   Dip a skewered fig half into the caramel. Lift it out and hold it so that the tapered end is pointing down. Place the skewer under the ruler so that it extends out from the work surface and the caramel will drip onto the parchment paper on the floor. Repeat this procedure to make 14 candied fig halves.

4.   When the caramel on the figs is cooled and hardened, use a scissor to cut the caramel tail that has formed to the desired length. Leave the skewer in the figs until ready to plate. [This dipping procedure should be done as close as possible to service since moisture in the figs can cause the caramel to liquefy.]

ASSEMBLY:

Pulled-sugar tiger lily flowers

1. Unmold a maple panna cotta onto a dessert plate, off center, such that the point of the tear drop is near the back of the plate. Decoratively sauce the plate with cranberry coulis and orange sauce.

2. Place a pulled-sugar tiger lily flower on top of the panna cotta and arrange a candied dried fig half next to the panna cotta with the point facing up.

Manjari Mousse and Kumquat Cake

NORMAN LOVE

RITZ-CARLTON HOTEL
COMPANY
NAPLES, FL

The sweet-tart jolt of kumquat blends with the full flavor of Manjari chocolate for this sublime, surprising, streamlined cake. Chocolate sponge, flavored with Pur Caraibe and not cocoa, is layered with kumquat compote and Manjari mousse, and chocolate glazed. A marbled chocolate forms an off-center base, and the plate is finished with a pulled sugar ribbon, chocolate cigarettes, and kumquat compote.

SPECIAL EQUIPMENT: *Fourteen ring molds, 3" [7.6 cm] diameter × 1.5" [3.8 cm] high*

PUR CARAIBE CHOCOLATE SPONGE:

6.3 oz [180 g] Pur Caraibe chocolate, chopped

3 oz [85 g] unsalted butter

6.3 oz [180 g] egg whites

1.8 oz [50 g] granulated sugar

2.5 oz [70 g] egg yolks, at room temperature

1.   Preheat oven to 350°F [175°C]. Over a double boiler, melt the chocolate with the butter to approximately 110°F [43°C].

2.   In a mixer whip the egg whites with the sugar to medium peaks. Add the egg yolks and whisk just until they are incorporated. Fold in the chocolate mixture. Pipe the batter into 3" [7.6 cm] circles on half sheet pans lined with silicone baking mats. Bake for 9 to 11 minutes or until the cake springs back when gently pressed with a finger.

MANJARI MOUSSE:

4.2 oz [120 g] egg yolks

3.5 oz [100 g] granulated sugar

1.7 liq oz [50 ml] water

9.9 oz [280 g] Manjari chocolate, melted and kept warm

22 liq oz [651 ml] heavy cream, whipped to soft peaks

In a mixer whip the egg yolks until they are very light. At the same time, cook the sugar with the water to 250°F [121°C]. With the mixer on low speed, carefully pour the hot sugar into the whipping yolks. Beat in the melted chocolate. When the mixture has cooled slightly, lighten it with one-third of the whipped cream. Gently fold in the remaining whipped cream.

CHOCOLATE GLAZE:

53 oz [1.5 k] Cocoa Barry Noire pâte à glacer, finely chopped

13.2 oz [375 g] Valrhona 70% chocolate couverture, finely chopped

17 liq oz [500 ml] milk

12.7 liq oz [375 ml] heavy cream

8 liq oz [237 ml] water

8.8 oz [250 g] granulated sugar

8.8 oz [250 g] glucose

1. Combine the pâte à glacer and the chocolate in a large mixing bowl. In a saucepan, combine the milk, cream, water, sugar, and glucose. Bring the mixture to a boil and pour it over the chopped chocolates. Whisk until the glaze is completely smooth.

2. Let the glaze cool to 95°F [35°C].

KUMQUAT COMPOTE:

1 gal [3.8 l] fresh orange juice

4 liq oz [118 ml] Grand Marnier

4 liq oz [118 ml] grenadine syrup

2 vanilla beans, split and scraped

8 oz [227 g] granulated sugar

1 oz [28 g] cornstarch

2.5 lb [1.1 k] sliced kumquats

1. In a stockpot combine the orange juice, Grand Marnier, grenadine, vanilla beans, and sugar and bring the mixture to a boil. Make a slurry with the cornstarch and add it to the pot. Continue to boil for another minute.

2. Remove the pot from the heat. Add the sliced kumquats and allow them to steep until assembly time.

MARBLED CHOCOLATE SQUARES:

Pink oil-based food coloring, as needed

1 lb [454 g] cocoa butter, tempered

1 lb [454 g] white chocolate, tempered

1. Add just enough food coloring to the cocoa butter to tint it a uniform pink color and drizzle some of it onto a sheet of acetate. Immediately, before the cocoa butter has begun to set, pour some of the white chocolate over it. Use an offset spatula to even out the chocolate into a thin layer. As the cocoa butter and chocolate spread they will form a marble pattern.

2. When the chocolate has begun to set, cut it into 3″ [7.6 cm] squares. Let set completely.

ASSEMBLY:

Pulled sugar bows

Pulled sugar twists

Chocolate cigarettes

1. Line the ring molds with acetate and fill them about halfway with the mousse. Chill for a few minutes until the mousse has just begun to set.

2.   Fill the rings almost to the top with the kumquat compote. Place a chocolate sponge disc on top of the compote and press down gently. Chill until completely set.

3.   Cover a sheet pan with waxed paper and place a dipping screen on top of it. Invert the cakes so that the sponge is on the bottom and unmold them onto the dipping screen. When the glaze has cooled to 95°F [35°C], pour it over the cakes to coat them completely. Let the glaze set.

4.   Place a marbled chocolate square on each dessert plate with a mousse cake overlapping on top of it. Top each cake with a pulled sugar bow and twist. Garnish the plates with chocolate cigarettes and kumquat compote.

cakes, tarts, and pies

CHAPTER 3

Chocolate Marquise

YIELD: *72 servings*

D. JEMAL EDWARDS

NEW YORK, NY

A near-classic marquise is presented in the form of a pavé—cut into cubes and dusted—and paired with curry crème anglaise, pistachio crème anglaise, and pistachio brittle. The alteration in the classic marquise formula is a bow to sanitation. "Most marquises use raw egg yolks," says Jemal Edwards. "In France, they can. The eggs themselves and the sanitation of the eggs are better." Edwards took the precaution of making a pâte à bombe and a sugar syrup, which he drizzled over the eggs to cook them. "It doesn't change the texture or the color of the marquise," he says. He values Valrhona Guanaja for its high cocoa content and low sugar content—and because it stands up well to the curry powder used in the crème anglaise. He recommends madras curry powder: "It's one of the spiciest curry powders around. And it blends very well with the pistachio."

SPECIAL EQUIPMENT: *One 10″ [25.4 cm] square × 1½″ [3.8 cm] high baking pan*

CHOCOLATE MARQUISE:

26.25 oz [744 g] unsalted butter

29.75 oz [843 g] Valrhona Guanaja [70%] chocolate, chopped

6 liq oz [177 ml] water

12 oz [340 g] granulated sugar

13.25 oz [376 g] whole eggs

15.75 oz [447 g] egg yolks

5.25 oz [149 g] cocoa powder

35 liq oz [1035 ml] heavy cream, whipped to firm peaks

1. Place the butter and chopped chocolate in a bowl set over simmering water and melt together. Remove from the heat and keep warm.

2. In a saucepan, combine the water and sugar. Bring to a boil, making sure the sugar is completely dissolved, and cook to 240°F [116°C].

3. Meanwhile, in a mixer fitted with a whisk attachment, whip the eggs and yolks, until they reach full volume. Slowly add the hot syrup to the eggs while whipping. Add the cocoa powder and whip until well blended. Add the melted chocolate mixture and mix until combined.

4. With a rubber spatula, gently fold the whipped cream into the chocolate-egg mixture. Scrape the mixture into the 10″ [25.4 cm] square baking pan. (The mixture will be 1½″ [3.8 cm] in depth.)

5. Refrigerate the marquise overnight. Unmold and cut into 1½″ [3.8 cm] cubes.

CURRY CRÈME ANGLAISE:

16 liq oz [473 ml] heavy cream

16 liq oz [473 ml] milk

4 oz [113 g] granulated sugar

2 Tbs [30 g] curry powder

5.2 oz [147 g] egg yolks

1. In a saucepan, combine the heavy cream, milk, sugar, and curry powder and bring to just under the boil; remove the pan from the heat and allow to steep for 10 minutes.

2. In a bowl, whisk the egg yolks until blended. Return the cream mixture to the heat and bring to just under the boil; remove the pan from the heat. Temper the yolks with

the hot cream mixture and pour the yolk-cream mixture back into the saucepan. Cook over low heat until the mixture reaches the custard stage.

3. Immediately strain the custard through a fine chinois into a bowl set over an ice bath and cool completely. Refrigerate until cold.

PISTACHIO CRÈME ANGLAISE:

16 liq oz [473 ml] heavy cream

16 liq oz [473 ml] milk

4 oz [113 g] granulated sugar

5.4 oz [153 g] Delipaste ground pistachio nuts

5.2 oz [147 g] egg yolks

1. In a saucepan, combine the heavy cream, milk, sugar, and pistachio paste and bring to just under the boil; remove the pan from the heat.

2. In a bowl, whisk the egg yolks until blended. Temper the yolks with the hot cream mixture and pour the yolk-cream mixture back into the saucepan. Cook over low heat until the mixture reaches the custard stage.

3. Immediately strain the custard through a fine chinois into a bowl set over an ice bath and cool completely. Refrigerate until cold.

PISTACHIO BRITTLE:

4 tsp [20 g] salt

8 liq oz [237 ml] water

16 oz [454 g] granulated sugar

8 liq oz [237 ml] corn syrup

9.25 oz [262 g] raw Sicilian pistachio nuts

¼ tsp [.25 tsp] baking soda

.5 oz [14 g] unsalted butter

1. Dissolve the salt in a small amount of water.

2. In a saucepan, combine the water, sugar, and corn syrup and bring to a boil, making sure the sugar is completely dissolved. Cook until the syrup reaches 245°F [118°C]. Stir in the dissolved salt. Continue cooking the syrup until it reaches 265°F [129°C]. Stir in the nuts and cook until the pistachios are well-toasted and the syrup is golden brown. Remove from the heat and immediately add in the baking soda and butter. Mix well.

3. Pour the mixture onto a well-oiled marble surface and allow to set.

4. Break the brittle into 3″ to 4″ [7.6 cm × 10 cm] long shards.

ASSEMBLY:

Cocoa powder

Finely chopped Sicilian pistachio nuts

Tempered chocolate decorations

1. Dust a marquise cube with cocoa powder. Place the cube onto the center of a dessert plate.

2. Garnish the plate with curry anglaise, pistachio anglaise, and chopped pistachio nuts.

3. Insert a shard of pistachio brittle and two chocolate decorations into the marquise.

Chai-Spiced Mascarpone Honey Cake

YIELD: *8 servings*

JAMES FORAN
SILK'S
SAN FRANCISCO, CA

Honey cake encircles a portion of mascarpone mousse; the plate is finished with a generous drizzle of pumpkin rum raisin crème anglaise, wine-sautéed pears, pear chips, and a caramel stick. The subtle flavors in the cake and mousse are spiked with the rum-soaked raisins. This honey cake, says James Foran, is similar to a ginger cake, "but with something else." That something else is the Chai tea flavor; Foran's favorite blend for this recipe is "spicy, with orange zest and a little pepper in it."

HONEY CAKE:

7.7 oz [218 g] brown sugar

1.75 oz [50 g] granulated sugar

6.5 oz [184 g] all-purpose flour

1 tsp [5 g] baking powder

2 tsp [10 g] baking soda

3.5 oz [99 g] eggs

1.3 oz [37 g] egg yolks

8 liq oz [237 ml] strongly brewed Chai*

1 tsp [4 g] vanilla extract

2.9 oz [82 g] chestnut honey

5 oz [142 g] unsalted butter, melted

8 liq oz [237 ml] buttermilk, at room temperature

*A blend of black tea and spices; available at Middle Eastern markets.

1.   Preheat oven to 375°F [190°C]. Sift together the brown sugar, granulated sugar, flour, baking powder, and baking soda. In a separate bowl whisk together the remaining ingredients. Add the liquid mixture to the dry ingredients and whisk until thoroughly combined.

2.   Pour the batter into a well-greased 9″ × 13″ [23 cm × 33 cm] cake pan and bake for 35 to 40 minutes or until the cake is set and a tester comes out clean. Immediately invert the cake onto a rack and cool completely.

MASCARPONE MOUSSE:

1.3 oz [37 g] egg yolks

2 oz [57 g] granulated sugar

.08 oz [2.5 g] gelatin, bloomed

1 Tbs [19 g] Poire William

Pinch of salt

10 oz [283 g] mascarpone cheese, at room temperature

1.   Place the egg yolks in the bowl of an electric mixer and whip on high speed until they are very light and thick. Meanwhile, place the sugar in a small saucepan and add enough water to cover. Heat the sugar to 240°F [116°C]. With the mixer on low speed, carefully pour the syrup onto the whipping yolks. Melt the gelatin in the hot saucepan

[do not return it to the heat] and add it to the egg mixture. Add the Poire William and salt. Continue to whip until cool.

2.   Add the mascarpone and whip on medium speed to medium peaks, being careful not to overwhip. Refrigerate for several hours.

SAUTÉED PEARS:

4 large Bosc pears, ripe but slightly firm

1.75 oz [50 g] granulated sugar

2 tsp [10 g] lemon juice

2 liq oz [59 ml] dry white wine

1.   Peel and core the pears and cut them into eighths. In a large sauté pan, caramelize the sugar. Add the pears and lemon juice.

2.   Remove the pan from the heat and add the wine. Simmer over a low flame until the pears are soft.

PUMPKIN RUM RAISIN CRÈME ANGLAISE:

1.5 oz [43 g] black raisins

1 oz [28 g] yellow raisins

3 liq oz [89 ml] spiced rum

8 liq oz [237 ml] milk

8 liq oz [237 ml] heavy cream

2 whole cloves

1 small cinnamon stick

2.6 oz [74 g] egg yolks

3 oz [85 g] granulated sugar

½ tsp [2 g] vanilla extract

Pinch of salt

3 oz [85 g] fresh pumpkin purée

1.   In a small bowl combine the black raisins, yellow raisins, and rum, and soak overnight.

2.   In a saucepan, scald the milk, cream, cloves, and cinnamon stick. Cover the pan and let it steep for 10 minutes.

3.   Whisk together the egg yolks and sugar and temper them into the milk mixture. Cook gently, stirring, until the mixture coats the back of a wooden spoon. Strain and mix in the vanilla extract and salt.

4.   While the mixture is still hot, pour it into a blender and process with the pumpkin purée until smooth. Strain and chill over an ice bath.

5.   Add the raisins to the cooled cream.

PEAR CHIPS:

1 firm Bosc pear

1.5 oz [43 g] confectioners' sugar

1. Preheat a convection oven to 200°F [95°C]. Using a mandoline or deli slicer, cut the pear into slices about the thickness of a dime.

2. Dust a silicone baking mat with half of the sugar. Place the pear slices on top and dust with the remaining sugar. Bake for 30 to 40 minutes or until the pears are dry.

ASSEMBLY:

Caramel sticks

1. Cut the cake into eight 3″ [7.6 cm] circles and cut a 1″ [2.5 cm] circle from the center of each. Sauce each dessert plate with the pumpkin rum raisin crème anglaise and place a cake circle in the center. Fill the hole in the cake with the mascarpone mousse.

2. Arrange 4 pear slices on top of the cake. Place a small quenelle of mousse on the pears. Garnish with a pear chip and a caramel stick.

Chocolate Velvet in a Sugar Dome

YIELD: *12 servings*

JOHN HUI

CAESAR'S PALACE
CASINO HOTEL
LAS VEGAS, NV

Rum and Kahlua accent the fathoms-deep chocolate flavor of the mousse in this contemporary classic. Accompanying the chocolate-glazed gianduja-mousse-and-chocolate sponge cakes are sauces of white chocolate, raspberry, and fresh berries, with sugar flowers and a dome to add a visual accent. Classic flavor combinations starring chocolate, ease of production, and the stabilizing effects of liquor make this a perfect dessert for banquets.

SPECIAL EQUIPMENT: *Twelve 3" [7.6 cm] demisphere molds*

CHOCOLATE SPONGE:

6.8 oz [193 g] egg yolks

11 oz [312 g] egg whites

8 oz [227 g] granulated sugar

2 tsp [8 g] vanilla extract

3 oz [85 g] cake flour

1 oz [28 g] unsweetened cocoa powder

1. Preheat oven to 400°F [205°C]. In a mixer whip the egg yolks to the ribbon stage. In a separate mixer bowl beat the egg whites at medium speed until foamy. Gradually beat in the sugar and beat at high speed until stiff peaks form. Fold the yolks and vanilla into the meringue. Sift the flour and cocoa over the egg mixture and gently fold until incorporated.

2. Divide the batter evenly between two parchment-lined half sheet pans. Bake for 7 to 9 minutes or until the cake springs back when gently pressed with a finger. Immediately remove the cake from the pans and cool completely.

3. Cut one sheet into 2½" [6.4 cm] circles and the other sheet into 3" [7.6 cm] circles.

CHOCOLATE VELVET:

22 oz [624 g] semisweet chocolate

10 oz [283 g] gianduja chocolate

2 oz [57 g] unsalted butter

12 liq oz [355 ml] heavy cream

1.3 oz [37 g] egg yolks

2 oz [57 g] confectioners' sugar

2.1 oz [60 g] egg whites

.5 oz [14 g] granulated sugar

1½ tsp [7 g] rum

1 tsp [6 g] Kahlua

1. In a double boiler melt together the chocolates and the butter. Remove from heat and add the cream. In a mixer whip the egg yolks and confectioners' sugar until they are thick enough to hold peaks, and add to the chocolate mixture.

2. In a mixer make a French meringue from the egg whites and granulated sugar. Fold the chocolate mixture, rum, and Kahlua into the meringue.

3. Fill the demisphere molds halfway with chocolate velvet. Place a 2.5″ [6.4 cm] circle of chocolate sponge on top and press it into the velvet. Fill the molds almost to the top and cover with a 3″ [7.6 cm] circle of chocolate sponge. Chill to set.

CHOCOLATE GLAZE:

10 oz [283 g] semisweet chocolate, finely chopped

8 liq oz [237 ml] heavy cream

2 oz [57 g] corn syrup

1. Place the chocolate in a large bowl. In a saucepan bring the cream and corn syrup to a boil. Pour the cream mixture over the chopped chocolate.

2. Whisk until the chocolate is completely melted and smooth.

RASPBERRY SAUCE:

1 oz [28 g] Clear Gel starch

10 liq oz [296 ml] water, divided

1 lb [454 g] granulated sugar

1 lb [454 g] raspberry purée

1. Dilute the Clear Gel in 2 liq oz [59 ml] of cold water. In a saucepan boil the remaining 8 liq oz [237 ml] of water. Whisk in the Clear Gel mixture and cook until thickened. Remove the pan from the heat. Add the sugar and stir until it dissolves. Mix in the raspberry purée.

2. Strain through a chinois and cool.

WHITE CHOCOLATE SAUCE:

1 lb [454 g] white chocolate, finely chopped

1 pt [473 ml] heavy cream

1. Place the chocolate in a large bowl. In a saucepan bring the cream to a boil. Pour the hot cream over the chopped chocolate.

2. Whisk until the chocolate is completely melted and smooth.

ASSEMBLY:

Tempered chocolate rectangles, made on gold-flecked transfer sheets
Pulled sugar roses
Sugar half domes
Fresh berries

1.   Unmold the chocolate velvet cakes and place them on a dipping screen over a sheet pan. Pour the chocolate glaze on top and chill to set.

2.   Place gold-flecked chocolate rectangles around the bottom and a pulled sugar rose on top of each velvet cake.

3.   Decorate each dessert plate with the white chocolate and raspberry sauces. Place a chocolate velvet in the center of each plate with a sugar half dome behind it and fresh berries on the side.

Gâteau St. Honoré

YIELD: *10 servings*

EN-MING HSU

RITZ-CARLTON HOTEL
CHICAGO, IL

The classic St. Honoré, notes En-Ming Hsu, historically involves puff pastry and pâte à choux with caramel and chiboust cream. For this individual presentation, "We just built it a different way," she says. "We also added chocolate to the chiboust and flavored the pastry cream with Grand Marnier." Candied kumquats fill the role of the traditional fresh fruit garnish.

SPECIAL EQUIPMENT: *Ten 3½" [8.9 cm] flan rings; Wagner airless paint sprayer*

CHOCOLATE CHIBOUST:

4.6 liq oz [135 ml] milk

3.2 liq oz [95 ml] heavy cream

4.1 oz [115 g] egg yolks

.5 oz [15 g] pastry cream powder

4.8 oz [137 g] granulated sugar, divided

2 gelatin sheets, bloomed

8.5 oz [240 g] Valrhona Manjari chocolate, melted and kept warm

6.5 oz [185 g] egg whites

1 Tbs [15 ml] water

1.   Line a sheet pan with plastic wrap and arrange ten 3½" [8.9 cm] flan rings on top. In a saucepan, bring the milk and heavy cream to a boil. Whisk together the egg yolks, pastry cream powder, and 2 oz [57 g] of the sugar, and temper in the hot milk mixture. Cook the pastry cream, whisking constantly, until it has bubbled for about 2 minutes, then transfer it to a mixing bowl. Squeeze the excess water from the gelatin and add it to the hot pastry cream, mixing until it has completely dissolved. Mix in the melted chocolate. Cover the surface of the pastry cream with plastic wrap and keep it warm.

2.   Place the egg whites and .7 oz [20 g] of sugar in a mixer bowl. In a saucepan, combine the remaining 2.1 oz [60 g] of the sugar with the water and cook to 250°F [121°C]. When the sugar is almost ready, turn on the mixer and whip the egg whites to soft peaks. With the mixer on low speed, carefully pour the hot sugar into the egg whites. Continue to whip for several more minutes until the meringue has cooled slightly. Try to time the meringue so that it is ready at about the same time as the pastry cream.

3.   Fold the meringue into the pastry cream and fill the flan rings to the top. Chill until set.

PÂTE À CHOUX:

4.9 oz [140 g] unsalted butter

7.8 liq oz [230 ml] milk

7.8 liq oz [230 ml] water

.7 oz [20 g] granulated sugar

¾ tsp [5 g] salt

9.2 oz [260 g] pastry flour, sifted

14 oz [397 g] eggs

1. Preheat oven to 400°F [205°C]. In a saucepan combine the butter, milk, water, sugar, and salt, and bring to a boil. Add the flour all at once and stir vigorously with a wooden spoon for 1 minute or until the mixture comes together into a ball. Transfer the mixture to a mixer bowl and beat with the paddle attachment while slowly adding most of the eggs, incorporating after each addition. Only add the last few ounces of egg if the batter seems too stiff.

2. Weigh out 10.6 oz [300 g] of the paste and spread it evenly onto a parchment-lined half sheet pan. On another parchment-lined half sheet pan pipe 70 rounds, about ¾″ [19 mm] in diameter. Brush the rounds with egg wash. Bake both trays until golden and crisp, about 8 to 10 minutes for the puffs and 10 to 12 minutes for the sheet. With a 3½″ [8.9 cm] diameter cutter, cut 10 circles from the sheet.

3. Fill a parchment cone with some of the remaining paste. Pipe ten 3½″ [8.9 cm] lattices onto a sheet pan lined with a silicone baking mat. Bake for 5 to 7 minutes or until golden. Cool completely.

GRAND MARNIER PASTRY CREAM:

17 liq oz [500 ml] milk

1 vanilla bean, scraped

3.5 oz [100 g] granulated sugar

3.5 oz [100 g] egg yolks

1.6 oz [45 g] pastry cream powder

2 liq oz [60 ml] Grand Marnier

8.5 liq oz [250 ml] heavy cream, whipped to soft peaks

1. In a saucepan, combine the milk and the vanilla bean and bring to a boil. In a bowl whisk together the sugar, egg yolks, and pastry cream powder, and temper in the hot milk. Cook the pastry cream, whisking constantly until it has bubbled for 2 minutes. Transfer the pastry cream to a mixing bowl. Cover the surface with plastic wrap and cool completely.

2. Mix the Grand Marnier into the cooled pastry cream. Gently fold in the whipped cream.

GRAND MARNIER CRÈME ANGLAISE:

8 liq oz [237 ml] heavy cream

8 liq oz [237 ml] milk

1 vanilla bean, split and scraped

2 oz [56 g] granulated sugar, divided

8 oz [227 g] egg yolks

5 liq oz [148 ml] Grand Marnier

1. In a saucepan, combine the cream, milk, vanilla bean, and 1 oz [28 g] of the sugar, and bring to a boil. In a bowl whisk together the egg yolks and the remaining 1 oz [28 g] of the sugar. Temper in the hot milk mixture and cook gently, stirring, until the mixture coats the back of a wooden spoon. Strain over an ice bath and cool completely. Refrigerate the sauce for 5 hours or overnight.

2. Whisk in the Grand Marnier.

SPRAY MIXTURE:

8.8 oz [250 g] bittersweet chocolate

8.8 oz [250 g] cocoa butter

1. Melt together the chocolate and cocoa butter.

2. Keep in a warm, dry place until needed for spraying.

ASSEMBLY:

Caramel

Confectioners' sugar

Candied kumquats, cut in half

Mint sprigs

1. Fill the cream puffs with the pastry cream and dip the tops in caramel. Let them sit until the caramel hardens.

2. Unmold the chiboust discs by carefully warming the sides of the rings. Spray the discs with the warm spraying mixture.

3. Place a pâte à choux disc on each dessert plate and place a chiboust disc on top. Arrange 7 cream puffs around the top of the chiboust. Dust the lattices with confectioners' sugar and place one on top of the puffs.

4. Fill a candied kumquat half with the Grand Marnier crème anglaise and a small mint sprig and place it alongside the St. Honoré. Decorate the plate with dots of the Grand Marnier crème anglaise.

White Chocolate Key Lime Tart

YIELD: *12 servings*

SUZANNE SILVERMAN

MAIN STREET
RESTAURANT GROUP
PHILADELPHIA, PA

A pecan shortbread shell is coated with white chocolate and topped with Key lime curd, fresh fruit, apricot glaze, and meringue, then browned. The plate is finished with a raspberry sauce—simple, which is the way Suzanne Silverman likes it. She creates desserts for several restaurants; they are shipped from her central, commissary bakery and are often plated by servers, so a minimum of fine finish work is involved. "The beauty of a dessert is the flow," she says. "There should be a natural line to it—not too crazy."

SPECIAL EQUIPMENT: *Twelve 3¼" [8.25 cm] tart shells*

PECAN SHORTBREAD SHELL:

10 oz [283 g] unsalted butter, softened

3 oz [85 g] granulated sugar

3.5 oz [99 g] eggs

Pinch of kosher salt

9 oz [255 g] pecans, ground

12.5 oz [354 g] all-purpose flour

1.   Preheat the oven to 325°F [165°C].

2.   In a mixing bowl, cream together the butter and sugar. Add the eggs, one at a time, and then the salt. Add ground pecans and flour. Let rest for 30 minutes.

3.   Press into twelve greased 3¼" [8.25 cm] tart rings. Freeze until firm. Bake until lightly browned, about 20 minutes.

KEY LIME CURD:

7.8 oz [221 g] egg yolks

14 oz [397 g] sweetened condensed milk

4 liq oz [118 ml] Key lime juice

1 oz [28 g] unsalted butter

8 liq oz [237 ml] heavy cream, whipped to a soft peak

1.   Combine the egg yolks, condensed milk, and Key lime juice, and heat over a double boiler until thickened. Stir in the butter until melted. Let cool.

2.   Fold in the whipped cream; chill.

MERINGUE:

8.4 oz [238 g] egg whites

7 oz [198 g] granulated sugar

Pinch of cream of tartar

In a mixer, using the whisk attachment, combine all the ingredients and beat until stiff, but not dry.

ASSEMBLY:

White chocolate, melted

Assorted fresh fruit

Apricot glaze

Raspberry sauce

1. Coat the inside of the tart shells with white chocolate. Let set.

2. Fill the shells with lime curd. Top with the assorted fruit and glaze. Pipe the meringue on top of the fruit and brown. Serve with raspberry sauce.

Chocolate Marble Toadstool Cake

FOUR SEASONS HOTEL
AND RESORT
PALM BEACH, FL

Inspired by the dew that glistens off a mushroom on a sunny morning, Tom Worhach has created a triple chocolate [milk, white, and dark] mousse cake. "By pressing them into the mold, and cutting them different ways, it gives a marbled effect," he says. With a brownie acting as the stem and various fruit sauces as forest floor decor, Worhach has also decorated his plate with guava and nasturtium, both edible, but rather hard-to-find, flowers.

SPECIAL EQUIPMENT: *Forty 3" [7.6 cm] diameter demisphere molds*

CHOCOLATE CAKE:

4 oz [113 g] unsalted butter, at room temperature

7 oz [198 g] granulated sugar

3.8 oz [108 g] light brown sugar

5.25 oz [149 g] eggs

7.5 oz [213 g] all-purpose flour

1.5 oz [43 g] unsweetened cocoa powder

1.5 tsp [8 g] baking soda

¼ tsp [2 g] salt

10.7 liq oz [316 ml] buttermilk

1 tsp [4 g] vanilla extract

1.   Preheat oven to 375°F [190°C]. In a mixer with the paddle attachment, cream together the butter, granulated sugar, and brown sugar. Gradually add the eggs, scraping down the side of the bowl after each addition.

2.   Sift together the flour, cocoa powder, baking soda, and salt; reserve. Combine the buttermilk and vanilla extract. Alternately add the sifted dry ingredients and the liquid ingredients to the butter mixture, beginning and ending with the dry mixture. Mix until all of the ingredients are incorporated and the batter has a smooth consistency.

3.   Spread the batter evenly onto 3 greased half sheet pans. Bake for 8 to 10 minutes or until the cake springs back when gently pressed with a finger. Invert the cakes onto cool pans.

CHOCOLATE BROWNIE SURPRISE:

12 oz [340 g] unsalted butter

24 oz [680 g] granulated sugar

1 lb [454 g] cake flour

4 oz [113 g] unsweetened cocoa powder

7 oz [198 g] eggs

4 oz [113 g] light corn syrup

8 oz [227 g] candy, nuts, and/or peanut butter [any combination]

CAKES, TARTS, AND PIES   135

1.   Preheat oven to 350°F [175°C]. In a mixer with the paddle attachment, cream together the butter and sugar. Sift together the cake flour and cocoa powder and add to the butter mixture, mixing just until combined. Gradually add the eggs and mix on low speed for 5 minutes. Mix in the corn syrup and any combination of candy, nuts, and peanut butter.

2.   Spread the batter evenly onto a greased half sheet pan. Bake for 25 to 35 minutes or until a cake tester comes out clean.

PASTRY CREAM:

1 qt [946 ml] milk

5.25 oz [149 g] eggs

1.3 oz [37 g] egg yolks

8 oz [227 g] granulated sugar

6.4 oz [181 g] all-purpose flour

3.2 oz [91 g] unsalted butter, softened and cut into cubes

1.   In a saucepan, bring the milk to a boil. In a bowl, whisk together the eggs, egg yolks, sugar, and flour, and temper in the hot milk. Cook on low heat, whisking constantly, until the mixture has bubbled for 2 minutes.

2.   Remove the pan from the heat and whisk in the butter. Cool completely.

THREE MOUSSES:

6 oz [170 g] semisweet chocolate

28.5 oz [808 g] pastry cream, divided

39 liq oz [1.2 l] heavy cream, divided

6 oz [170 g] white chocolate

6 oz [170 g] milk chocolate

1.   Melt the semisweet chocolate over a pot of simmering water. Mix the melted chocolate into 9.5 oz [269 g] of the pastry cream. In a mixer, whip 13 liq oz [384 ml] of the heavy cream to soft peaks. Gently fold the whipped cream into the pastry cream.

2.   Repeat the procedure 2 more times, with the white chocolate and then with the milk chocolate.

ASSEMBLY:

Rum-flavored simple syrup

Tempered dark chocolate

Assorted tropical fruit coulis

White chocolate squiggles

1. Spread the semisweet chocolate mousse evenly onto a plastic-lined half sheet pan. Place one of the chocolate cake sheets on top, pressing down gently. Generously soak the cake with rum-flavored simple syrup. Repeat 2 more times, with the white chocolate and then the milk chocolate. Refrigerate for at least 12 hours.

2. Trim the edges of the cake and cut it into 2″ [5.1 cm] squares. Place each square into a demisphere mold and press it down firmly. Freeze for 2 hours.

3. Pipe a design onto the dessert plates with tempered dark chocolate and assorted tropical fruit coulis. Cut the brownies into 1″ [2.5 cm] diameter circles and place one in the center of each dessert plate. Unmold the cakes and place one on each brownie "stem." Garnish the plates with white chocolate squiggles.

Old-Fashioned Plum Tart

YIELD: *10 servings*

JEAN MARC VIALLET

RITZ-CARLTON
HUNTINGTON
HOTEL & SPA
PASADENA, CA

"This is a hearty dessert," comments Jean Marc Viallet. "It has a lot of flavors. I see it as a winter menu item, more than summer." By hearty, and by flavors, Viallet must be referring to the cognac in the sweet dough and hazelnut cream, the curaçao in the fruit compote, and the cabernet in the raspberry and citrus reduction. Still, the plums are not lost amid the nutty and fruity flavors of this intoxicating tart.

SPECIAL EQUIPMENT: *Ten tartlet pans, 4½" [11.4 cm] diameter*

ALMOND SWEET DOUGH:

9 oz [255 g] unsalted butter

6.5 oz [184 g] granulated sugar

1.75 oz [50 g] eggs

.65 oz [18 g] egg yolks

2.5 oz [71 g] almond flour

13.5 oz [383 g] all-purpose flour

1 Tbs [15 ml] vanilla extract

2 Tbs [30 ml] cognac

1.   In a mixer with the paddle attachment, cream together the butter and sugar. Mix in the eggs and egg yolks and scrape down the side of the bowl. Add the almond flour and all-purpose flour, then the vanilla extract and cognac. Transfer the dough to a sheet pan and chill for at least 2 hours.

2.   On a floured surface, roll out the dough to ⅛" [3 mm] thickness. Line the tartlet pans with the dough.

HAZELNUT CREAM:

8 oz [227 g] unsalted butter

8 oz [227 g] granulated sugar

7 oz [198 g] eggs

8 oz [227 g] hazelnut flour, well toasted

2 liq oz [59 ml] cognac

7 fresh dark plums, cut into wedges

1.   Preheat oven to 350°F [175°C]. In a mixer with the paddle attachment, cream together the butter and sugar. Scrape down the side of the bowl, then add the eggs. Mix in the hazelnut flour followed by the cognac. Beat on medium speed for 10 minutes.

2.   Fill the tartlet shells about two-thirds of the way with the cream. Arrange five plum wedges in a spoke pattern on top. Bake the tartlets for 25 minutes or until the tops are golden. Cool on a wire rack.

KUMQUAT, PEAR, AND RASPBERRY COMPOTE:

4 oz [113 g] fresh kumquats, blanched

1 pear, poached in light syrup

Handful of fresh raspberries

3 liq oz [89 ml] water

2 oz [57 g] granulated sugar

1 orange, juiced

1.5 tsp [7 ml] curaçao

1.   Dice the kumquats and cut the pear into batonnets. Cut the raspberries in half. Toss all the fruit together in a mixing bowl.

2.   In a saucepan, combine the water, sugar, orange juice, and curaçao, and cook until all of the sugar has dissolved. Pour the hot syrup over the fruit and macerate for several hours.

CABERNET RASPBERRY SAUCE:

25.4 liq oz [750 ml] cabernet sauvignon

12 oz [340 g] brown sugar

1 vanilla bean, split and scraped

½ lemon, zested and juiced

½ orange, zested and juiced

2 cinnamon sticks

16 liq oz [473 ml] raspberry purée

1.   In a saucepan, combine the cabernet sauvignon, brown sugar, vanilla bean seeds, lemon zest and juice, orange zest and juice, and cinnamon sticks. Bring the mixture to a boil, then reduce the heat and simmer until it is reduced by half.

2.   Remove the cinnamon sticks and mix in the raspberry purée.

ASSEMBLY:

Thinly sliced pears, poached in light syrup

1.   Place half a tartlet standing on its cut side in the center of a dessert plate and place one quarter of a tartlet in front of it. Arrange 3 poached pear slices along the front of the plate.

2.   Garnish the plate with the compote and the cabernet raspberry sauce.

Apple Cream Tart

YIELD: *16 servings*

MARTIN HOWARD
NEW YORK, NY

*A sophisticated, lush varia-
tion of America's favorite,
apple pie and ice cream.
Applejack cream accompa-
nies a warm apple tart in a
puff pastry shell rolled in
sugar and hazelnut flour. "It
makes it crunchy," says
Martin Howard. "I cook the
apples separately, then keep
them warm over a water
bath, so the shell stays nice
and crisp. The applejack
cream is a version of a classic
cream called sapphire cream,
which is traditionally a light,
classic filling for a bombe,"
he continues. "For this
recipe, I've eliminated the
brandy and flavored the
cream with applejack and
nutmeg."*

APPLE FILLING:

1 oz [28 g] unsalted butter

8 oz [227 g] brown sugar

1 oz [28 g] honey

½ tsp cinnamon

⅛ tsp nutmeg

12 apples, peeled and cut into large dice

1. In a large sauté pan, melt the butter. Add the brown sugar, honey, cinnamon, and nutmeg, and stir until the mixture is smooth and starts to bubble.

2. Add the apples and cover the pan. Cook until the apples are soft, 5 to 7 minutes.

APPLEJACK CREAM:

3.5 oz [99 g] eggs

3.25 oz [92 g] egg yolks

7.2 oz [204 g] granulated sugar, divided

1.5 liq oz [44 ml] water

¼ whole nutmeg, grated

.25 oz [7.5 g] gelatin

3 liq oz [89 ml] applejack

24 liq oz [710 ml] heavy cream

1. In a mixer bowl, combine the eggs, egg yolks, and 2.2 oz [62 g] of the sugar. In a saucepan combine the remaining 5 oz [142 g] of sugar with the water and heat over a high flame. At the same time, whip the egg mixture until it is very light. When the sugar reaches 235°F [113°C], turn the mixer to low speed and add the syrup in a slow, steady stream. Whip until the syrup is incorporated. Mix in the grated nutmeg.

2. Bloom the gelatin in cold water. Wring out the excess water and add the applejack. Melt the gelatin over simmering water and add it to the egg mixture.

3. In a mixer, whip the cream to medium peaks and fold it into the egg mixture. Refrigerate until ready to use.

PUFF PASTRY SHELLS:

2 oz [57 g] granulated sugar, or as needed

2 oz [57 g] hazelnut flour, or as needed

17 oz [482 g] frozen all-butter puff pastry, thawed

1. Preheat oven to 350°F [175°C]. Sprinkle a rolling surface with sugar and hazelnut flour. Roll out the puff pastry to a ⅛" [3 mm] thickness. Sprinkle the top with additional sugar and hazelnut flour.

2. Cut sixteen 4" [10.2 cm] circles from the dough and place them on a parchment-lined sheet pan. Bake for 15 to 20 minutes or until they are puffed and golden.

APPLESAUCE:

6 tart apples, thinly sliced [unpeeled]

4 oz [113 g] granulated sugar

½ lemon

1 cinnamon stick

1. Combine all of the ingredients in a saucepan and cook over low heat until the apples are very soft, about 20 minutes.

2. Remove the lemon and cinnamon stick. Purée the sauce and strain it through a chinois. Place the sauce in a squeeze bottle.

ASSEMBLY:

Thinly sliced apple wedges

Cotton candy

Drizzle some of the applesauce onto a dessert plate. Cut each puff pastry shell in half crosswise. Place the bottom half on the plate. Spoon some of the warm apple filling into the shell. Top with some of the chilled applejack cream. Place the other half of the pastry shell on top. Garnish the plate with thinly sliced apple wedges and cotton candy.

Bittersweet Chocolate Passion Tart

YIELD: *15 servings*

KEEGAN GERHARD

DEAN & DELUCA
CHARLOTTE, NC

Everyone has a flourless chocolate tart on their menu, notes Keegan Gerhard, "and I've tried all of them," he says. His favorite was Joel Robuchon's because, with a 70% cocoa content chocolate, it was very bitter. Though he modeled this one on Robuchon's, "I put a little sugar in it, for the sake of the customers," says Gerhard. He flavors the tart with passion fruit, "for a modern-day twist," and accompanies it with a rum-laced creole sauce and banana passion fruit sorbet. "The creole sauce has an underlying acid—lemon juice—and with saffron and banana, it ties the flavors together. People who love chocolate will love this tart," promises Gerhard.

SPECIAL EQUIPMENT: *Ice cream machine; fifteen 3½" [8.9 cm] diameter flan rings*

BANANA PASSION FRUIT SORBET:

6.3 oz [180 g] granulated sugar

10 liq oz [296 ml] water

1.7 oz [50 g] trimoline

8.4 oz [240 g] banana purée

11.6 oz [330 g] passion fruit purée

1 Tbs [15 ml] orange juice

1. In a medium saucepan, bring the sugar and water to a boil. Add the trimoline and return to a boil. Remove the pan from the heat.

2. Combine the fruit purées and orange juice. Pour the hot mixture over the purées and blend. Refrigerate until completely chilled.

3. Process in an ice cream machine according to the manufacturer's instructions.

ALMOND SABLÉ:

10.5 oz [300 g] unsalted butter, at room temperature

Pinch of salt

7.9 oz [225 g] confectioners' sugar

2.6 oz [74 g] almond flour

4.4 oz [125 g] whole eggs

20.7 oz [588 g] cake flour, divided

1. In a mixer, using the paddle attachment, combine the butter, salt, confectioners' sugar, almond flour, eggs, and 5.3 oz [150 g] of the cake flour. Blend well.

2. Add the remaining flour and blend just until incorporated. Wrap the dough in plastic wrap and refrigerate for approximately 2 hours, until firm.

3. Preheat oven to 350°F [175°C]. Line a sheet pan with parchment paper. Place fifteen 3½" [8.9 cm] diameter flan rings on the lined sheet pan. Roll the almond sablé dough out to a thickness of ¹⁄₁₆″ [.16 cm]. Dust your fingers with flour and line the sides and bottoms of each ring with the dough. Line each ring with parchment paper and fill with dried beans or pie weights. Bake until set, about 8 minutes, remove the beans and parchment, and return to the oven. Bake until light golden brown. Cool completely.

CHOCOLATE PASSION TART FILLING:

12 oz [340 g] dark chocolate, 56%, finely chopped

4 oz [113 g] dark chocolate, 70%, finely chopped

1 lb [454 g] unsalted butter

8 oz [227 g] granulated sugar

9 oz [255 g] passion fruit purée

14 oz [397 g] eggs

1.   Preheat oven to 350°F [175°C]. Place the chopped chocolates in a heatproof bowl. Combine the butter and sugar in a saucepan and heat until the sugar has completely dissolved. Pour the hot butter mixture over the chocolate. Stir gently to combine.

2.   Add the fruit purée to the chocolate and blend. Whisk the eggs together and gently whisk them into the chocolate mixture.

3.   Pour the mixture into the pre-baked shells and bake for about 11 minutes, until set.

CREOLE SAUCE:

17.6 oz [500 g] heavy cream

14 oz [400 g] banana, pureed

8 oz [227 g] granulated sugar

27.7 liq oz [820 ml] water

3.6 liq oz [108 ml] rum

2 lemons, juiced

1 lemon, zested

Pinch of saffron

Combine all the ingredients in a saucepan and bring to a boil. Strain and cool.

ASSEMBLY:

Chocolate ribbons

Place each tart on a plate and garnish the plate with dots of creole sauce, chocolate ribbons, and a quenelle of banana passion fruit sorbet.

Warm Seckel Pear and Damson Plum Tart

YIELD: *12 servings*

JILL ROSE

URBAN HORIZONS
FOOD CO.
BRONX, NY

A flavorful embroidery of a simple pear tart, the dessert's foundation is classic as can be—German Riesling as the poaching liquid for the pears. From there, the plate is pure creation—cardamom short-bread with an almond filling is the neo-shell for the tart, which is a mix of poached pears and plum compote. A port wine reduction sauce, candied pecan ice cream, and a phyllo collar finish this symphony of provocative flavors.

POACHED PEARS:

12 Seckel pears, peeled and cored

25.4 liq oz [750 ml] German Spatlese Riesling

1 oz [28 g] unsalted butter, softened

2 oz [57 g] granulated sugar

1.   Preheat oven to 325°F [165°C].

2.   In a saucepan, poach the pears in the wine. Place in the oven to dry, about 2 minutes. Brush with the butter and sprinkle with sugar. Bake until tender, about 15 minutes.

CARDAMOM DOUGH:

18 oz [510 g] unsalted butter

13.5 oz [383 g] granulated sugar

1.75 oz [50 g] eggs

1 vanilla bean, split and scraped

1.5 lb [680 g] pastry flour

¼ tsp [2 g] salt

¼ tsp [1 g] ground cardamom

1.   Preheat oven to 325°F [165°C].

2.   In mixing bowl, cream together the butter and sugar. Add the eggs and vanilla bean. Add the remaining ingredients and mix until combined. Refrigerate until firm, about ½ hour.

3.   Roll out the dough. Cut out twelve 2⅞" [7.3 cm] circles.

4.   Place the circles in 4 oz [118 ml] Flexipan demisphere molds. Prebake until light brown, about 7 minutes.

ALMOND CREAM:

6 oz [175 g] unsalted butter

6 oz [175 g] granulated sugar

6 oz [175 g] almond flour

2.6 oz [75 g] all-purpose flour

5.25 oz [149 g] eggs

In a mixing bowl, cream together the butter and sugar. Add the flours and eggs and mix until combined.

PASTRY CREAM:

33.8 liq oz [1 lt] milk

17.6 oz [500 g] granulated sugar, divided

2 vanilla beans, split and scraped

7.8 oz [221 g] egg yolks

4.2 oz [120 g] all-purpose flour

8.8 oz [250 g] unsalted butter

1.   In a saucepan, bring the milk, 8.8 oz [250 g] of the sugar, and vanilla beans to a boil.

2.   In mixing bowl combine the egg yolks, the remaining 8.8 oz [250 g] of granulated sugar, and flour. Temper and add to the milk mixture. Cook until thickened, stirring constantly. Stir in the butter. Remove from heat.

3.   Transfer to the mixer stand and beat until cool.

ALMOND FILLING:

1.8 oz [51 g] almond cream

1.2 oz [34 g] pastry cream

2 Tbs [27 g] Poire William

.3 oz [8 g] sliced almonds, toasted

1.   Preheat the oven to 325°F [165°C].

2.   In a mixing bowl combine all the ingredients. Place the filling in the prebaked tart shells. Bake until light brown, about 8 minutes.

DAMSON PLUM COMPOTE:

1 lb [454 g] Damson plums, seeded and chopped

7 oz [200 g] granulated sugar

3.5 oz [100 g] lemon juice

In a saucepan, bring all the ingredients to a boil. Simmer until thickened. Let cool.

CANDIED PECAN ICE CREAM:

33.8 liq oz [1 lt] milk

33.8 liq oz [1 lt] heavy cream

4 vanilla beans, split and scraped

21 oz [595 g] eggs

7.8 oz [221 g] egg yolks

14 oz [400 g] granulated sugar

1 lb [454 g] brown sugar

8 oz [227 g] unsalted butter

2 lb [907 g] pecans, toasted and crushed

1. In a saucepan, bring the milk, cream, and vanilla beans to a boil.

2. In a separate bowl, combine the eggs, yolks, and granulated sugar. Gradually whisk about half of the milk mixture into the yolk mixture. Return this mixture to the saucepan and cook over low heat to 185°F [85°C], stirring constantly. Strain and cool in an ice bath. Process in an ice cream machine according to the manufacturer's instructions.

3. Put the pecans in a greased hotel pan. In a saucepan, caramelize the brown sugar. Stir in the butter. Pour the caramel over the pecans. Let cool.

4. Crumble the caramelized pecans and fold into the ice cream.

PORT WINE SAUCE:

10.1 liq oz [300 ml] red port wine

In a saucepan, reduce the wine to a thin syrupy consistency. Let cool.

PHYLLO TRIANGLES:

6 phyllo sheets

2 oz [57 g] unsalted butter, melted

1.8 oz [50 g] granulated sugar

2 Tbs [18 g] poppy seeds

1. Preheat oven to 400°F [205°C].

2. Brush the top only of 2 layered sheets of phyllo with butter and sprinkle with sugar. Bake between 2 silicone baking mats on a sheet pan until browned, about 8 minutes.

3. Sprinkle with the poppy seeds. Cut the phyllo into 5″ × 8″ [12.7 cm × 20.3 cm] triangles. Shape each triangle into a ring while still hot, with the poppy seeds facing inward. Repeat with remaining sheets.

ASSEMBLY:

Place an almond tart on a dessert plate and top with some plum compote and a poached pear. Place the phyllo ring around the tart. Serve with the candied pecan ice cream and port wine sauce.

Bittersweet Chocolate Marjolaine with Cocoa Meringue, Caramelized Bananas, and Pecan Crust

YIELD: *40 servings*

KEITH JEANMINETTE

MASA'S

SAN FRANCISCO, CA

"Classically, marjolaine is layers of hazelnut meringue and praline buttercream," says Keith Jeanminette. "This is pecan crust, rum chocolate mousse, slices of bananas, cocoa meringue, and two layers of banana Bavarian. I do marjolaine because it's one of those can't-miss combinations of crunchy, nutty, and creamy that keeps your palate playing with different textures and flavors. The pecan layer stays crispy, but the meringues absorb the moisture of the Bavarian and they get soft. When you eat it, it doesn't explode—the dessert eats very easily." This is important to Jeanminette. "I like things to keep their integrity," he says. "If you're eating a dessert and it stays intact at least for the first two or three bites, it's another form of stimulation. If you have to knock it over or pull it apart, it loses points for me. I won't do a napoleon, because I don't like the way it eats."

SPECIAL EQUIPMENT: *Forty ring molds, 1½" [3.8 cm] diameter × 3" [7.6 cm] high*

COCOA MERINGUE CIRCLES:

1.5 oz [43 g] cornstarch

.5 oz [14 g] unsweetened cocoa powder

1 oz [28 g] confectioners' sugar

7.4 oz [210 g] egg whites

3 oz [85 g] granulated sugar

1.   Preheat oven to 225°F [105°C]. Sift together the cornstarch, cocoa powder, and confectioners' sugar. In a mixer whip the egg whites to soft peaks. Gradually add the sugar and continue whipping to stiff peaks. Fold the sifted mixture into the egg whites.

2.   On parchment-lined baking sheets pipe the meringue into 1½" [3.8 cm] diameter circles. Bake for 90 minutes or until the circles are very dry.

PECAN CRUST:

7 oz [198 g] pecan halves

1 Tbs [12 g] granulated sugar

2 oz [57 g] unsalted butter, melted

4 oz [113 g] bittersweet chocolate, melted

1.   Preheat oven to 325°F [165°C]. In a food processor combine the pecans and sugar, and process until the pecans are coarsely chopped. Transfer the mixture to a bowl and toss with the melted butter.

2.   Place a 1½" [3.8 cm] diameter cookie cutter on a parchment-lined sheet pan. Place a small amount of the pecan mixture inside the cutter and press it down firmly to form a thin layer the size of the cutter. Remove the cutter, and repeat with the remaining pecan mixture. Bake for 8 to 10 minutes or until the crust is barely golden in color. Cool completely.

3.   Flip the circles over. Lightly brush the bottoms with melted chocolate and let set.

HONEY TUILES:

8 oz [227 g] unsalted butter, melted

8 oz [227 g] confectioners' sugar

5.9 oz [167 g] wildflower honey

8.5 oz [241 g] all-purpose flour

8.5 oz [241 g] egg whites, at room temperature

1.   Preheat oven to 350°F [175°C]. In a mixer with the paddle attachment, beat together the butter and confectioners' sugar just until combined. Mix in the honey. Add the flour alternately with the egg whites, and beat until smooth.

2.   On a lightly greased sheet pan, spread the batter thinly over a teaspoon-shaped stencil. Bake for 7 to 9 minutes, or until the tuiles are golden. Immediately remove them from the pan and place them on the backs of real teaspoons. Cool until set.

STRAWBERRY SORBET:

7 oz [198 g] granulated sugar

8 liq oz [237 ml] water

2 drops lemon juice

3 pt [1.4 lt] fresh strawberries, washed and hulled

1.5 oz [43 g] corn syrup

1.   In a saucepan, combine the sugar, water, and lemon juice, and bring the mixture to a boil. Remove the pan from the heat and let the syrup cool completely.

2.   Purée the strawberries in a blender. Add the corn syrup and 2 liq oz [59 ml] of the syrup. Taste the mixture and, if necessary, add up to 2 liq oz [59 ml] of additional syrup. Process in an ice cream machine according to the manufacturer's instructions.

GANACHE:

1 lb [454 g] Valrhona Caraque chocolate, chopped

10 liq oz [296 ml] heavy cream

8 liq oz [237 ml] half-and-half

Splash of dark rum

1.   Place the chopped chocolate in a mixing bowl. In a saucepan, scald the heavy cream and half-and-half. Pour the hot cream mixture over the chocolate and whisk until the chocolate is completely melted and smooth.

2.   Whisk in the rum.

CHOCOLATE RUM MOUSSE:

8 oz [227 g] Valrhona Pur Caraibe chocolate

2.6 oz [74 g] pasteurized egg yolks

2.2 oz [62 g] orange flower honey

1 liq oz [30 ml] dark rum

20 liq oz [591 ml] heavy cream, whipped to soft peaks

1.   Melt the chocolate and set it aside.

2.   In a mixer with the whisk attachment, whip the egg yolks until they are light in color and fluffy. In a saucepan, bring the honey to a boil. With the mixer on low speed, carefully pour the honey into the egg yolks. Continue to whip for 5 more minutes.

3.   Transfer the mixture to a large mixing bowl. Whisk in the rum, then the melted chocolate. Lighten the mixture with about one-fourth of the whipped cream, then gently fold in the remaining cream.

BANANA ANGLAISE:

6 very ripe bananas, peeled and split lengthwise

1 qt [946 ml] half-and-half

1 vanilla bean, split and scraped

1 cinnamon stick, lightly toasted

3.5 oz [99 g] granulated sugar, divided

7.8 oz [221 g] egg yolks

1.   In a saucepan, combine the bananas, half-and-half, vanilla bean, cinnamon stick, and 1.75 oz [50 g] of the sugar. Bring the mixture to a simmer over medium heat. Remove the pot from the heat and steep for 30 minutes.

2.   Strain the mixture into a clean saucepan and return it to a simmer. In a bowl, whisk together the egg yolks and the remaining 1.75 oz [49 g] of sugar and temper in the hot liquid. Cook over low heat, stirring, until the mixture coats the back of a wooden spoon. Strain over an ice bath and cool completely.

BAVARIAN:

.44 oz [12.5 g] gelatin, bloomed and drained

2 liq oz [59 ml] Frangelico

16 liq oz [473 ml] banana anglaise, chilled

16 liq oz [473 ml] heavy cream, whipped to soft peaks

1.   In a mixing bowl, combine the gelatin and Frangelico and place over simmering water just until the gelatin has melted.

2.   Whisk the chilled banana anglaise into the melted gelatin. Fold in the whipped cream.

MARJOLAINE ASSEMBLY:

Tempered milk chocolate

Tempered dark chocolate

Tempered white chocolate

Fresh bananas, sliced

Confectioners' sugar

1.   Cut strips of acetate to fit around the inside of the ring molds. Place tempered milk and dark chocolates into parchment cones and pipe diagonal lines on the acetate. When the chocolate has just begun to set, cover the entire strip with tempered white chocolate. Place the acetate in the ring molds with the chocolate facing inside. Let set completely.

2.   Place a disc of pecan crust in the bottom of each ring mold, chocolate side down. Pipe a layer of mousse over the crust and top the mousse with a meringue disc.

3.   Dust banana slices with confectioners' sugar and caramelize the sugar with a heat torch. Place two banana slices on top of the meringue. Pipe a layer of Bavarian over the bananas and top with another meringue, then another layer of Bavarian. Chill for at least 1 hour.

4.   Unmold the marjolaines and remove the acetate. Spread a thin layer of melted ganache on top.

DESSERT ASSEMBLY:

Crème anglaise

Heavy cream, whipped

Chocolate butterflies

Confectioners' sugar

Orange segments

Fresh blueberries

Mint sprigs

Mango coulis

Strawberry coulis

1.   Make a pool of crème anglaise in the center of each dessert plate and place a marjolaine in it. Top the marjolaine with a quenelle of whipped cream and a chocolate butterfly.

2.   Place a small scoop of strawberry sorbet next to the marjolaine. Dust a spoon-shaped tuile with confectioners' sugar and stick the tip into the sorbet.

3.   Garnish the plate with orange segments, fresh blueberries, and a mint sprig. Place dots of mango coulis and strawberry coulis around the plate.

Coconut Cream Pie with Bananas and Caramel Sauce

YIELD: *10 servings*

MARTIN HOWARD

NEW YORK, NY

Martin Howard, known for his visual extravagance, is in classic, restrained mode with this coconut cream pie. Chocolate cookie dough serving as the tart shell is the neoclassic flavor and textural twist. Fully edible visual enhancements include the starfish formed from meringue and a milk and dark chocolate palm tree.

CHOCOLATE CRUST:

8 oz [237 g] unsalted butter

6 oz [170 g] granulated sugar

½ tsp [3 g] salt

1.3 oz [37 g] egg yolks

1 tsp [4 g] vanilla extract

4 oz [113 g] almond flour

1.5 oz [43 g] bread or cake crumbs

10 oz [283 g] cake flour

9 oz [255 g] melted bittersweet chocolate, divided

1.   In a mixer with the paddle attachment, cream together the butter, sugar, salt, egg yolks, and vanilla extract. Combine the almond flour, crumbs, and cake flour and add to the butter mixture. Mix just until the dough comes together. Mix in 4 oz [113 g] of the melted chocolate. Wrap the dough and chill for at least 1 hour.

2.   Preheat oven to 350°F [175°C]. On a floured surface, roll out the dough, one-half at a time, to a ⅛″ [3 mm] thickness, and line ten 4″ [10 cm] tartlet pans. Prick the bottoms well and bake for 12 to 15 minutes, or until they just begin to color. Cool completely.

3.   Brush the insides of the shells with the remaining 5 oz [142 g] of melted chocolate and let set.

CARAMEL SAUCE:

12 oz [340 g] granulated sugar

1 tsp [5 g] lemon juice

8 liq oz [237 ml] heavy cream

.5 oz [14 g] unsalted butter

1.   In a heavy saucepan, combine the sugar and lemon juice, rubbing with your fingers to insure that they are well incorporated. Heat over a high flame until the sugar just starts to melt, then stir slowly with a wooden spoon. Continue cooking until the sugar turns golden brown.

2.   Remove the pan from the heat and add the cream slowly and carefully. Return to the heat and stir until smooth. Whisk in the butter.

FILLING:

1 qt [946 ml] milk, divided

3.5 oz [99 g] eggs

3.3 oz [94 g] granulated sugar, divided

.5 oz [14 g] cornstarch

.5 oz [14 g] unsalted butter

3.1 oz [88 g] grated coconut, toasted and cooled

4 oz [113 g] Coco Lopez cream of coconut

7.5 oz [213 g] gelatin, bloomed

2 Tbs [28 g] dark rum

1 pt [473 ml] heavy cream

1 tsp [4 g] vanilla extract

1. In a saucepan, bring 24 liq oz [709 ml] of the milk to a boil. Whisk together the eggs and the remaining 8 liq oz [237 ml] of the milk. Combine 2 oz [57 ml] of the sugar with the cornstarch and whisk into the eggs. Temper the egg mixture into the hot milk and cook, whisking constantly, until it comes to a boil. Remove from heat and whisk in the butter. Transfer the pastry cream to a clean bowl and whisk in the toasted coconut and cream of coconut.

2. Combine the bloomed gelatin with the rum and melt the gelatin over simmering water. Mix it into the pastry cream and let cool.

3. In a mixer, whip the cream, vanilla extract, and the remaining 1.3 oz [37 g] of sugar to medium peaks and fold it into the pastry cream.

COCONUT MERINGUE STARFISH:

4.2 oz [120 g] egg whites

8 oz [227 g] superfine sugar

Toasted coconut, as needed

1. Preheat oven to 225°F [105°C]. Line a sheet pan with parchment paper. In a mixer fitted with the whisk attachment, beat the egg whites until very stiff. Add one-half of the sugar and beat for 30 seconds more. Fold in the remaining sugar. Fill a pastry bag fitted with a #2 plain tip with the meringue. Pipe out 10 starfish shapes onto the sheet pan. Sprinkle the starfish with the toasted coconut.

2. Bake the starfish for 1½ to 2 hours, until dry and crisp. Cool completely.

ASSEMBLY:

4 bananas, sliced

1 pt [473 ml] heavy cream

1 tsp [4 g] vanilla extract

.8 oz [23 g] granulated sugar

Chocolate palm tree garnish

1.   Arrange the banana slices on the bottoms of the tartlet shells, then divide the filling evenly between them. Refrigerate to set.

2.   In a mixer, whip the cream, vanilla extract, and sugar to stiff peaks and pipe it on top of the filling. Serve with caramel sauce and garnish with the coconut meringue starfish.

french classics

CHAPTER 4

Profiteroles with Crunchy Peanut Butter Ice Cream and Warm Chocolate Sauce

YIELD: *10 servings*

LINCOLN CARSON

PICASSO
LAS VEGAS, NV

The classic profiterole is filled with pastry cream, but Lincoln Carson uses ice cream, the better to contrast with the warm chocolate sauce. And for crunch? Chocolate is melted and mixed with feuilletine ["Fancy crunchy stuff," is Carson's description], then pulverized and incorporated into the peanut butter ice cream. "The flavors are tried and true," says Carson. "It's not hard to see where this came from—Americans grew up loving peanut butter cups." A chocolate cookie, two chocolate sauces, and a chocolate cigarette finish the plate.

CHOCOLATE CRUNCH:

4 oz [113 g] bittersweet chocolate, melted

2 oz [57 g] feuilletine

1.   Fold the feuilletine into the melted chocolate. Spread a thin, even layer of the chocolate mixture onto a parchment-lined baking pan. Allow to cool completely.

2.   Break up the chocolate feuilletine layer into small pieces and place them in the bowl of a food processor fitted with a metal blade. Pulse until the pieces are about ⅛" [.3 cm] square. Alternatively, use a chef's knife to cut the chocolate layer into the small squares.

CRUNCHY PEANUT BUTTER ICE CREAM:

16 liq oz [473 ml] heavy cream

27 liq oz [798 ml] half-and-half

9 oz [255 g] granulated sugar

16 oz [454 g] egg yolks

17 oz [482 g] smooth peanut butter

3 liq oz [89 ml] Grand Marnier

6 oz [170 g] chocolate crunch

1.   In a saucepan, combine the heavy cream, half-and-half, and sugar and bring to a boil; remove the pan from the heat.

2.   In a bowl, whisk the egg yolks until blended. Temper the yolks with about half of the hot cream mixture and pour the yolk-cream mixture back into the saucepan. Cook over low heat until the mixture reaches the custard stage.

3.   Immediately strain the custard into a bowl set over an ice bath and cool completely.

4.   Place the peanut butter in a large bowl. Whisk in about 1 cup of the cooled custard. When the mixture is smooth, whisk in the remaining custard and the Grand Marnier.

5.   Refrigerate until cold or, preferably, overnight.

6.   Process the mixture in an ice cream machine according to the manufacturer's instructions. Fold in the chocolate crunch as the ice cream is coming out of the machine.

CHOCOLATE TUILES:

3 oz [85 g] all-purpose flour, sifted

4 oz [113 g] confectioners' sugar, sifted

1.5 oz [43 g] Valrhona cocoa powder, sifted

4 oz [113 g] egg whites

4 oz [113 g] unsalted butter, melted

1.   Combine the sifted dry ingredients in a mixer fitted with a paddle attachment. Gradually add in the egg whites and beat at medium speed until smooth. Slowly drizzle in the butter and mix until the butter is absorbed and the batter is well blended. Refrigerate for at least 1 hour.

2.   Preheat oven to 300°F [150°C]. Line a baking sheet with a silicone baking mat. Cut a triangular stencil, 9″ [22.9 cm] high with a 2″ [5.1 cm] base, that tapers off to a hook at the top.

3.   Place the stencil over the silicone mat and spread a thin layer of chocolate tuile batter through the stencil. Remove the stencil and bake for 9 to 12 minutes or until the tuile is set and dry. Bend the tuile at the "neck" of the hook. Allow to cool completely. Repeat to make 10 tuiles.

CHOCOLATE DISCS:

8 oz [227 g] unsalted butter, softened

8 oz [227 g] granulated sugar

1.75 oz [50 g] whole eggs

8 oz [227 g] Valrhona cocoa powder

1.5 liq oz [44 ml] water

5 oz [142 g] all-purpose flour

Confectioners' sugar for dusting

1 oz [28 g] large crystal sugar

1.   In a mixer fitted with a paddle attachment, beat the butter at medium speed until smooth. Gradually add the sugar and continue beating until the mixture is light.

2.   Add the eggs and mix until incorporated. Reduce the speed to low and mix in the cocoa powder. Mix in the water, then the flour. Mix until an even-colored mass of dough has formed. Divide the dough into thirds; shape each third into a disc and wrap each disc with plastic wrap. Refrigerate for at least 1 hour. [Note: two of the discs will not be needed for this recipe and may be frozen for future use.]

3.   On a work surface that has been dusted with confectioners' sugar, roll out one disc of dough to about ¹⁄₁₆″ [.16 cm] thick. Just before the desired thickness is reached, sprinkle the dough generously with the large crystal sugar [you may not need all of the sugar]. Very gently roll the sugar into the dough. Using a 1½″ [3.8 cm] round cutter, stamp out 30 rounds of dough. Place them on a parchment-lined baking pan; cover with plastic wrap and chill for at least 1 hour.

PROFITEROLES:

4 liq oz [118 ml] milk

4 liq oz [118 ml] water

4 oz [113 g] unsalted butter, cut into cubes

Pinch of salt

5.25 oz [149 g] bread flour

8.75 oz [248 g] whole eggs, lightly beaten

1.   Preheat oven to 375°F [190°C]. Line a sheet pan with parchment paper.

2.   In a saucepan, combine the milk, water, butter, and salt. Cook over low heat until the butter is completely melted; increase the heat and bring to a full boil. Reduce the heat to low; add the flour all at once and stir the mixture with a wooden spoon for 2 to 3 minutes, until it is well-blended and smooth and comes away from the side of the pan.

3.   Transfer the paste to a mixer fitted with a paddle attachment and mix on low speed until the paste is no longer hot, but still warm, about 2 to 3 minutes. Still at low speed, add the beaten eggs in 5 additions, incorporating as much of the beaten eggs as the paste will absorb and still hold its shaped when piped.

4.   Scrape the paste into a pastry bag fitted with a medium-large plain tip [Ateco #7]. Pipe out 30 mounds of paste, about 1½″ [3.8 cm] in diameter, onto the prepared pan. Top each mound with a chocolate disc. [At this point the chocolate-dough topped profiteroles may be frozen and then baked off directly from the freezer.] Bake the profiteroles for 25 to 30 minutes or until golden brown. Transfer to a rack to cool completely.

DARK CHOCOLATE SAUCE:

4 oz [113 g] unsweetened cocoa powder, such as Valrhona

1.75 oz [50 g] Valrhona extra-bittersweet chocolate, finely chopped

16 liq oz [473 ml] water

16 oz [454 g] granulated sugar

1.   Place the cocoa powder in a large bowl. Place the chopped chocolate in another large bowl.

2.   In a saucepan, bring the water and sugar to a boil. Remove the pan from the heat and slowly whisk enough of the syrup into the cocoa powder to create a smooth, thick paste. Slowly whisk in the remaining syrup and then return the entire mixture to the saucepan, whisking until smooth. Bring the sauce to a boil.

3.   Pour the hot sauce over the chopped chocolate. Allow the mixture to stand for 3 minutes to melt the chocolate. Whisk the mixture until smooth and pass the sauce through a fine sieve. Refrigerate until cold.

WARM CHOCOLATE SAUCE:

9 oz [255 g] Valrhona Manjari chocolate, finely chopped

4 oz [113 g] light corn syrup

16 liq oz [473 ml] heavy cream

1. Place the chopped chocolate and corn syrup in a large bowl.

2. In a saucepan, bring the cream to a boil. Pour the hot cream over the chocolate and corn syrup. Allow the mixture to stand for 3 minutes to melt the chocolate. Whisk until smooth.

ASSEMBLY:

Striped cigarettes

1. Place a pool of warm chocolate sauce off-center on a dessert plate. Squeeze some dark chocolate in a pattern emanating from the center of the pool.

2. Split three profiteroles in half horizontally and sandwich a scoop of crunchy peanut butter ice cream between the top and bottom halves of each one. Place the 3 filled profiteroles in the pool of warm chocolate sauce.

3. Garnish the dessert with a striped cigarette inserted in the hook of a chocolate tuile.

Trio of Asian Brûlées

YIELD: *20 servings*

JOHN DEGNAN

THE LODGE AT KOELE, HI

Green tea, chocolate ginger, and citrus crème brûlées are served in sake cups and decorated with pulled sugar orchids. "If you infuse green tea too long it becomes bitter," advises John Degnan. "Only infuse it for two to three minutes, then all the tannin of the tea comes out in the custard. Citrus is fairly easy, but if you add too much citrus the acid tends to curdle the custard. Whenever I make a confit of any zest, I bring it to a boil two or three times with plain water first. That gets the bitterness out, and after that you can cook it in your syrup. As for chocolate, the timing is tricky— people tend to overbake it and it cracks."

SPECIAL EQUIPMENT: *60 sake cups*

CITRUS CRÈME BRÛLÉE:

2 lemons

2 oranges

1 grapefruit

1 pt [473 ml] whole milk

1 pt [473 ml] heavy cream

10 oz [283 g] egg yolks

4.25 oz [120 g] granulated sugar

1. Preheat oven to 300°F [150°C]. Remove the rinds of the lemons, oranges, and grapefruit. Place the rinds in a saucepan and fill with water. Bring to a boil, strain, and boil the rinds again in fresh water. Repeat this process one more time to make sure that all of the bitterness has been removed from the rinds.

2. Put the milk and heavy cream in a saucepan with the boiled citrus rinds and bring to a boil.

3. Place the egg yolks and sugar in a bowl and whisk together. Temper the yolk mixture with the hot cream mixture.

4. Remove the mixture from the heat and allow to steep until cool; strain. Evenly distribute the mixture among 20 sake cups and bake in a water bath for about 15 minutes, until set.

CHOCOLATE GINGER CRÈME BRÛLÉE:

4.5 oz [128 g] bittersweet chocolate couverture

1 pt [473 ml] whole milk

1 pt [473 ml] heavy cream

2.5 oz [71 g] fresh ginger, grated

10 oz [283 g] egg yolks

4.25 oz [120 g] granulated sugar

1. Preheat oven to 300°F [150°C]. Finely chop the couverture and place in a heatproof bowl. Bring the milk, heavy cream, and ginger to a boil in a saucepan.

2. Place the egg yolks and sugar in a medium bowl and whisk together. Temper the yolk mixture with the hot cream mixture.

3. Pour the mixture over the chocolate and allow to steep until cool.

4. Evenly distribute the mixture among 20 sake cups and bake in a water bath for about 15 minutes, until set.

GREEN TEA CRÈME BRÛLÉE:

1 pt [473 ml] whole milk

1 pt [473 ml] heavy cream

2½ tsp [3 g] green tea

10 oz [283 g] egg yolks

4.25 oz [120 g] granulated sugar

1.   Preheat oven to 300°F [150°C]. Place the milk, heavy cream, and green tea in a saucepan and bring to a boil. Allow to steep for 3 minutes. Strain and return the mixture to the saucepan.

2.   Whisk together the egg yolks and sugar in a bowl. Temper the yolk mixture with the reheated milk mixture.

3.   Evenly distribute the mixture among 20 sake cups and bake in a water bath for about 15 minutes, until set.

ASSEMBLY:

Candied orange zest

Thin chocolate ribbons

Spun sugar

Arrange one of each type of the three crème brûlées on a plate. Garnish the top of the citrus crème brûlée with some candied orange zest. Garnish the top of the chocolate ginger crème brûlée with a few thin chocolate ribbons. Garnish the top of the green tea crème brûlée with some spun sugar.

Sabayon Charlotte

**LAS VEGAS HILTON
LAS VEGAS, NV**

A champagne-egg brandy sabayon is presented inside a demisphere of a joconde raspberry roulade, which has been imprinted with a polka-dot silkscreen; the dessert is accompanied by a brunoise of mango, kiwi, cantaloupe, and strawberries in a raspberry coulis. "It is very refreshing and light, a perfect choice after a heavy dinner," comments Stan Ho. Egg brandy is a product of Germany and is difficult, but not impossible, to find in the States, admits Ho; just as it sounds, it is a product of eggs cured or processed with brandy, and the egg flavor is subtle.

SPECIAL EQUIPMENT: *Polka-dot design silkscreen stencil; fifteen 4 oz [118 ml] metal or Flexipan demisphere molds*

CHOCOLATE STENCILING:

Cocoa Barry Krem d'Arome, as needed

Line a full sheet pan with a silicone baking mat. Place the polka-dot silkscreen stencil over the mat. Evenly spread some of the Krem d'Arome over the polka dots. Allow to set for a few minutes. Remove the silkscreen and freeze for about 1 hour, or until completely set.

BISCUIT JOCONDE:

12.75 oz [361 g] almond flour

12.75 oz [361 g] confectioners' sugar

4.5 oz [128 g] all-purpose flour

17.25 oz [489 g] whole eggs

17.25 oz [489 g] egg whites

3 oz [85 g] granulated sugar

3 Tbs [18 g] dried egg whites

½ tsp [1.5 g] cream of tartar

3 oz [85 g] unsalted butter, melted

1. Preheat the oven to 400°F [204°C]. Line 2 full sheet pans with silicone baking mats.

2. In a bowl, combine the almond flour, confectioners' sugar, and all-purpose flour. Sift together twice; set aside.

3. In a mixer with a whisk attachment, whip the eggs on high speed until doubled in volume.

4. With the mixer on low speed, add the sifted dry ingredients in three additions.

5. In a mixer with a whisk attachment, combine the egg whites, one-third of the granulated sugar, the dried egg whites, and the cream of tartar. Beat the mixture to soft peaks. Slowly add the remaining granulated sugar and beat until firm peaks form. Gently fold the meringue into the egg-flour mixture; fold in the melted butter.

6. Remove the sheet pan with the frozen chocolate silkscreen design from the freezer.

7. Divide the joconde batter among the 3 prepared pans and spread an even layer of batter over each. Bake for 10 to 14 minutes or until the cake is lightly golden in color and springs back when gently pressed with a finger.

8.   Let cool for a couple of minutes, then run a knife around the edge of each pan and invert the cakes onto a cooling rack. Carefully peel off the silicone mats and let cool completely.

9.   Using a 4″ [10.2 cm] round cutter, cut out 15 discs from the polka-dot silkscreen joconde.

RASPBERRY ROULADE:

18 oz [510 g] raspberry jam

Cut the plain biscuit joconde into twelve 4½″ × 10½″ [11.4 cm × 26.7 cm] strips. Spread a thin layer of raspberry jam over the strips. Place each strip of biscuit on a piece of parchment slightly larger than the strip. Use the parchment to roll each strip into a 10½″ [26.7 cm] long cylinder. At the end of the rolling process, place a ruler on the exterior of the parchment sheet, at an angle to the roulade. Apply pressure on the ruler, while pulling on the bottom parchment, to tighten the roulade. The diameter of the roulade will be about ¾″ [1.9 cm]. Indivdually wrap the roulades tightly in plastic wrap and refrigerate until needed. [There may be more roulade than is needed for this recipe. Freeze any excess for future use.]

CHAMPAGNE-EGG BRANDY SABAYON:

3 liq oz [89 ml] water

3 oz [85 g] granulated sugar

.5 oz [14 g] gelatin sheets, softened in cold water

8.5 oz [241 g] egg yolks

½ tsp [1 g] finely grated orange zest

½ tsp [1 g] finely grated lemon zest

7 liq oz [207 ml] champagne

2 liq oz [59 ml] egg brandy

12 liq oz [355 ml] heavy cream, whipped to soft peaks

1.   In a small saucepan, combine the water and sugar. Bring to a boil, making sure the sugar is completely dissolved. Remove from heat and whisk in the gelatin.

2.   Meanwhile, in a mixer with a whisk attachment, whip the yolks to the ribbon stage. Slowly pour the hot syrup into the whipping yolks and then immediately add the orange and lemon zests. Continue whipping until the mixture is light in texture and increased in volume. Mix in the champagne and egg brandy.

3.   Place the mixture over an ice bath and stir gently with a rubber spatula until it begins to congeal. Remove the bowl from the ice bath and fold in one-third of the whipped cream. Fold in the remaining whipped cream in 2 additions and chill.

SABAYON CHARLOTTE ASSEMBLY:

Light apricot glaze, as needed

1. Cut the raspberry roulades into ³⁄₁₆″ [.5 cm] thick slices.

2. Place the demisphere molds on a sheet pan. Line the molds with raspberry roulade slices.

3. Fill the lined molds with champagne sabayon to within ³⁄₁₆″ [.5 cm] of the top. Place a layer of roulade slices over the sabayon, pressing down sligtly. The charlottes may either be refrigerated for at least 3 hours or made ahead and frozen for future use. [If using the Flexipan molds, the charlottes must be frozen in order to facilitate unmolding.] If frozen, first unmold, then allow to defrost in the refrigerator.

4. Unmold the charlottes and coat with apricot glaze shortly before serving.

RASPBERRY COULIS:

17.5 oz [496 g] raspberry purée
4.5 oz [128 g] granulated sugar

1. In a food processor fitted with the metal chopping blade, combine the raspberry purée and sugar and process until blended.

2. Place the purée in a stainless steel bowl, cover with plastic wrap, and chill thoroughly.

ASSEMBLY:

Fresh mango, kiwi, cantalope, and strawberries, cut into brunoise
Pulled sugar flower with spikes and leaves

1. Place a polka-dot silkscreen disc onto the center of a dessert plate.

2. Remove a glazed sabayon charlotte from the refrigerator and center it on the disc.

3. Place a sugar ornament on top of the charlotte. Drizzle raspberry coulis and arrange some brunoise of assorted fruit around the dessert.

Vanilla Charlotte

YIELD: *20 servings*

NORMAN LOVE

RITZ-CARLTON HOTEL
COMPANY
NAPLES, FL

The classic elements are in place—Bavaroise, ladyfinger, and fruit—but Charlotte has been given a beauty makeover for individual plating: placed in a ring mold, topped with glaze and surrounded by sugar work, chocolate forms, mint sprigs, and lychee nuts.

LADYFINGERS:

17.6 oz [500 g] all-purpose flour

.9 oz [25 g] baking powder

20 oz [567 g] egg whites

17.6 oz [500 g] granulated sugar

10 oz [283 g] egg yolks, warm

1. Preheat oven to 400°F [205°C].
2. Sift together the flour and baking powder.
3. In a mixing bowl, whip the egg whites and sugar to stiff peaks. Fold in the yolks, then the sifted flour and baking powder.
4. Pipe the batter onto a parchment-lined sheet pan. Bake until lightly browned, about 8 minutes.

VANILLA BAVAROISE:

1.1 qt [1 lt] milk

3 vanilla beans, split and scraped

9.9 oz [280 g] egg yolks

8.8 oz [250 g] granulated sugar

10 [25 g] gelatin sheets, bloomed and strained

16.9 liq oz [.5 lt] heavy cream, whipped to soft peaks

1. In a saucepan, bring the milk and vanilla beans to a boil.
2. In a mixing bowl, combine the egg yolks and sugar. Temper and add to the hot milk mixture. Cook to 185°F [85°C]. Remove from the heat. Add the gelatin. Strain and cool in an ice bath.
3. Fold in the whipped cream.

ASSEMBLY:

Assorted fresh fruit

Neutral glaze

Pulled sugar ribbons and sticks

Chocolate curls and sticks

Lychee nuts

Mint sprigs

1. Place twenty 3½″ [8.9 cm] ring molds on a parchment-lined sheet pan. Line with ladyfingers. Fill with vanilla Bavaroise. Refrigerate until set.

2. Remove charlottes from rings. Decorate the top of the charlotte with fruit. Glaze. Wrap with pulled sugar ribbon. Garnish with chocolate curls, pulled sugar, chocolate sticks, lychee nuts, and mint.

Banana Feuillettes with Caramel Sauce

NICK MALGIERI

PETER KUMP'S NEW YORK
COOKING SCHOOL

The classic, time-consuming puff pastry formula of folding, refrigerating, and folding is streamlined for this presentation: only two folds, rather than six, are involved, and only one refrigeration interval is required. Nick Malgieri's "quickest" puff pastry "is very straightforward, comes out like standard puff pastry, and can be done in five minutes," says Malgieri. Two layers of this puff loosely enclose bananas that have been tossed with rum and sugar, with a topping of whipped cream and generous drizzles of caramel sauce, which Malgieri has substituted for the more familiar pastry cream.

QUICK PUFF PASTRY:

10 oz [284 g] unsalted butter, cold, divided

4 liq oz [118 ml] cold water

1 tsp [7 g] salt

9 oz [255 g] unbleached, all-purpose flour

1.   Cut 8 oz [227 g] of the butter into ¼″ to ½″ [.6 cm to 1.27 cm] dice. Place the cubed butter on a plate and refrigerate. Mix the water and salt together and set aside. Coarsely dice the remaining 2 oz [57 g] of butter. Set aside.

2.   Combine the 2 oz [57 g] of coarsely diced butter and the flour in the bowl of a food processor fitted with the metal chopping blade. Pulse about 10 to 12 times, until the butter is completely blended in.

3.   Add the remaining cubed butter to the mixture in the food processor and pulse once or twice just to distribute. Add the water and salt mixture and pulse an additional 3 to 4 times, until the dough begins to come together. Do not over-process the dough.

4.   Dust a work surface with flour. Transfer the dough to the floured surface and shape it into a rough rectangle. Place the rectangle of dough between two pieces of plastic wrap and roll out into a 12″ × 18″ [30 cm × 46 cm] rectangle.

5.   Peel off the plastic wrap and invert the dough onto the floured surface. Peel away the second piece of plastic wrap and fold the dough into thirds to form a 4″ × 18″ [10 cm × 46 cm] rectangle. Roll up the dough from one 4″ [10 cm] side to the other. Press the roll into a square. Wrap it in plastic wrap and refrigerate for 1 hour or until firm.

6.   Line a half sheet pan with parchment paper and have ready another piece of parchment and a half sheet pan. Remove the dough from the refrigerator and divide it in half. Wrap one half and freeze it for another use. On a floured surface roll out the other half of the dough into a 10″ × 15″ [25 cm × 38 cm] rectangle and place it on the parchment-lined half sheet pan. Cover the dough and return it to the refrigerator for an hour to rest and chill.

7.   Preheat the oven to 350°F [175°C]. Remove the pan with the dough from the refrigerator, uncover it, and place the other piece of parchment and half sheet pan over the dough. Bake it for 30 minutes until the pastry is deep golden brown. Allow it to cool on a rack between the 2 half sheet pans.

CARAMEL SAUCE:

8 oz [227 g] granulated sugar

1 tsp [5 ml] water

6 liq oz [177 g] heavy cream

1. Stir the sugar and water together in a medium saucepan. Place the saucepan over low heat and allow the sugar to melt and caramelize, stirring occasionally.

2. In a separate pan, heat the heavy cream to a simmer. When the sugar is a deep amber color, add it to the simmering heavy cream in 4 additions. After all the sugar has been added, stir the mixture once or twice and bring it to a full boil. Strain the sauce through a fine chinois and let it stand to cool.

BANANA FILLING:

1.5 lb [680 g] bananas [3 large]

1.5 oz [43 g] granulated sugar

1 liq oz [30 ml] dark rum

1. Peel the bananas and cut them into ¼″ [.63 cm] thick slices.

2. Combine the bananas with the sugar and dark rum. Cover tightly with plastic and refrigerate.

WHIPPED CREAM:

8 liq oz [237 g] heavy cream

1 oz [28 g] granulated sugar

1 tsp [4 g] vanilla extract

In the mixer combine the cream, sugar, and vanilla extract. Whip on high speed to soft peaks. Cover and reserve in the refrigerator.

ASSEMBLY:

Confectioners' sugar for dusting

1. Use a 3″ [7.6 cm] round cutter to cut 16 circles from the puff pastry.

2. Pour the caramel sauce into a squeeze bottle and streak the dessert plate with the sauce. Place a 3″ [7.6 cm] puff pastry round in the center of the plate and cover it with several slices of banana. Pipe a large spiral of whipped cream on top of the bananas. Top the whipped cream with another puff pastry round and press it down gently. Dust the pastry with confectioners' sugar.

Tropical Pavé

JEAN MARC VIALLET

RITZ-CARLTON
HUNTINGTON
HOTEL & SPA
PASADENA, CA

Glazed rather than frosted, this pavé contains layers of flourless chocolate biscuit, chocolate macadamia truffle mousse, and white chocolate and passion fruit truffle mousse, with fresh fruits and berries, rum caramel sauce, bubble sugar, pulled sugar leaves, and poured sugar pyramids to finish the presentation. "A bitter chocolate goes well with passion fruit," says Viallet, "and the acidity of the passion fruit cuts very well with the sweetness of the white chocolate. It's a nice combination, I believe."

FLOURLESS CHOCOLATE BISCUIT:

7 oz [198 g] almond paste

5.5 oz [156 g] egg yolks

10.5 oz [298 g] egg whites

8 oz [227 g] granulated sugar

6 oz [170 g] Valrhona Manjari chocolate, melted and kept warm

1 oz [28 g] unsweetened cocoa powder

1.   Preheat oven to 375°F [190°C]. In a mixer with the paddle attachment, beat the almond paste while gradually adding the egg yolks. Continue beating until the mixture is light and airy. In a separate mixer bowl, whip the egg whites to soft peaks while gradually adding the sugar. Lighten the almond mixture with one-third of the egg whites. Fold in the melted chocolate, then another third of the egg whites. Sift the cocoa powder over the almond mixture and fold it in, followed by the remaining egg whites.

2.   Spread the batter evenly onto 2 half sheet pans lined with silicone baking mats. Bake for 9 to 11 minutes or until the cake springs back when gently pressed with a finger.

RED CURRANT AND PINEAPPLE SORBET:

1 medium pineapple, well ripened

8 liq oz [237 ml] water

9 oz [255 ml] granulated sugar

8 oz [227 g] red currants, fresh or individually quick-frozen [defrosted]

2 liq oz [59 ml] light rum

1.   Peel, core, and dice the pineapple. Purée it in a blender to yield 24 liq oz [710 ml] of pulp. In a saucepan, combine the water and sugar and cook just until all of the sugar has dissolved. Remove the pan from the heat and cool over an ice bath.

2.   Add 12 liq oz [355 ml] of the syrup to the pineapple purée. Mix in the red currants and the rum. Process in an ice cream machine according to the manufacturer's instructions.

CHOCOLATE MACADAMIA TRUFFLE MOUSSE:

8 oz [227 g] Valrhona Manjari chocolate, finely chopped

4.5 oz [128 g] Valrhona Jivara lactée, finely chopped

22.4 liq oz [663 ml] heavy cream, divided

6 oz [170 g] macadamia nuts, roasted, patted dry, and chopped

1.   Place the dark and milk chocolates in a large mixing bowl. In a saucepan, bring 12 liq oz [355 ml] of the heavy cream to a boil. Pour the hot cream over the chopped chocolate and whisk until the chocolate is completely melted and smooth. Let cool to 100°F [38°C].

2.   In a mixer, whip the remaining 10.4 liq oz [308 ml] of heavy cream to soft peaks and gently fold it into the chocolate mixture. Fold in the chopped nuts.

WHITE CHOCOLATE AND PASSION FRUIT TRUFFLE MOUSSE:

12 oz [340 g] Valrhona Ivoire chocolate, finely chopped

8 liq oz [227 ml] passion fruit purée

24 liq oz [710 ml] heavy cream, whipped to soft peaks

1.   Place the chopped chocolate in a large mixing bowl. In a saucepan, heat the passion fruit purée until it bubbles. Pour the hot purée over the chopped chocolate and whisk until the chocolate is completely melted and smooth. Let cool.

2.   Gently fold the whipped cream into the chocolate mixture.

ABSOLUT CHOCOLATE GLAZE:

9.25 oz [262 g] Valrhona pâte à glacer noire, finely chopped

4 oz [113 g] Valrhona Manjari chocolate, finely chopped

8 liq oz [237 ml] half-and-half

1.75 oz [50 g] brown sugar

1.5 oz [43 g] corn syrup

1½ Tbs [21 g] Absolut lemon vodka

Place the chopped pâte à glacer and chocolate in a large mixing bowl. In a saucepan, combine the half-and-half, brown sugar, and corn syrup. Bring the mixture to a boil and pour it over the chocolate. Whisk until the mixture is completely smooth. Whisk in the vodka.

RUM CARAMEL SAUCE:

14 oz [397 g] granulated sugar

7.7 oz [218 g] brown sugar

8 liq oz [237 ml] water

3 liq oz [89 ml] passion fruit purée

4 liq oz [118 ml] heavy cream

2 liq oz [59 ml] dark rum

In a saucepan, combine the granulated sugar, brown sugar, and water, and cook to a medium caramel. Deglaze the pan with the passion fruit purée, then add the cream slowly and carefully. Remove the pan from the heat and stir in the rum.

ASSEMBLY:

Tempered Valrhona Manjari chocolate

Simple syrup flavored with La Grande Passion liqueur

Pulled-sugar sticks

Poured-sugar pyramids

Bubble sugar

Pulled-sugar leaves

Assorted fresh fruits and berries

1.   Spread a thin coat of tempered chocolate over 1 sheet of the biscuit. When the chocolate has set, place the biscuit, chocolate side down, on a half sheet pan. Soak the cake with simple syrup. Spread a thin layer of the chocolate macadamia truffle mousse over the biscuit. Cover the mousse with the other sheet of biscuit and soak it with simple syrup. Spread all of the white chocolate and passion fruit truffle mousse over the biscuit and let it set in the freezer for 15 minutes.

2.   Spread the remaining chocolate macadamia truffle mousse on top and let it set in the freezer for 2 hours. Cover with melted Absolut chocolate glaze.

3.   Cut the pavé into 30 ovals and place 2 on each dessert plate. Insert 2 pulled-sugar sticks into each oval. Place a poured-sugar pyramid in front. Top it with a piece of bubble sugar and a small scoop of the red currant and pineapple sorbet with a pulled-sugar leaf. Garnish the plate with assorted fresh fruits and berries and the rum caramel sauce.

Lemon Chiffon Bombe

YIELD: *20 servings*

SUSAN NOTTER

ALBERT USTER IMPORTS
GAITHERSBURG, MD

Though the bombe is classic, and chiffon is classic, Susan Notter likes to characterize this dessert as "a lighter cheesecake" with cherry, lemon, and white chocolate as a pleasing color scheme. Between discs of white chocolate-coated almond sablé is a lemon bombe with a kirsch-soaked sponge at its center and sour cherries "to cut the flavors of the cheese and sour cream," says Notter. The bombe is served with a sour cherry sauce and white chocolate rose petals. A pastry cutter is dragged through tempered white chocolate "at exactly the right moment, so they curl, not crack," says Notter. The former teacher says that "the inspiration was simply to show the chocolate technique."

SPECIAL EQUIPMENT: *Twenty 5 oz [148 ml] demisphere molds*

ALMOND SABLÉ DISCS:

8.5 oz [241 g] unsalted butter, softened

6.5 oz [184 g] confectioners' sugar

3.5 oz [99 g] whole eggs

2.0 oz [57 g] almond flour

16 oz [454 g] all-purpose flour, sifted

1. In a mixer with a paddle attachment, cream the butter and confectioners' sugar on medium speed until smooth. Slowly add the eggs, and mix until incorporated; then mix in the almond flour.

2. Reduce the speed to low and add the all-purpose flour, mixing until the flour is just barely combined. Turn the mixture out onto a work surface and knead until all the flour is incorporated and the dough is smooth. Shape the dough into a disc; wrap with plastic wrap and refrigerate until firm.

3. Preheat oven to 400°F [205°C]. Line a baking sheet with parchment paper.

4. On a work surface that has been lightly dusted with flour, roll the dough out to ⅛" [.3 cm] thick. Use a round cutter, with a diameter slightly less than that of the demisphere mold, to stamp out 20 rounds of dough. Place the rounds on the prepared pan; cover with plastic wrap and chill until firm, at least 1 hour.

4. Bake the discs for 7 to 10 minutes or until lightly colored. Allow to cool completely on a wire rack.

ALMOND SPONGE CAKE:

5.5 oz [156 g] cake flour, sifted

2 oz [57 g] cornstarch

8 oz [227 g] almond paste [50% sugar, 50% almond]

4 oz [113 g] egg yolks

7.5 oz [213 g] granulated sugar

11.5 oz [326 g] whole eggs

1 Tbs [6 g] lemon rappé [grated lemon zest]

Pinch of salt

2 oz [57 g] unsalted butter, melted and warm

1. Preheat oven to 400°F [205°C]. Line a half sheet pan with parchment paper.

2. In a bowl, combine the sifted cake flour and cornstarch and set aside.

3. In a mixer with a paddle attachment, beat the almond paste and the egg yolks until smooth. Add the sugar, whole eggs, lemon rappé, and salt. Beat for 9 minutes on high speed. By hand, fold in the dry ingredients; then gently fold in the butter.

4. Spread the batter evenly in the prepared pan and bake for 20 to 25 minutes or until the cake is lightly golden in color and springs back when gently pressed with a finger.

5. Let cool for a couple of minutes, then run a knife around the edge of the pan, and invert the cake onto a cooling rack. Carefully peel off the parchment paper and let cool completely.

LEMON CHIFFON FILLING:

15 oz [425 g] cream cheese, at room temperature

15 oz [425 g] sour cream

4 liq oz [118 ml] fresh lemon juice

.5 oz [14 g] gelatin sheets, softened in cold water

2 liq oz [59 ml] water

5 oz [142 g] sugar

4 oz [113 g] egg yolks

1 Tbs [6 g] lemon rappé

20 liq oz [591 ml] heavy cream, whipped to soft peaks

1. In a mixer with a paddle attachment, beat the cream cheese at low speed until it is completely smooth. Add the sour cream and beat until just combined.

2. In a small nonreactive bowl, set over a pan of simmering water, warm the lemon juice. Drain the gelatin and add it to the lemon juice, stirring until the gelatin is completely melted. Remove the bowl from the heat and set aside.

3. In a small saucepan, combine the water and sugar. Bring to a boil, making sure the sugar is completely dissolved, and cook to 248°F [120°C].

4. Meanwhile, in a mixer with a whisk attachment, whip the egg yolks to the ribbon stage. When the syrup reaches 248°F [120°C], slowly add the hot syrup to the whipping egg yolks and whip until the mixture is cool. Add the lemon-gelatin liquid to the yolks along with the lemon rappé. Add the cream cheese-sour cream mixture. By hand, gently fold in the whipped cream. If the lemon cream cheese filling is very loose, refrigerate it until it has set just slightly.

BOMBE ASSEMBLY:

33.8 liq oz [1 lt] cherries in kirsch

7 oz [198 g] white chocolate couverture, melted and warm

1. Place the cherries with their syrup in a sieve set over a bowl and allow them to drain thoroughly. Reserve 60 cherries for assembling the bombe and the remainder of the cher-

ries for the sour cherry sauce [see below]. Reserve 4 liq oz [118 ml] of the cherry syrup for soaking the sponge rounds and the remainder of the syrup for the sour cherry sauce [see below].

2.   Brush both sides of the cooled almond sablé discs with the melted chocolate and place on a rack to set the chocolate.

3.   Using a cutter with a diameter slighty smaller than that of the sablé disc, stamp out 20 rounds of almond sponge cake. Cut each round in half horizontally and liberally brush both sides of the sponge round with cherry syrup.

4.   Arrange the 20 demisphere molds on a sheet pan. Pipe a small amount of lemon chiffon filling into each of the molds. Arrange three drained cherries over the filling and place a soaked sponge round over the cherries. Pipe in more filling almost to the top of the mold, making sure that the sponge round is completely surrounded with the filling. Top with a white chocolate-coated almond sablé disc.

5.   Freeze the filled molds for several hours or overnight, until firm.

SOUR CHERRY SAUCE:

Reserved liquid and cherries from above

1 Tbs [7 g] arrowroot

1.   In a saucepan, bring the cherry syrup to a boil. Dissolve the arrowroot in a small amount of water and whisk some of the arrowroot solution into the boiling syrup.

2.   Continue to boil for a few minutes or until thickened, adjusting the amount of solution, if necessary, to reach a coating consistency. Add the reserved cherries and keep warm.

WHITE CHOCOLATE PETALS:

3 lb [1361 g] white chocolate couverture, melted and tempered

Spread some of the tempered white chocolate in a thin even layer on a marble work surface. When the chocolate just begins to set, create petals by drawing a round metal cutter across the chocolate in a circular motion. The temperature of the chocolate is very important: if the couverture is too warm, it will gather up too much; if it is too cool, it will break.

ASSEMBLY:

Cocoa powder

Candied lemon zest

1.   To unmold, run the demisphere mold under warm water just until the sides loosen.

2.   Place a frozen bombe onto the center of a dessert plate. Surround the bombe with white chocolate petals, dusted with cocoa powder. Place some warm sour cherry sauce aound the bombe and garnish the top with a sprinkling of candied lemon zest.

Ginger and Quince Napoleon

YIELD: 25 servings

ALBERT USTER IMPORTS
GAITHERSBURG, MD

"It's not the classic shape," admits Susan Notter, referring to the napoleon, "but there's puff pastry in there." In fact, there are several playful elements in this neo-napoleon, including taking a ginger purée and adding gelatin, then making an Italian meringue and adding whipped cream to it, all to make the flavorful ginger cream. Notter took quinces, which are not often seen on American menus but are very traditional in her native England, and made a tart jelly with them, first marinating them in lemon juice. Paired with ginger cream, marinated orange segments, and blueberries, this napoleon is "very tart and very refreshing."

SPECIAL EQUIPMENT: *Twenty-five oval ring molds, 3" [7.6 cm] long × 2" [5.1 cm] wide × 1¼" [3.2 cm] high*

PUFF PASTRY LAYERS:

40 oz [1 kg, 134 g] puff pastry dough

5 oz [142 g] confectioners' sugar

1. Preheat oven to 375°F [190°C]. Line 3 sheet pans with parchment paper.

2. Divide the dough into thirds. On a lightly floured work surface, roll out each piece of dough to a thickness between ¹⁄₁₆" [.16 cm] and ⅛" [.32 cm]. Place the rolled-out dough on the parchment-lined pan and allow to rest in the refrigerator for at least 2 hours.

3. Dock the pieces of dough very well on both sides and return them to the prepared pans. Cover each piece of dough with another piece of parchment and another sheet pan.

4. Bake the layers of dough for 15 to 20 minutes or until the dough is golden brown and baked through. During the baking process, invert the double-pan assembly at least once to insure that the pastry bakes evenly. Allow the pastry to cool, sandwiched in the pans, on a wire rack.

5. Use one of the oval ring molds as a cutter to stamp out 75 ovals of puff pastry.

6. Dust the puff pastry ovals with an even layer of confectioners' sugar and place them on sheet pans.

7. Place the pans of sugared ovals under a broiler or salamander until the sugar caramelizes. [This will take a very short time, so watch constantly.]

QUINCE JELLY:

32 liq oz [946 ml] water

1.5 liq oz [44 ml] fresh lemon juice

4 quinces

50 liq oz [1479 ml] simple syrup

16 oz [454 g] Clear Gel

5 liq oz [148 ml] white wine

1. In a large bowl, combine the water and lemon juice.

2. Peel the quinces and immerse them in the lemon-water mixture.

3. In a large saucepan, bring the simple syrup to a boil. Drain the quinces and add them to the syrup. Adjust the heat so that the syrup is simmering and poach the quinces until they are tender.

4. Remove the pan from the heat and allow the quinces to cool in the poaching liquid.

5. Drain the cooled quinces. Reserve 4 liq oz [118 ml] of the poaching liquid. Cut the drained quinces into very small dice and reserve 6 oz [170 g] of the diced quince for the ginger cream [see below].

6. In a saucepan, combine the Clear Gel, white wine, and reserved quince poaching liquid and cook over medium heat, stirring constantly, until the Clear Gel is melted. Bring the mixture to a boil. Remove the pan from the heat and allow to cool for a few minutes.

7. Line a half sheet pan with plastic wrap and place the remaining diced quince in an even layer in the prepared pan. Pour the Clear Gel mixture over the quince. Allow to cool, then refrigerate until set.

8. Cut the quince jelly into 1″ [2.54 cm] squares.

GINGER CREAM:

4 oz [113 g] ginger purée

.5 oz [14 g] gelatin sheets, softened in cold water

2 liq oz [59 ml] water

4 oz [113 g] sugar

2 oz [57 g] glucose

10 oz [283 g] egg yolks

16 liq oz [473 ml] heavy cream, whipped to soft peaks

6 oz [170 g] reserved diced quince [from quince jelly]

1. In a small nonreactive bowl, set over a pan of simmering water, warm the ginger purée. Drain the gelatin and add it to the purée, stirring until the gelatin is completely melted. Remove the bowl from the heat and set aside.

2. In a small saucepan, combine the water, sugar, and glucose. Bring to a boil, making sure the sugar is completely dissolved, and cook to 248°F [120°C].

3. Meanwhile, in a mixer with a whisk attachment, whip the yolks to the ribbon stage. When the syrup reaches 248°F [120°C], slowly add the hot syrup to the whipped egg yolks and whip until the mixture is tepid. Add the ginger-gelatin liquid to the egg yolks. By hand, gently fold in the whipped cream. Fold in the reserved cooled, chopped quince. Refrigerate the ginger cream until set.

NAPOLEON ASSEMBLY:

Arrange the ring molds on a parchment-lined sheet pan. All the pastry ovals will be placed in the rings sugared-side facing up. Place one pastry oval in the bottom of each mold. Pipe a layer of ginger cream over the pastry, to just under the halfway mark. Smooth the layers and top each with a second piece of puff pastry, gently pressing down on the pastry. Pipe in more ginger cream to come almost to the top of the molds and top with another oval. Chill the napoleons for 2 hours.

MARINATED ORANGE SEGMENTS:

14 liq oz [414 ml] fresh orange juice

6 liq oz [177 ml] water

18 oz [510 g] granulated sugar

3 liq oz [89 ml] orange-flavored liqueur

10 navel oranges, peeled and cut into segments

1. In a saucepan, cook the orange juice until it comes to a simmer. Remove the pan from the heat.

2. In another saucepan, combine the water and sugar. Cook over medium heat, stirring constantly until the mixture comes to a boil and the sugar dissolves, washing down the side of the pan as necesary to prevent crystals from forming. Continue to boil the syrup until it reaches a medium brown caramel. Remove the pan from the heat.

3. While stirring constantly, slowly and carefully pour the warm orange juice into the caramel. Return the pan to low heat and stir until the syrup is well blended and smooth and any hardened caramel is melted. Cool slightly; then stir in the liqueur. Refrigerate until cold.

4. Add the orange segments to the cold syrup and allow them to marinate at least 1 hour.

SUGAR CAGES [OPTIONAL]:

6 lb [2.7 kg] Isomalt sugar

32 liq oz [946 ml] water

1. Lightly oil a 5″ [12.7 cm] diameter ladle. Place the Isomalt sugar and water in a large heavy saucepan and stir to combine. Cook over low heat until the Isomalt is dissolved.

2. Increase the heat to medium and cook the syrup to 340°F [171°C]; immediately plunge the bottom of the pan into a pan of cold water. Allow the syrup to cool until a steady thread is formed when the prongs of a fork are dipped into the syrup and lifted over the pan.

3. Quickly spin a small amount of caramel over the oiled ladle. Cut away excess sugar with a sharp knife, and carefully remove the cage from the ladle. Place the cage on a parchment-lined sheet pan. Repeat to form 25 cages. Store the cages in a cool, dry place.

ASSEMBLY:

Confectioners' sugar

Fresh blueberries

1. Place a chilled napoleon on a heatproof work surface. Use a propane torch to warm the outside of the ring; lift the ring off the dessert. Dust the top thickly with confectioners' sugar. Heat a metal rod and burn a crisscross pattern over the sugar. Carefully transfer the napoleon to a dessert plate and place it off-center.

2. Decoratively arrange the quince jelly squares, marinated orange segments, and blueberries on the plate.

3. Place an Isomalt cage over the napoleon.

Raspberry Rhubarb Crème Brûlée

YIELD: *8 servings*

KIM O'FLAHERTY

THE FOUR SEASONS
HOTEL
NEW YORK, NY

'Yes, it's overdone, yes, everyone has crème brûlée on their menu; you can't take it off," admits Kim O'Flaherty. And then another confession: "But I'm not one to talk, because I love it." Her custard is classic but is accompanied by enough textural and flavor variations to haul it into the new century: a pastry base of shredded phyllo [kataifi], a compote with a variation of the familiar combination of strawberry and rhubarb, raspberry sauce, and wholly unexpected brown sugar puff pastry straws.

SPECIAL EQUIPMENT: *Eight 4" [10 cm] flan rings*

RASPBERRY RHUBARB COMPOTE:

1 oz [29 g] unsalted butter

1.75 oz [50 g] granulated sugar

12 oz [340 g] rhubarb, diced

2 liq oz [59 ml] raspberry purée

In a sauté pan, melt the butter with the sugar. Add the rhubarb and cook until crisp-tender. Stir in the raspberry purée. Remove the pan from the heat; let the mixture cool.

RASPBERRY SAUCE:

8 liq oz [237 ml] raspberry purée

2 Tbs [41 g] corn syrup

1 tsp lemon juice

In a small bowl, combine all the ingredients.

KATAIFI DISCS:

4 oz [113 g] kataifi

4 oz [113 g] butter, melted and cooled

1.75 oz [50 g] granulated sugar

1.   Preheat oven to 350°F [175°C]. Place the kataifi in a bowl and separate the strands. Add the butter and sugar, and toss to coat strands evenly.

2.   Place eight 4" [10 cm] flan rings on a parchment-lined sheet pan. Divide the kataifi among the flan rings, gently pressing the strands into an even layer. Bake for 10 minutes, or until golden brown.

CRÈME BRÛLÉE:

24 liq oz [710 ml] heavy cream

8 liq oz [237 ml] milk

7 oz [200 g] granulated sugar

1 Tahitian Gold vanilla bean, split

3.9 oz [111 g] large egg yolks

1.75 oz [50 g] large eggs

1.   Preheat oven to 300°F [150°C]. Place eight 4″ [10 cm] flan rings in a hotel pan. Cut eight 6″ [15.25 cm] squares of plastic wrap. Secure the plastic wrap over one side of the ring with a rubber band. Place the rings, plastic side down, in the pan.

2.   In a saucepan combine the cream, milk, sugar, and vanilla bean and bring to a boil. Turn off the heat and let the vanilla bean steep for 3 to 5 minutes. Whisk the eggs in a bowl; temper the eggs with some of the hot cream. Return the egg-cream mixture to the remaining cream in the pan. Strain the mixture and pour into the prepared ring molds. Place the hotel pan in the preheated oven; fill the pan with ¾″ [19 mm] hot water. Bake for 25 minutes, or until the custard is completely set.

BROWN SUGAR STRAWS:

One 6″ [15.25 cm] square of puff pastry ⅛″ [3 mm] thick

1.05 oz [30 g] large egg whites, lightly beaten

2 Tbs [14 g] brown sugar

1.   Preheat oven to 375°F [190°C]. Line a sheet pan with parchment paper. Brush the pastry with egg whites and sprinkle the brown sugar over it. Use an offset spatula to spread the sugar over the pastry. Fold the dough in half and flatten slightly with a rolling pin.

2.   Slice the dough into ¼″ [.63 cm] strips. Using both hands, twist the strips in opposite directions. Cut each strip in half [approximately 6″ [15.25 cm] long] and place on the prepared sheet pan. Allow the dough to rest 10 minutes before baking. Bake for 10 to 12 minutes, until golden brown.

ASSEMBLY:

Granulated sugar, as needed

Place a spoonful of raspberry sauce on a dessert plate; arrange a kataifi disc over the sauce. Top the kataifi disc with crème brûlée. Sprinkle granulated sugar over the crème brûlée and caramelize it with a torch. Form 3 quenelles of raspberry rhubarb compote and arrange them around the crème brûlée. Garnish with raspberry sauce and brown sugar straws.

Banana "Snickers" Napoleon

YIELD: *10 servings*

KIM O'FLAHERTY

FOUR SEASONS HOTEL
NEW YORK, NY

There is always an elegant story behind the creation of a sophisticated plate like this one. Kim O'Flaherty: "A friend of mine told me his favorite dessert was to hold a Snickers bar in one hand and a banana in the other and to bite into one, and say, 'Isn't that so good,' and bite into the other, 'Mmm, this is delicious.' So I made a dessert for him." Puff pastry, the classic pastry base of the napoleon, is cut into neoclassic forms to set the stage for a frozen banana parfait garnished with banana caramel sauce, chocolate sauce, roasted peanuts, fresh bananas, and whipped cream.

SPECIAL EQUIPMENT: *Ten 2 oz [59 ml] silicone molds or aluminum cups*

FROZEN BANANA PARFAIT:

14 oz [397 g] bananas, peeled

½ tsp [2.5 ml] fresh lemon juice

1 Tbs [15 ml] Myer's dark rum

8 oz [237 ml] heavy cream

1.75 oz [50 g] granulated sugar

½ tsp [2 g] Tahitian Gold vanilla extract

1.25 oz [35 g] roasted peanuts, chopped

1. Purée the bananas in a food processor; strain. Transfer the purée to a bowl and stir in the lemon juice and rum. Set aside.

2. Combine the heavy cream, sugar, and vanilla extract in a bowl; whip until the mixture holds soft peaks. Fold the cream into the banana purée.

3. Using a pastry bag fitted with a large plain tip, pipe the mixture into ten 2 oz [59 ml] silicone molds or aluminum cups. Sprinkle the banana mixture with chopped peanuts and freeze.

BANANA CARAMEL SAUCE:

1 qt [946 ml] heavy cream

13 oz [380 g] bananas, split lengthwise

8 oz [230 g] granulated sugar

1. Place the cream and bananas in a saucepan and bring to a boil; cover and remove pan from the heat. Let steep for 20 minutes. Strain and set aside.

2. In a heavy saucepan, caramelize the sugar over high heat until it turns deep amber. Stir in the heavy cream and bring to a boil. Strain and cool the sauce.

CHOCOLATE SAUCE:

8 oz [230 g] bittersweet chocolate, chopped

12 liq oz [355 ml] heavy cream

4 liq oz [118 ml] corn syrup

Place the chopped chocolate in a bowl. In a saucepan, bring the cream and corn syrup to a boil. Pour the cream mixture over the chocolate. Stir to combine; cool.

PUFF PASTRY CUTOUTS:

One 12" × 18" [30 cm × 46 cm] sheet of puff pastry, cut into 4 pieces

Confectioners' sugar for dusting

1.   Roll out 1 piece of dough at a time, keeping the remainder in the refrigerator, until it is paper-thin and almost transparent. Place the rolled-out sheets of puff pastry on a sheet pan between pieces of parchment paper and freeze for 30 minutes.

2.   Preheat oven to 375°F [190°C]. Using the template on page 241 as a guide, cut 30 shapes from the dough. Remove the center from 10 of the cutouts; these will be the top layer of the napoleons. Place the cutouts on inverted sheet pans lined with parchment paper. Place a sheet of parchment paper over the cutouts; put 2 sheet pans over the parchment to weigh down the cutouts and prevent them from rising. Bake for 12 to 15 minutes, until golden but still slightly undercooked.

3.   Preheat the broiler. Dust the baked cutouts with confectioners' sugar and transfer to unlined sheet pans. Lightly caramelize the sugar under the broiler to give the pastry a shiny glaze.

ASSEMBLY:

Roasted peanuts

Whipped cream

Bananas, peeled and sliced

1.   Invert the frozen banana parfait onto a dessert plate. Drizzle with the banana caramel sauce and the chocolate sauce. Sprinkle the parfait with peanuts.

2.   Place a thin layer of whipped cream on a solid cutout. Arrange banana slices over the whipped cream. Place a solid cutout on top and repeat process. Top with a cutout that has its center removed. Arrange the napoleon on the plate with the parfait and serve.

Kugelhopf Glacé 2000

JACQUY PFEIFFER

THE FRENCH
PASTRY SCHOOL
CHICAGO, IL

The traditional Alsatian dessert, kugelhopf ["No, I didn't sneeze," says Jacquy Pfeiffer, "it's the actual name."] has been lightened and spiffed up for the new millennium. "It's a sweet dough, kind of like a brioche, but with less butter and less egg," says Pfeiffer. Though the classic star of the dessert, kirschwasser, remains, it is featured in a parfait, with a kugelhopf chip as a chewy accompaniment and a flambéed cherry mixture to drive the theme home.

SPECIAL EQUIPMENT: *Kugelhopf mold; twelve mini-kugelhopf molds*

KUGELHOPF CHIP:

16.5 liq oz [488 ml] warm milk, divided

1.1 oz [30 g] fresh yeast

5.3 oz [150 g] granulated sugar, divided

2.2 lb [1 kg] all-purpose flour

5.3 oz [149 g] eggs

1.8 oz [50 g] kirsch

12.3 oz [350 g] unsalted butter, softened

7.1 oz [200 g] raisins

3 oz [85 g] whole almonds

1. Preheat oven to 350°F [175°C]. Grease the kugelhopf mold.

2. Combine 3.3 liq oz [98 ml] of the warm milk, yeast, and 1.8 oz [50 g] of the sugar in a mixing bowl. Cover with flour. Let sit for 1 hour.

3. Add the eggs, kirsch, and the remaining 13.2 liq oz [390 ml] of milk. Mix until the dough clears the sides of the bowl. Mix in the softened butter and raisins. Let rise until doubled. Arrange the whole almonds on the bottom of the kugelhopf mold.

4. Form the dough into a ball and make a hole in the center. Place the dough in the mold. Let rise until doubled.

5. Bake until dry in the center, about 1 hour. Unmold on a wire rack. Cover with plastic wrap after 30 minutes.

6. Refrigerate for 8 hours. Cut very thin slices on a slicer and toast slightly. Keep in an airtight container.

KIRSCH PARFAIT:

8 liq oz [237 ml] milk

2 vanilla beans, split and scraped

6.4 oz [181 g] granulated sugar

5.8 oz [164 g] egg yolks

1.4 oz [40 g] invert sugar

16.2 liq oz [479 ml] heavy cream, whipped to soft peaks

2.4 oz [68 g] kirsch

1.   Combine the milk, vanilla beans, sugar, and egg yolks in a saucepan. Cook, stirring constantly, to 183°F [85°C]. Strain.

2.   Pour into mixing bowl and whip until cool. Add the invert sugar and whipped cream. Add the kirsch. Pipe into 12 small kugelhopf molds, leaving a hole in the center. Freeze until set.

CHERRY MIXTURE:

3 oz [85 g] granulated sugar

8 liq oz [237 g] cherry juice

1 oz [28 g] candied lemon peel, chopped

1 lb [454 g] cherries, pitted

2 oz [57 g] unsalted butter

Pinch of cornstarch

1 oz [28 g] kirsch

Cook the sugar in a saucepan to the caramel stage. Add the cherry juice, candied lemon peel, cherries, and butter. Bring to a simmer and reduce slightly. Thicken with a little cornstarch. Remove from heat and flambé with the kirsch.

ASSEMBLY:

Confectioners' sugar

Caramel sugar rods

Remove each kugelhopf from its mold and place on a plate. Serve with the flambéed cherry mixture. Garnish with a kugelhopf chip, confectioners' sugar, and a caramel sugar rod.

Lemon Macadamia Nut Brûlée

YIELD: *8 servings*

BRIAN SCHOENBECK

WESTIN RIVER NORTH
CHICAGO, IL

Crème brûlée is given a complete makeover—the bruléed, lemon-accented custards are frozen, then served at room temperature, layered with macadamia nut biscuit, for a delicate, crunchy, and creamy experience. The caramel-vanilla bean sauce echoes the nutty flavor of the biscuit, and caramelized lemon slices round out the lemon in the custard. The dessert is further contemporized with silkscreen work on the tuile.

SPECIAL EQUIPMENT: *Silkscreen [pattern of your choice]*

CARAMELIZED LEMON SLICES:

48 oz [1 kg, 350 g] granulated sugar

33.8 liq oz [1 lt] water

1 lemon, thinly sliced

1. Combine the sugar and water in a saucepan and bring to a boil. Pour the syrup over the lemon slices. Cover with plastic wrap and refrigerate overnight.

2. Preheat oven to 210°F [99°C]. Line a half sheet pan with a silicone baking mat. Place the lemon slices on the pan and dry in the oven for 2 hours. Store in an airtight container.

CARAMEL-VANILLA BEAN SAUCE:

16.4 oz [465 g] granulated sugar

3 oz [60 g] glucose

18 liq oz [540 ml] water

2 vanilla beans, scraped

Cook the sugar, glucose, and 6 liq oz [177ml] of the water to a caramel color. Heat the remaining water with the vanilla bean scrapings and slowly whisk into the hot sugar syrup. Refrigerate overnight.

LEMON CRÈME BRÛLÉE:

15.9 oz [450 g] egg yolks

11.6 oz [330 g] granulated sugar

53 liq oz [1.5 lt] heavy cream

6.35 oz [180 g] frozen lemonade concentrate

6 lemons, zested

Turbinado sugar, as needed

1. Preheat oven to 250°F [121°C]. Beat the egg yolks and sugar in a mixer until thick.

2. Bring the heavy cream, lemonade concentrate, and lemon zest to a boil in a saucepan.

3. Temper the egg yolk mixture with the hot cream mixture. Pour into a half sheet pan lined with plastic wrap. Bake with a pan of water in the oven for about 30 minutes.

4. Sprinkle the top of the crème brûlée with turbinado sugar and caramelize using a torch. Freeze the crème brûlée.

MACADAMIA NUT BISCUIT:

4.69 oz [133 g] whole eggs

1 oz [28 g] egg yolks

8.3 oz [238 g] granulated sugar, divided

4.9 oz [140 g] almond flour

4.9 oz [140 g] unsalted butter [preferably 82% butterfat], melted and kept warm

3.9 oz [112 g] pastry flour, sifted

8.9 oz [252 g] egg whites

3 oz [85 g] macadamia nuts, ground

1.   Preheat oven to 400°F [205°C]. Line a half sheet pan with a silicone baking mat. In a mixer, using the whisk attachment, beat the whole eggs, egg yolks, 4.9 oz [139 g] of the sugar, and the almond flour until thick.

2.   Fold the melted butter in the egg mixture. Fold in the pastry flour.

3.   In a mixer, using a whisk attachment, whip the egg whites and the remaining sugar to soft peaks. Fold the beaten egg whites into the batter.

4.   Evenly spread the batter in the prepared pan. Sprinkle the ground macadamia nuts on the batter. Bake for 5 to 7 minutes, until the cake springs back when lightly touched.

TUILES:

Cocoa Barry Krem d'Arome cocoa, as needed

4.8 oz [136 g] egg whites

4.8 oz [136 g] confectioners' sugar

4.8 oz [136 g] unsalted butter [preferably 82% butterfat], at room temperature

4.8 oz [136 g] pastry flour, sifted

1.   Preheat oven to 400°F [205°C]. Make a 2″ × 6″ [5 cm × 15.25 cm] rectangular stencil. Place a silkscreen on a silicone baking mat. Spread a thin, even layer of the Krem d'Arome cocoa over the silkscreen and freeze.

2.   In a mixer, using the paddle attachment, mix the remaining ingredients together, until well combined.

3.   Stencil the batter over the strip template on the silk-screened baking mat, making one for each finished dessert. Bake until golden brown.

4.   Carefully remove the strips from the pan while still hot and allow them to cool draped over a 3¼″ [8.25 cm] diameter cylinder.

ASSEMBLY:

1.   Using a 3″ [7.6 cm] round cutter, cut out 16 rounds each of the biscuit and brûlée. Stack 2 of the brûlée rounds and 2 of the biscuit rounds in alternate layers.

2.   Place the layered dessert on the plate and place the tuile in front on it. Garnish the plate with the caramelized lemon slices and the caramel-vanilla bean sauce.

Praline Parfait Napoleon

YIELD: *12 servings*

BRIAN SCHOENBECK

WESTIN RIVER NORTH
CHICAGO, IL

Brian Schoenbeck devises a devilish twist to the traditional napoleon, substituting chocolate for the puff pastry and praline parfait for the pastry cream. Caramelized hazelnuts and cinnamon biscotti add decisive crunch and flavor complements to the creamy parfait, and sun-dried cherry sauce, served warm, adds a pleasing tang and temperature contrast.

SPECIAL EQUIPMENT: *Silicone baking mat; acetate sheets; cutoff whisk; 5-wheel adjustable dough divider*

CARAMELIZED HAZELNUTS:

21 oz [600 g] hazelnuts

7.8 oz [225 g] granulated sugar

1.3 liq oz [37 ml] water

.8 oz [23 g] unsalted butter [preferably 82% butterfat]

1.   Warm the hazelnuts in the oven. In a copper bowl, combine the sugar and water and cook to 240°F [116°C]. Add the nuts and cook, stirring constantly, until the sugar coats and caramelizes the nuts. Add the butter and stir until melted. Pour out on a silicone baking mat and separate the nuts.

2.   Allow to cool completely. Store in an airtight container.

PRALINE PARFAIT FILLING:

8 liq oz [237 ml] whole milk

6.5 oz [186 g] granulated sugar

2.25 oz [64 g] egg yolks

1.4 oz [40 g] invert sugar

12.6 oz [360 g] praline paste

31 oz [886 g] reserved caramelized hazelnuts, chopped

1 pt [473 ml] heavy cream [35% butterfat], whipped to soft peaks

1.   Chill a half sheet pan and line it with parchment paper. Whisk the milk, granulated sugar, and egg yolks together in a double boiler and heat to 185°F [85°C]. Strain the mixture into the bowl of a mixer and whip with the whisk attachment until cool.

2.   Add the invert sugar and the praline paste to the egg mixture and mix until blended.

3.   Fold the hazelnuts into the mixture. Gently fold in the whipped cream.

4.   Pour the mixture in the prepared pan and freeze.

CINNAMON PRALINE BISCOTTI:

13.5 oz [383 g] pastry flour

1 Tbs [15 g] baking powder

2½ Tbs [15 g] ground cinnamon

6 oz [170 g] unsalted butter

6 oz [170 g] turbinado sugar

3.5 oz [99 g] large eggs

1½ Tbs [22 ml] bitter almond essence

11 oz [312 g] praline grains

Confectioners' sugar, as needed

1.   Preheat the oven to 400°F [205°C]. Line a sheet pan with parchment paper. Sift together the pastry flour, baking powder, and cinnamon.

2.   In a mixer, using the paddle attachment, cream the butter and turbinado sugar. Add the eggs, one at a time, incorporating well after each addition.

3.   Add the bitter almond essence, the sifted dry ingredients, and the praline grains. Mix just until combined.

4.   Roll out the dough into a rectangle ¼" [.63 cm] thick and 7" [17.8 cm] wide. Place on the prepared pan and bake for 10 to 12 minutes. Remove from oven and allow to cool slightly. Cut into ¼" [.63 cm] wide strips.

5.   Place the cookies back on the sheet pan and return to the oven for approximately 10 minutes. Allow to cool and dust with confectioners' sugar.

CHOCOLATE NAPOLEON LAYERS:

1 lb, 8 oz [680 g] bittersweet couverture chocolate, such as Valrhona Caraibe

1.   Dampen the back of 2 sheet pans and adhere a large sheet of acetate to each. Temper the chocolate.

2.   Dip a cutoff whisk into the tempered chocolate and move it back and forth quickly across one of the sheet pans. Repeat the process until the pan is sufficently and evenly covered. Repeat with the second sheet pan.

3.   When the chocolate has slightly set, using a 5-wheel adjustable divider set at 3½" [8.9 cm] spaces, cut the chocolate into squares.

4.   Line 2 sheet pans with parchment paper. Remove the acetate from the sheet pan and turn it upside-down on one of the parchment-lined sheet pans. Place another sheet pan on top to prevent the squares from curling. Repeat with the second sheet of squares.

SUN-DRIED CHERRY SAUCE:

11.8 liq oz [350 ml] red wine

12 oz [341 g] dried tart cherries

12 oz [341 g] granulated sugar

8.4 liq oz [250 ml] water

8.4 liq oz [250 ml] orange juice

2 Tbs [15 g] arrowroot

5 liq oz [150 ml] Cherry Marnier

1.   Combine the red wine, cherries, sugar, water, and orange juice in a saucepan and bring to a boil. Remove from the heat, cover with plastic wrap, and refrigerate overnight.

2.   Strain the mixture to remove the cherries. Heat the liquid and thicken with the arrowroot. Allow the sauce to cool and add the Cherry Marnier.

ASSEMBLY:

Dried cherries

1.   Line up 12 chocolate squares on a parchment-lined sheet pan. Using a 2½″ [6.3 cm] diameter, plain, round cutter, cut 24 circles from the frozen parfait.

2.   Place one parfait round on each chocolate square. Place a chocolate square off-center on top of the parfait rounds. Layer another round and square in the same manner.

3.   Place a napoleon on each plate. Garnish the plates with the sun-dried cherry sauce, dried cherries, and cinnamon praline biscotti.

Savarins with Strawberry Tartar, Crème Fraîche Ice Cream, and Chocolate Beignets

TOM VACCARO

TRUMP PLAZA
CASINO HOTEL
ATLANTIC CITY, NJ

A savarin is an ideal medium in which to infuse any flavor a chef chooses. "The classic soak is rum, and it's usually served with fruit and ice cream, so this is not far from that," says Tom Vaccaro. His savarin is soaked in orange juice and Grand Marnier, a flavor that pairs well with the dense chocolate of the beignets. "The feuille de brick basket itself is neutral, the ice cream is not too sweet, and very refreshing." All of this plays nicely with the pleasingly tangy strawberry tartar. With the fritter batter raised with baking powder rather than yeast, "the beignet is a bit of a play on the classic," notes Vaccaro.

SPECIAL EQUIPMENT: *Thirty savarin molds, 2" [5 cm] diameter*

SAVARINS:

.5 oz [14 g] fresh yeast

4 liq oz [118 ml] milk, lukewarm

.5 oz [14 g] granulated sugar

7 oz [198 g] eggs

12 oz [340 g] high-gluten flour

.25 oz [7 g] salt

6 oz [170 g] unsalted butter, melted and cooled

1. In a medium bowl dissolve the yeast in the milk. Add the sugar and eggs and whisk until thoroughly combined.

2. In a large bowl mix together the flour and salt. Add the yeast mixture and the melted butter and mix together with a wooden spoon. Cover the bowl and keep it in a warm place until the dough has doubled in size.

3. Punch down the dough and let it proof again until doubled.

4. Punch down the dough and transfer it to a pastry bag. Pipe the dough into greased savarin molds so that they are filled halfway. Let them proof until doubled.

5. Preheat oven to 375°F [190°C] and bake the savarins for 7 to 9 minutes or until they just turn golden. Remove from the molds immediately and let cool on a wire rack.

CHOCOLATE BEIGNETS:

15.75 oz [447 g] eggs

4 liq oz [118 ml] vegetable oil

1 lb [454 g] granulated sugar

1 pt [473 ml] milk

28 oz [794 g] bread flour

8 oz [227 g] unsweetened cocoa powder

.5 oz [14 g] baking powder

.3 oz [9 g] salt

7 oz [198 g] bittersweet chocolate, melted

Oil for deep frying

1. In a large mixing bowl, combine the eggs, oil, sugar, and milk. Add the flour, cocoa powder, baking powder, and salt, and mix to combine. Stir in the melted chocolate. Refrigerate the batter overnight.

2. Form the batter into 90 balls using a 1 oz [29 ml] scoop as a measure. Deep fry at 350°F [175°C] for 4 to 5 minutes or until they are just slightly moist in the center. Drain on paper towels.

CRÈME FRAÎCHE ICE CREAM:

1 pt [473 ml] heavy cream

1 pt [473 ml] milk

6 oz [170 g] granulated sugar

7.8 oz [221 g] egg yolks

8.5 oz [241 g] crème fraîche

1. In a saucepan, combine the cream, milk, and sugar and bring to a boil. Temper in the egg yolks. Cook gently, stirring until the mixture coats the back of a wooden spoon. Cool completely over an ice bath.

2. Fold in the crème fraîche and process in an ice cream machine according to the manufacturer's instructions.

CRISPY CRÊPES:

30 sheets feuille de brick

Oil for deep frying

1. Press a sheet of feuille de brick into a 4 oz ladle, about 3″ [7.5 cm] in diameter, so that it forms a cup. Leave the feuille de brick in the ladle and deep fry at 365°F [185°C] until golden brown. Drain on paper towels.

2. Repeat with the remaining feuille de brick.

SOAKING SYRUP:

1 lb [454 g] granulated sugar

1 pt [473 ml] water

4 liq oz [118 ml] Grand Marnier

8 liq oz [237 ml] orange juice

½ vanilla bean, split and scraped

1 cinnamon stick

1. In a saucepan, combine all the ingredients and bring to a simmer. Remove the pan from heat and let cool.

2. Soak the savarins, a few at a time, until they are one and one-half times their original size.

TUILES:

4 oz [113 g] unsalted butter, melted

4 oz [113 g] granulated sugar

4 oz [113 g] all-purpose flour, sifted

4 oz [113 g] egg whites

.25 oz [7 g] unsweetened cocoa powder

1.   In a mixer with the paddle attachment, beat the butter, sugar, flour, and egg whites just until smooth. Divide the batter equally into 2 bowls. Sift the cocoa powder into 1 bowl and mix well. Chill the batter until it is firm enough to pipe.

2.   Preheat oven to 375°F [190°C]. Place the light batter in 1 parchment cone and the dark batter in another. Cut openings about ⅛" [3 mm] wide. Pipe 12" [30.5 cm] lines of light batter onto a sheet pan lined with a silicone baking mat. Pipe a line of dark batter directly alongside each line. Carefully flatten with a small offset spatula so that each tuile is about ½" [13 mm] wide. Bake for 5 to 6 minutes or until the light part is just barely golden.

3.   Remove the tuiles from the oven and immediately wrap each one around a dowel ½" [13 mm] in diameter. Let set.

STRAWBERRY TARTAR:

2 pt [1 lt] fresh strawberries

4 oz [113 g] granulated sugar

20 sprigs fresh mint

1.   Chop the strawberries into small pieces. Add the sugar and place in a chinois until all the liquid has drained.

2.   Finely chop the mint leaves and fold them into the strawberries.

ASSEMBLY:

1.   Place a feuille de brick cup to one side of each dessert plate. Put a savarin in the cup. Top it with some strawberry tartar, a scoop of crème fraîche ice cream, and a tuile.

2.   Place 3 chocolate beignets around the plate.

Puff Melba

AMERNICK
WHEATON, MD

*"Peach Melba was created by
Escoffier, and was a silver
dish filled with vanilla ice
cream, poached peaches, and
crushed raspberries," says
Ann Amernick. "I've taken
traditional Peach Melba and
added puff pastry to it." On a
sponge cake circle are placed
the traditional ingredients—
"pure vanilla ice cream," says
Amernick. "That's the classic, and I recommend it." She
has topped it with puff pastry
that has been allowed to rise,
rather than weighing it down
as one would for napoleon
layers. "What I wanted was
something fragile, without
the shattering texture. It's
napoleon-like." The juices
soak into the sponge cake but
not the puff. "You don't want
the juices to imbue into the
puff. It loses the texture."*

PUFF PASTRY:

8 oz [227 g] all-purpose flour

8 oz [227 g] cake flour

¼ tsp [1.7 g] salt

1 lb [454 g] unsalted butter, chilled, divided

6 liq oz [177 ml] ice water

Confectioners' sugar, as needed

1.   In a mixing bowl, combine the flours, salt, and 4 oz [113 g] butter cut into small pieces. Mix until the consistency of coarse meal.

2.   Slowly add the ice water until the dough comes together. Refrigerate until firm, about 1 hour.

3.   Form the remaining 12 oz [341 g] butter into two 6″ × 8″ [15.25 cm × 20.3 cm] rectangles and refrigerate for ½ hour.

4.   Roll the dough into a rectangle 18″ [46 cm] long. Place 1 rectangle of butter in the center. Fold one flap of dough over the butter. Place the second rectangle of butter on top. Cover with the remaining flap of dough. Roll out into an 18″ [46 cm] long rectangle and fold in thirds. Refrigerate for ½ hour. Give the dough 4 turns, resting after the first 2. Let rest overnight.

5.   Cut the dough into 6 strips. Roll each strip into a 6½″ × 16″ [16.5 cm × 40.6 cm] rectangle, ⅛″ [3 mm] thick. Dock the dough. Cut 2″ × 5″ [5 cm × 12.7 cm] strips from the rectangle. Place the strips on a parchment-lined sheet pan. Refrigerate for 1 hour.

6.   Preheat oven to 375°F [190°C].

7.   Sprinkle the tops of the strips with confectioners' sugar. Bake for 15 minutes. Lower oven to 350°F [175°C] and bake 10 to 15 minutes, until browned and baked through.

VANILLA ICE CREAM:

36 liq oz [1 lt] milk

36 liq oz [1 lt] heavy cream

2 vanilla beans, split and scraped

15.6 oz [442 g] egg yolks

10.5 oz [298 g] granulated sugar

1.   In a saucepan, bring the milk, cream, and vanilla beans to a boil.

2.   In separate bowl, combine the egg yolks and sugar. Temper and add to the milk mixture. Cook over low heat to 185°F [85°C], stirring constantly.

3. Strain and cool in an ice bath.

4. Process in an ice cream machine according to the manufacturer's instructions.

SPONGE CAKE:

28 oz [792 g] eggs

17 oz [484 g] granulated sugar

2 tsp [8 g] vanilla extract

14 oz [400 g] cake flour

3 oz [90 g] almond flour

1. Preheat oven to 350°F [175°C]. Line 3 half sheet trays with greased parchment paper.

2. In a mixing bowl, combine the eggs, sugar, and vanilla extract. Heat until warm over a water bath.

3. Whip until light and triple in volume.

4. Combine the flours and sift. Fold into the egg mixture.

5. Pour into the prepared pans. Bake until browned, about 15 minutes. Let cool.

6. Cut out twenty-four 3″ [7.6 cm] circles. Set aside.

RASPBERRY SAUCE:

2 lb [907 g] raspberries

2 Tbs [32 g] eau de framboise

to taste granulated sugar

In a food processor, purée the raspberries. Strain. Add the eau de framboise and sugar. Refrigerate.

ASSEMBLY:

Peaches

Raspberries

Confectioners' sugar

1. Place a sponge cake circle on a plate. Place a slightly smaller metal ring mold on top of the sponge cake.

2. Chop some of the peaches and toss with granulated sugar and lemon juice. Fill the ring with the chopped peaches to a height of about 1″ [2.5 cm].

3. Let stand for ½ hour to allow the juices to soak the sponge cake. Remove the mold.

4. Place some sliced peaches around the sponge cake and arrange raspberries in between each slice.

5. Place a scoop of vanilla ice cream on top of the chopped peaches and sponge cake. Place a piece of puff pastry to the side. Sprinkle with confectioners' sugar. Drizzle the raspberry sauce over the ice cream.

Five-Spice Crème Brûlée

DIDIER GOLLER

RITZ-CARLTON HOTEL
PALM BEACH, FL

For yet another variation of the best-selling custard dessert, Didier Goller has added Chinese five-spice powder for flavor buzz, and white and dark chocolate strips for presentation and further crowd-pleasing taste dimension. The plate is finished with raspberry and mango coulis, chocolate cigarettes, a sugar spiral, and chocolate piping. "The mixing method and ingredients of this recipe make it ideal for changing the flavor," says Goller. "You don't have to use Chinese five-spice. I have used this recipe and flavored it with Key lime, Grand Marnier, and chocolate."

SPECIAL EQUIPMENT: *Eight 5 oz [148 ml] ramekins; acetate strips; decorating comb*

FIVE-SPICE CRÈME BRÛLÉE:

1 qt [946 ml] heavy cream

7 oz [198 g] granulated sugar

1 vanilla bean, split

10 oz [283 g] egg yolks

1 tsp [2 g] Chinese five-spice powder

1.   Preheat oven to 350°F [175°C]. Combine the heavy cream, half of the sugar, and the vanilla bean in a large saucepan and bring to a boil.

2.   In a mixer beat the egg yolks and remaining sugar until the egg yolks are pale yellow and the sugar has dissolved.

3.   Whisking the egg yolks continuously, slowly pour the hot cream mixture into the egg yolks. Whisk in the five-spice powder. Cool the mixture in an ice bath.

4.   Evenly divide the cooled mixture among the 5 oz [148 ml] ramekins. Bake in a water bath for approximately 25 minutes, until set.

ASSEMBLY:

4 oz [113 g] dark chocolate, tempered

4 oz [113 g] white chocolate, tempered

As needed mango purée

As needed raspberry purée

1.   Spread the dark chocolate on an acetate strip. Comb through the chocolate to create clean lines. Allow the chocolate to partially set and spread a thin layer of white chocolate on top. Allow the chocolate to partially set. Wrap around the crème brûlée and allow to set completely. Peel off the acetate.

2.   Put each fruit purée into a squeeze bottle. Place each crème brûlée on a plate and garnish with dots of each purée, mint, and berries.

frozen desserts

CHAPTER 5

Frozen Kir Royale

D. JEMAL EDWARDS

NEW YORK, NY

D. Jemal Edwards dubs this a "neoclassic edible cocktail. Kir Royale is a classic. We have champagne sorbet, and the cassis flavors the sabayon." The lemon sorbet also found in the blown sugar goblet is perhaps the twist. "We julienne the mint very fine. I like the appearance of it, and it refreshes even more." As a libation, says Edwards, "I don't like champagne that much, but it's great for dessert—it makes a fine sorbet, granité, or sabayon and it goes with fruit very well."

CHAMPAGNE GRANITÉ:

25 liq oz [750 ml] champagne

8 oz [227 g] granulated sugar

28 liq oz [828 ml] water

.5 oz [14 g] fresh mint leaves, finely chopped

1. Place a shallow metal baking pan into the freezer to chill. The size of the pan should be such that the depth of the mixture is between ½" [1.3 cm] and ¾" [1.9 cm].

2. Combine all the ingredients in a nonreactive bowl and stir constantly until the sugar is completely dissolved.

3. Pour the champagne mixture into the chilled pan. Place the pan in the freezer and freeze for about 30 minutes or until there is a rim of ice around the edge [the exact amount of time it takes for the rim of ice to form will depend upon the temperature of the freezer]. Using a fork, scrape the ice from the sides of the pan into the center of the mixture. Freeze again for about 1 hour or until more ice crystals form, and again scrape the crystals into the center of the mixture. Repeat the freezing and scraping process until the entire mixture is the consistency of large ice crystals.

LEMON SORBET:

5 liq oz [148 ml] water

1 oz [28 g] trimoline

3 oz [85 g] light corn syrup

11 oz [312 g] granulated sugar

16 liq oz [473 ml] lemon juice

1. Combine all the ingredients in a medium saucepan. Cook over medium heat, stirring constantly, until the sugars are completely dissolved. Remove the pan from the heat and allow the mixture to cool. Refrigerate until chilled.

2. Process in an ice cream machine according to the manufacturer's instructions. Store the sorbet covered in the freezer.

CASSIS SABAYON:

1.95 oz [55 g] egg yolks

4 oz [113 g] confectioners' sugar

8 liq oz [237 ml] cassis liqueur

.1 oz [3 g] gelatin sheets, softened in cold water

8 liq oz [237 ml] heavy cream, whipped to firm peaks

1. In a nonreactive bowl, combine the egg yolks, confectioners' sugar, and cassis. Whisk until blended. Place the bowl over a pan of simmering water and whip the mixture until light and fluffy, about 15 minutes.

2. Remove the bowl from the heat. Drain the softened gelatin and whisk it into the cassis sabayon until the gelatin is completely melted.

3. Place the sabayon over an ice bath and stir gently with a rubber spatula until cooled. Remove the bowl from the ice bath and fold in the whipped cream.

4. Refrigerate covered until ready to use.

ASSEMBLY:

Blown sugar champagne glasses

Curved sugar sticks

Lemon zest, cut into very fine strips

1. Cover the base of a dessert plate with cassis sabayon.

2. Fill the "champagne glass" with champagne granité and top with a small scoop of lemon sorbet to one side.

3. Garnish the dessert with a sugar stick and strips of lemon zest. Serve immediately.

Tri-Fruit Loop

YIELD: *30 servings*

MARTHA CRAWFORD

JOHNSON & WALES
UNIVERSITY
PROVIDENCE, RI

*Crawford chooses Bavarian
for a neoclassic exercise.
"It's a classic that you can
take to the next level," she
says. "You can shape it, mold
it. Flexipans work well with
Bavarian." The recipe has
flexibility too; Crawford has
substituted a portion of the
milk with a fruit purée.
Bavarian cream balls flavored
with passion fruit, blackberry,
and raspberry are served with
a passion fruit sauce, and enclosed in a loopy chocolate
frame. To ensure that the
Bavarians would fit exactly in
the chocolate cage, Crawford
modeled it in clay first and
shaped the plastic around it.
Hippen cookies offer texture
and visual interest, and dried
raspberry mixed with confectioners' sugar creates a tint
on the plate.*

SPECIAL EQUIPMENT: *Three Flexipan #1265 sheets of 1⅛" [3.5 cm] diameter; ¼ oz [7 ml] mini demi-sphere molds*

RASPBERRY BAVARIAN CREAM BALLS:

8 liq oz [237 ml] heavy cream,

1 Tbs [9 g] powdered gelatin

4 oz [113 g] raspberry puree, divided

4 liq oz [118 ml] milk

2 oz [27 g] granulated sugar, divided

2.5 oz [71 g] egg yolks

1 liq oz [30 ml] lemon juice

¼ tsp [1 g] lemon extract

1 liq oz [30 ml] kirsch

Confectioners' sugar, as needed

1. In a mixer with a whisk attachment, whip the heavy cream to soft peaks and chill until needed.

2. Soften the gelatin in 2 oz [57 g] of the raspberry purée for 10 minutes.

3. In a saucepan, bring the milk and 1 oz [28 g] of the sugar to a boil.

4. Combine the remaining sugar and the egg yolks in a bowl and whisk until blended. Temper the egg yolks into the hot milk. Cook gently, stirring constantly, to the custard stage [do not allow the mixture to boil].

5. Pour the custard through a chinois over the bloomed gelatin and whisk together until the gelatin is completely melted. Whisk in the remaining raspberry purée. Add the lemon juice, lemon extract, and kirsch.

6. Place the bowl of custard over an ice bath and stir until it is cool but not set. Adjust the flavorings to taste and sweeten with confectioners' sugar, if needed. Fold in the whipped cream.

7. Pipe the Bavarian cream into the demisphere molds and level off. Freeze.

8. Unmold the Bavarian cream when completely frozen. With a small metal spatula that has been heated, wipe over the flat sides of 2 demispheres and place the flat sides together to form a ball. Return to the freezer until ready to use. Repeat to make 30 balls.

FROZEN DESSERTS 221

BLACKBERRY BAVARIAN CREAM BALLS:

Follow the above recipe for Raspberry Bavarian Cream Balls, substituting blackberry purée for the raspberry purée.

PASSION FRUIT BAVARIAN CREAM BALLS:

Follow the above recipe for Raspberry Bavarian Cream Balls, substituting passion fruit purée for the raspberry purée.

PASSION FRUIT SAUCE:

3 oz [85 g] sugar

.75 oz [21 g] Triquel instant thickener

16 oz [454 g] passion fruit purée

1 Tbs [15 ml] lemon juice

¼ tsp [1 g] lemon extract

1 Tbs [15 ml] kirsch

In a bowl, combine the sugar and Triquel. Whisk the mixture into the passion fruit purée until thickened; adjust the sugar and thickener as needed. Add the lemon juice, lemon extract, and kirsch; adjust the flavorings to taste. Pour the passion fruit sauce into a squeeze bottle and refrigerate until needed.

HIPPEN PASTE COOKIES:

10.5 oz [298 g] almond paste

7 oz [198 g] confectioners' sugar

3.5 oz [99 g] bread flour

8.5 oz [241 g] egg whites

1.5 liq oz [44 ml] milk

1 tsp [4 g] vanilla extract

1.   Preheat the oven to 350°F [175°C]. Line a sheet pan with a silicone baking mat. Cut a rectangular stencil 8″ [20.3 cm] long and ¼″ [.6 cm] wide. Cut another stencil 6½″ [16.5 cm] long and ¼″ [.6 cm] wide.

2.   Using a mixer with a paddle attachment, combine the almond paste, confectioners' sugar, and bread flour and beat on medium speed until the mixture is uniform and crumbly in texture.

3.   In a bowl, combine the egg whites, milk, and vanilla extract. With the mixer on medium speed, add the egg white mixture in a very slow stream and beat until incorporated. If the paste is lumpy, strain it through a sieve.

4.   Place one of the stencils for the cookie on the prepared pan. Spread some of the batter evenly over the stencil; remove the stencil. Repeat to make 30 cookies. Bake for 4 to 6 minutes or until golden brown.

5.   Remove the cookies from the pan and bend them into a loop shape by pressing the ends together. Carefully place the cookies on a parchment-lined sheet pan to cool completely.

6.   Store the cookies in an airtight container until ready to use.

7.   Repeat steps 4 to 6 using the second stencil.

CHOCOLATE TEARDROP LOOPS:

16 oz [454 g] dark chocolate, melted and tempered

16 oz [454 g] white chocolate, melted and tempered

1.   Cut 30 strips of acetate 12″ [30 cm] long and 1″ [2.5 cm] wide.

2.   Place some of the dark chocolate in a parchment cone. Pipe diagonal lines of chocolate over one of strips. Place some of the white chocolate in a parchment cone and pipe diagonal lines [in the opposite direction] over the dark chocolate, making a crosshatch pattern. Let set slightly; form a teardrop-shaped loop by pressing the ends of the strip tightly together. This should form a shape that is large enough to accompany 3 Bavarian cream balls [see photo]. Allow to set completely at room temperature; carefully remove the acetate. Repeat with the remaining strips.

ASSEMBLY:

Confectioners' sugar flavored with dehydrated raspberry powder to taste

Fresh raspberries

1.   Place a chocolate teardrop loop on a dessert plate with the point of the loop facing towards the front of the plate. Dust the base of the plate around the chocolate loop with the flavored confectioners' sugar.

2.   Place three Bavarian fruit balls, one of each flavor, inside the chocolate loop. Place two hippen cookies, one of each size, in front of the Bavarian balls, so that they are resting on the balls.

3.   Arrange 6 fresh raspberries on the left side of the loop. Garnish the right side with 7 dime-size dots of passion fruit sauce.

Nougat Glacé with Lavender Honey and Candied Fruits

YIELD: *30 servings*

TODD JOHNSON

RITZ-CARLTON HOTEL
NAPLES, FL

A frozen nougat flavored with lavender honey and cluttered with toasted nuts and candied fruits is the centerpiece of this lavish presentation. "To bring it into the twenty-first century I have a piece of silkscreened joconde," says Todd Johnson. "The chocolate base, which is very thin, continues the pattern of the silkscreen. Obviously you're not going to eat all the chocolate on the plate. It's just for show." That chocolate includes cigarettes, ribbons, and a white chocolate butterfly. The dessert eats very easily: "There's enough sugar in the nougat so that it doesn't freeze entirely," says Johnson.

JOCONDE:

9 oz [255 g] Krem d'Arome cocoa paste

16.5 oz [468 g] eggs

11 oz [312 g] almond flour

3.5 oz [99 g] all-purpose flour

2.5 oz [71 g] unsalted butter, melted

12 oz [340 g] egg whites

10 oz [283 g] granulated sugar

1. Preheat oven to 450°F [225°C].

2. Spread the cocoa paste over a silkscreen design onto 2 silicone baking mats. Freeze.

3. In a mixing bowl, whip the eggs and almond and all-purpose flours. Add the melted butter.

4. In a mixing bowl, whip the egg whites and sugar to soft peaks. Fold into the almond mixture. Spread onto the silkscreened baking mats. Bake until it just begins to color, about 7 minutes. Invert immediately.

NOUGAT GLACÉ:

6 oz [170 g] granulated sugar, divided

8 oz [227 g] lavender honey

2 oz [57 g] glucose

10 oz [283 g] egg whites

2 oz [57 g] Cointreau

4 oz [113 g] slivered almonds, toasted

4 oz [113 g] pistachios, toasted

4 oz [113 g] candied fruit

4 oz [113 g] currants

1 qt [.9 lt] heavy cream, whipped to soft peaks

1. In a saucepan, combine 4 oz [113 g] of the sugar, honey, and glucose. Heat to 250°F [120°C].

2. Meanwhile, in a mixing bowl, whip the egg whites with the remaining 2 oz [57 g] of sugar. When the sugar syrup reaches 250°F [120°C], pour into the meringue. Whip until cooled.

3. Fold in the Cointreau, nuts, fruits, and whipped cream.

ASSEMBLY:

Tempered dark chocolate
Tempered white chocolate
Chocolate ribbons
Chocolate cigarettes
Chocolate butterflies
Berries

1. Line thirty 3″ × 2″ [7.6 cm × 5 cm] oval ring molds with the joconde. Fill with the nougat glacé. Freeze.

2. Spread the tempered dark chocolate over the silkscreen design onto the acetate sheet. Let set. Spread the tempered white chocolate over the design. Cut to the size of the inner portion of the plate when almost set. Place on the serving plate.

3. Place the frozen glacé on the plate. Garnish with chocolate ribbons, cigarettes, butterflies, and berries.

Frozen Chocolate Caramel Mousse

DANIEL JASSO

WESTERN CULINARY
INSTITUTE
PORTLAND, OR

Enclosed in a glaze of cardamom-infused chocolate ganache is frozen chocolate caramel mousse; it is accompanied by bittersweet chocolate sauce flavored with Chinese five-spice powder. "The praline nougatine is like an almond brittle without the fat," says Daniel Jasso. "I present it in the form of a fan because it is intended to be the vessel from which you eat the mousse. No fork or spoon is required." He describes the flavors as "spicy, nutty caramelly, and a whole lotta chocolate. The cardamom is a bit strong to counter the strong chocolate flavor. The five-spice is strong too, so there's only a hint of it."

SPECIAL EQUIPMENT: *Nine pointed oval ["football"] ring molds, 3½" [8.9 cm] long × 1¼" [3.2 cm] high × 2" [5.1 cm] wide*

FROZEN CARAMEL CHOCOLATE MOUSSE:

8 oz [227 g] bittersweet chocolate, finely chopped

13 liq oz [384 ml] heavy cream, divided

2 liq oz [59 ml] water

4 oz [113 g] granulated sugar

⅛ tsp [.5 g] cream of tartar

3.5 oz [99 g] eggs

1.   Place the chopped chocolate in a bowl. Set the 9 oval molds on a parchment-lined sheet pan.

2.   In a mixer fitted with the whisk attachment, whip 8 liq oz [237 ml] of the cream to soft peaks. Refrigerate until needed.

3.   Combine the water, sugar, and cream of tartar in a heavy saucepan and cook over medium heat, stirring constantly, until the sugar dissolves and the mixture comes to a boil. Continue to boil the syrup until it is golden amber in color. Remove the pan from the heat and immediately pour in the remaining heavy cream. Allow the mixture to bubble up and then settle.

3.   Return the pan to low heat and cook, stirring constantly, until the syrup is well blended and smooth and any hardened bits of caramel have dissolved.

4.   Pour the hot caramel over the chopped chocolate. Allow the mixture to stand for 3 minutes to melt the chocolate. Whisk until smooth. Whisk in the eggs and cool the mixture to room temperature.

5.   Gently fold the whipped cream into the chocolate-egg mixture. Fill the prepared molds with the mousse and freeze until serving.

NOUGATINE FANS:

4 oz [113 g] sliced almonds, chopped

2 oz [59 ml] water

8 oz [227 g] granulated sugar

1½ Tbs [22.5 ml] light corn syrup

⅛ tsp [.5 g] cream of tartar

1.   Slightly warm the almonds in an oven, making sure they do not color. Combine the water, sugar, corn syrup, and cream of tartar in a heavy saucepan and cook over medium heat, stirring constantly, until the sugar dissolves and the mixture comes to a boil. Continue to boil the syrup until it is light golden amber in color. Add the warmed almonds and stir over low heat until the almonds are completely coated with the caramel, about 1 minute.

2.   Pour the nut mixture onto a lightly greased marble work surface. Immediately spread the nougatine into a very thin, even layer.

3.   Use a sharp knife to cut the nougatine into nine 6″ [15.2 cm] high triangles. Shape each nougatine triangle, while still warm, over a rolling pin and let set. [If the nougatine becomes brittle before all the fans are shaped, the nougatine may be placed in a microwave oven for a few seconds, until malleable.]

CHOCOLATE FIVE-SPICE SAUCE:

5.5 oz [156 g] heavy cream

1 tsp [2 g] Chinese five-spice powder

4 oz [113 g] semisweet chocolate, finely chopped

1.   In a saucepan, combine the cream and five-spice powder and bring to a boil.

2.   Strain the hot cream through a chinois set over the bowl containing the chopped chocolate. Allow the mixture to stand for 3 minutes to melt the chocolate. Whisk until smooth. Pour the sauce into a squeeze bottle.

CHOCOLATE GANACHE:

10 liq oz [296 ml] heavy cream

¼ tsp [.5 g] ground cardamom

12 oz [340 g] semisweet chocolate, finely chopped

1.   In a saucepan, combine the cream and cardamom and bring to a boil.

2.   Strain the hot cream through a chinois set over the bowl containing the chopped chocolate. Allow the mixture to stand for 3 minutes to melt the chocolate. Whisk until smooth. Keep warm for assembly.

ASSEMBLY:

Milk chocolate filigrees

Gold pulled sugar curls, 3½" [8.9 cm] long

Gold pulled sugar leaves

Gold pulled sugar rods, 5" [12.7 cm] long

1. Gently rewarm the chocolate ganache, if necessary.

2. Remove a caramel chocolate mousse from the freezer and unmold onto a cold plate. Pour some warmed ganache over the mousse and spread to completely cover. Place the glazed mousse in the refrigerator to set the ganache, about 1 to 2 minutes.

3. Trim off any excess ganache and transfer the mousse to a dessert plate. Place a milk chocolate filigree on top of the mousse.

4. Garnish the dessert with a nougatine fan, the pulled sugar components, and the chocolate five-spice sauce.

Banana Split

YIELD: *14 servings*

PATRICIA MURAKAMI

AMBROSIA FINE FOODS
SACRAMENTO, CA

Classic or no classic, Pat Murakami followed her own Rule Number One when creating this dessert. "I don't put anything on it I don't like. A classic banana split is usually vanilla ice cream, bananas, strawberries, pineapple, caramel. But I don't like pineapple, so you won't find it here." The various twists and turns of this split, brilliant shadows of the original, include a frozen vanilla bean soufflé, crushed nuts, chocolate sauce served warm, fresh strawberries, strawberry sauce, sautéed bananas in butter, rum and brown sugar, and crème anglaise. "I love American desserts," says Murakami, "and I think people love our traditions. Just changing the format of them a little bit, making them a little more modern in design—people enjoy that."

SPECIAL EQUIPMENT: *Fourteen ring molds, 3" [7.6 cm] diameter × 1¾" [4.4 cm] high*

CRÈME ANGLAISE:

1 pt [473 ml] heavy cream

2 Tbs [25 g] granulated sugar

1 vanilla bean, split and scraped

2.6 oz [74 g] egg yolks

1. In a saucepan, combine the heavy cream, sugar, and vanilla bean seeds and bring to a boil; remove the pan from the heat.

2. In a bowl, whisk the egg yolks until blended. Temper the yolks with about half of the hot cream mixture and pour the yolk-cream mixture back into the saucepan. Cook over low heat until the mixture reaches the custard stage.

3. Immediately strain the custard into a bowl, set over an ice bath, and cool completely. Refrigerate until cold.

BUTTER COOKIES:

8.5 oz [241 g] all-purpose flour

2 oz [57 g] confectioners' sugar

8 oz [227 g] unsalted butter, cut into 1" [2.5 cm] chunks, at room temperature

1. Place the flour and confectioners' sugar in a food processor and pulse until combined. Add the softened butter and process until a ball of dough forms.

2. Shape the dough into a disc; wrap with plastic wrap and refrigerate for at least 1 hour.

3. Preheat oven to 350°F [175°C]. Line a baking pan with parchment paper.

4. On a work surface that has been lightly dusted with flour, roll the dough out to ¼" [.6 cm] thick. Since the cookies spread a little during baking, use a round cutter, with a diameter slightly less than that of the ring mold, to stamp out 14 rounds of dough. [A cutter with a 2¾" [69.9 mm] diameter works well here.] Place the rounds on the prepared pan; cover with plastic wrap and chill until firm, at least 1 hour.

5. Bake the cookies until lightly colored, about 12 to 14 minutes.

6. Let cool completely on a wire rack.

FROZEN VANILLA BEAN SOUFFLÉ:

6 oz [170 g] egg whites

2 oz [57 g] granulated sugar

1½ tsp [7 ml] vanilla extract

4 liq oz [118 ml] crème anglaise

16 liq oz [473 ml] heavy cream, whipped to soft peaks

1.   Line 14 ring molds with strips of parchment paper cut the same height as the molds. Place the molds on a parchment-lined tray. Place a cookie in the bottom of each of the prepared ring molds. Set aside.

2.   In a mixer fitted with a whip attachment, whip the egg whites with the sugar until stiff peaks form.

3.   In a large bowl, whisk the vanilla extract with the crème anglaise. Fold in the whipped cream, then fold in the whipped egg whites.

4.   Scrape the soufflé mixture into a pastry bag without a tip. Pipe the mixture into the prepared molds. Freeze the soufflés overnight.

5.   Unmold the frozen soufflés and peel off the parchment paper. Refreeze the soufflés until ready to use.

WARM CHOCOLATE SAUCE:

8 oz [227 g] bittersweet chocolate, finely chopped

8 liq oz [237 ml] heavy cream

1.   Place the chopped chocolate in a medium bowl.

2.   In a saucepan, bring the cream to a boil. Pour the hot cream over the chocolate. Allow the mixture to stand for 3 minutes to melt the chocolate. Whisk until smooth. Serve warm.

STRAWBERRY SAUCE:

24 oz [680 g] fresh strawberries, hulled

6 oz [170 g] granulated sugar

1.   Thickly slice the strawberries and sprinkle them, to taste, with the sugar, making sure all the berries are coated with sugar. [The exact amount of sugar will depend upon the sweetness of the berries.]

2.   Place the sugared strawberries in a large heavy-bottomed saucepan. Cook the mixture over medium-low heat until the berries begin to give off their juices and most of the sugar is dissolved, about 6 to 8 minutes. During the cooking process, use a rubber spatula to gently turn the berries once or twice to ensure even heating; do not bruise the berries.

3. Remove the pan from the heat and let the strawberry-sugar mixture macerate for 20 minutes.

4. Drain the mixture in a fine-meshed sieve set over a stainless steel bowl until all the juices have been released; do not press down on the berries, as this will cause the juice to become cloudy. Reserve the juice and discard the berries.

5. Refrigerate the strawberry sauce until needed.

BROWN SUGAR SAUCE FOR THE BANANAS:

6 oz [170 g] unsalted butter

4 oz [113 g] light brown sugar

2 liq oz [59 ml] dark rum

2 liq oz [59 ml] heavy cream

Combine all the ingredients in a medium saucepan and cook over medium-low heat, stirring occasionally, until the butter is melted and the sugar is dissolved. Raise the heat and bring to a full boil. Remove from the heat and set aside until ready to assemble.

ASSEMBLY:

Chopped nuts, such as walnuts, pecans, or macadamia nuts

Sliced strawberries

6 medium bananas, sliced ¼" [.6 cm] thick on the diagonal

1. Put the nuts around the sides of each soufflé.

2. Bring the brown sugar sauce to a boil. Add 5 slices of banana and cook until the banana slices are just warmed through, about 1 minute.

3. Place a frozen vanilla soufflé in the center of a dessert plate. Top with a few banana slices.

4. Spoon some of the crème anglaise around the soufflé. Garnish with warm chocolate sauce and strawberry sauce.

5. Arrange the strawberry slices around each soufflé.

Passion Fruit Baked Alaska
with Coconut Marshmallows

YIELD: *10 servings*

HEATHER HO

BOULEVARD
SAN FRANCISCO, CA

The classic Baked Alaska—cake and ice cream covered with meringue, oven-browned—is given a makeover for reasons of flavor and ease of production: "In a restaurant setting it's not that easy to do, even with a blowtorch," says Heather Ho. "The problem is storage—with all that meringue, you can't hold them anywhere. This way I can stack them up in a container and put it in the freezer. When you're ready, you cook them, unmold them, put the marshmallows on top, and out they go." Ho's version consists of coconut marshmallows [replacing the meringue] over passion fruit sorbet over coconut ice cream over devil's food cake. "I'm not a big fan of meringue," Ho confides. "To me the classic Baked Alaska tends to taste like meringue. It's too sweet and masks other flavors. This way, you can taste the passion fruit and coconut."

SPECIAL EQUIPMENT: *Ten mini loaf pans, 4" [10 cm] × 2" [5 cm]*

DEVIL'S FOOD CAKE:

2 oz [57 g] *unsweetened cocoa powder*

5.3 liq oz [157 ml] *boiling water*

4 liq oz [118 ml] *buttermilk, divided*

1.5 oz [43 g] *all-purpose flour*

3.5 oz [99 g] *cake flour*

½ tsp [2.5 g] *baking powder*

½ tsp [2.5 g] *baking soda*

Pinch of salt

1.75 oz [50 g] *mayonnaise*

7 oz [198 g] *light brown sugar*

1.75 oz [50 g] *eggs*

½ tsp [2 g] *vanilla extract*

1.   Preheat a convection oven to 300°F [150°C]. Whisk together the cocoa powder and boiling water to form a smooth paste. Cover with plastic wrap and cool to room temperature. Whisk in 2 liq oz [59 ml] of the buttermilk.

2.   Sift together the flours, baking powder, baking soda, and salt, and set aside. In a mixer with the paddle attachment, beat together the mayonnaise, brown sugar, eggs, and vanilla extract until the mixture has lightened slightly, about 4 to 5 minutes. Add the sifted dry ingredients and mix until almost incorporated. Add the remaining 2 liq oz [59 ml] of buttermilk and mix until smooth. Fold in the cocoa paste.

3.   Pour the batter onto a parchment-lined half sheet pan and spread it evenly with an offset spatula. Bake for 5 minutes or just until the cake springs back when lightly touched. Cool completely.

COCONUT ICE CREAM:

12 liq oz [355 ml] milk

12 liq oz [355 ml] heavy cream

2.25 oz [64 g] dessicated coconut

½ vanilla bean, split

2.3 oz [65 g] granulated sugar, divided

4.6 oz [130 g] egg yolks

1.   In a saucepan, combine the milk, cream, coconut, vanilla bean, and 1.2 oz [34 g] of the sugar and bring to a boil. Remove from heat, cover the pan, and let it steep for 30 minutes.

2.   In a mixing bowl, whisk together the remaining 1.1 oz [30 g] of sugar with the egg yolks until pale. Slowly whisk in the coconut mixture. Strain through a sieve, pressing hard on the solids to squeeze out all of the liquid. Let cool. Keep the mixture refrigerated until ready to process during the final assembly.

PASSION FRUIT SORBET:

4.5 oz [128 g] granulated sugar

9 liq oz [266 ml] water

1 tsp [5 g] egg whites

18 liq oz [532 ml] passion fruit purée

1.   In a small saucepan, heat the sugar and water until the sugar dissolves. Let the syrup cool completely.

2.   Whisk the syrup and egg whites into the passion fruit purée. Keep the mixture covered and chilled until ready to process during the assembly.

COCONUT SAUCE:

6 liq oz [177 ml] milk

6 liq oz [177 ml] heavy cream

1.5 oz [43 g] dessicated coconut

½ vanilla bean, split

2.3 oz [65 g] granulated sugar, divided

3.25 oz [92 g] egg yolks

1.   In a saucepan, combine the milk, cream, coconut, vanilla bean, and 1.2 oz [34 g] of the sugar and bring to a boil. Remove from heat, cover the pan, and let it steep for 30 minutes.

2.   Strain the mixture through a sieve, pressing hard on the solids to squeeze out all of the liquid. Transfer the sauce to a clean pan and bring it back to a boil. Whisk the egg yolks with the remaining 1.1 oz [31 g] of sugar and temper them into the hot milk mixture. Cook gently, stirring, until the mixture coats the back of a wooden spoon. Strain over an ice bath and cool completely.

COCONUT MARSHMALLOWS:

Confectioners' sugar for dusting

.13 oz [3.75 g] gelatin sheets

6.3 oz [179 g] egg whites

10.5 oz [298 g] granulated sugar

1 tsp [3.1 g] cream of tartar

2 tsp [18 g] corn syrup

.75 oz [21 g] dessicated coconut, lightly toasted and cooled

1.   Lightly sift confectioners' sugar over a parchment-lined sheet pan. Bloom the gelatin and squeeze out the excess water. Warm it in a small saucepan just until it melts.

2.   In the bowl of an electric mixer, combine the egg whites and sugar. Whisk over simmering water until the mixture is warm and the sugar has dissolved. Add the cream of tartar and transfer the bowl to the mixer. Whip to medium peaks. Add the corn syrup and whip to stiff peaks. Add the gelatin and pulse once or twice to partially incorporate it. Sprinkle the coconut on top and gently fold it in.

3.   Transfer the mixture to a pastry bag fitted with a medium plain tip. Working quickly, pipe the marshmallows into the desired shape, such as strips, squiggles, or dollops. Lightly sift confectioners' sugar over the marshmallows. Let dry at room temperature for 4 hours.

ASSEMBLY:

1.   Spray the 10 loaf pans with nonstick cooking spray. Line the pans with plastic wrap, fitting the plastic snugly into the corners and allowing enough of an overhang to cover the tops. Freeze the pans for at least 1 hour. Fit a pastry bag with a large plain tip and place it tip-down in a pitcher. Freeze for at least 1 hour.

2.   Invert the devil's food cake and cut from it 10 rectangles, each measuring 2″ × 4″ [5 cm × 10 cm]. Wrap the rectangles in plastic and freeze for at least 1 hour.

3.   Process the passion fruit sorbet in an ice cream machine until it is very firm, and extract it into the frozen pastry bag. Working quickly, pipe the sorbet into the frozen pans, filling them about one-third to one-half full. Return the loaf pans to the freezer. Clean out and dry the pastry bag and return it to the freezer.

4.   Process the coconut ice cream and repeat the procedure, extracting it into the frozen pastry bag and filling the loaf pans almost to the top. Place a devil's food cake rectangle on top of the ice cream. Cover the pans with the overhanging plastic wrap and freeze until solid, at least 4 hours.

5.   Gently tug on the plastic wrap to unmold the Alaskas and place them cake-side down on dessert plates. Using a small offset spatula dipped in confectioners' sugar or sprayed with nonstick cooking spray, carefully lift the marshmallows from the parchment and place on the tops of and beside the Alaskas. Brown the marshmallows with a heat torch. Serve with coconut sauce, adding a bit of cream if it has become too thick upon standing.

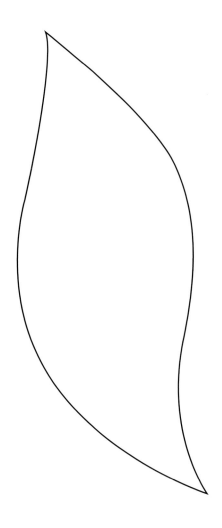

TEMPLATE FOR KIM O'FLAHERTY'S
BANANA "SNICKERS" NAPOLEON, PAGE 195

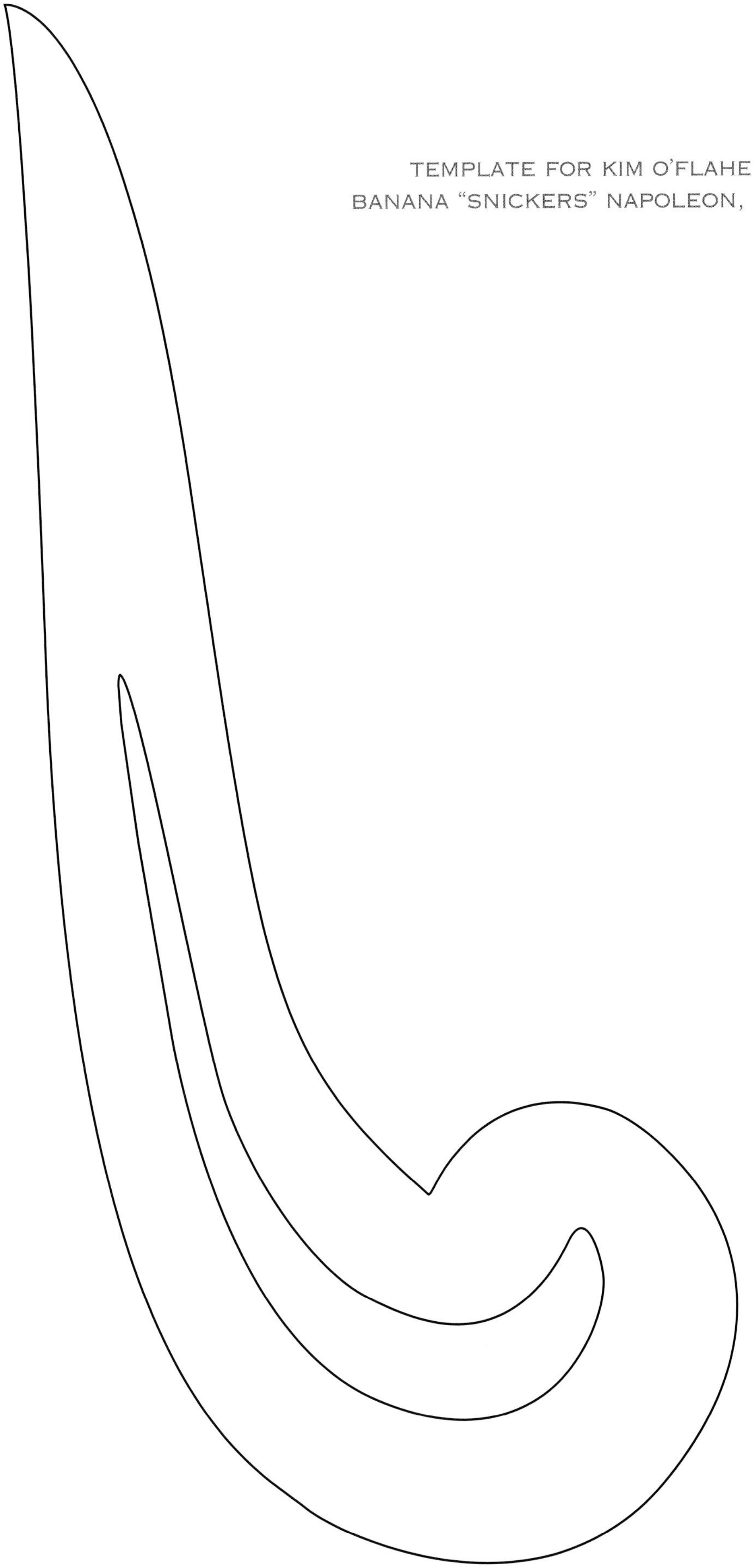

sugar work

CHAPTER 6

Sugar Garnishes

AN INTRODUCTION TO PRODUCTION

Is it edible? Is it necessary? These questions, which are often directed toward pulled and blown sugar pieces in plated desserts, are almost beside the point. The fact is that in many fine restaurants and hotels a pulled or blown sugar piece is commonly used as a visual accent to a dessert; it is seen as an inexpensive, elegant way to enhance the perceived value of a plate. Many of the desserts on display in the *Grand Finales* series include some sugar work. This is not to say that every pastry chef must know sugar inside and out, but, obviously, the more skills the chef brings to the table, the better.

Ewald Notter, owner and lead instructor of the Notter International School of Confectionery Arts in Gaithersburg, Maryland, is an acknowledged master of sugar work, and a renowned teacher of the craft. Here he provides a glimpse into the basics of creating sugar pieces as plate accents.

This is a primer, not a "how to" on making sugar garnishes. Experience, practice, and solid, one-on-one instruction are crucial to success with sugar, not only because of the many motor skills and cues that must be learned, but because of the endless variables of product, environment, and equipment involved with the discipline.

As an example, boiling time varies due to the quality of the sugar, the temperature and humidity in the shop, and the glucose—was it made from potatoes, or corn or wheat? If wheat, in what type of earth was it grown? Evaluating the sugar is an important step when Ewald Notter travels to give demonstrations. He allows himself a day to work with the sugar that is most accessible to the students in that market. The goal is to maximize the time the students can work with a sugar without it crystallizing.

Making the sugar

Chefs who present sugar work as garnishes will devote some time every few months to make finished pulled sugar—the raw material for the actual garnishes. Once it is cooked, colored, and cooled, it is segmented and stored for future use. Preboiled sugar is available from some pastry supply companies (see Sources, page 281), but it is better to learn how to cook it yourself. This knowledge can come in handy in emergencies.

The basic formulation for sugar to be pulled is 3 pounds of sugar, 1 pound of water, and 10 ounces of glucose. The sugar and water are first placed in a 2- or 3-quart pot. Use the highest flame possible, concentrated directly under the center of the pan. (If it reaches the outside of the pan, it could caramelize the sugar on the outside and make the sugar more yellow than you want.)

When the sugar and water mixture comes to a boil, scrape the glucose into the mixture. The glucose cools the sugar down and gives you a second chance to skim or clean the sugar. Once the glucose is added, the ideal boiling time is 15 minutes for 1 pound of sugar.

If you are pulling sugar, slowly add 10 drops of tartaric acid, making adjustments to this amount based on the sugar's texture. You can use lemon juice or vinegar rather than tartaric acid, but tartaric acid is the preferred choice because you can count the number of drops. If your stovetop has slow gas or low gas, the total boiling time of the sugar with the acid is longer, so you need less acid or the sugar will be soft. If your gas is too high or too hot, the sugar will boil more quickly. You'll need more acid or your sugar will be more brittle, or, in the worst case, the sugar will crystallize early. Continue to boil the sugar fast so that the color doesn't change. The longer you boil, the more the color will deepen.

Boil the sugar up to 320°F (170°C) as fast as possible and with the heat concentrated directly under the center of the pan. Once the sugar has reached that temperature, it is ready. Above that, it will caramelize.

TOOLS AND EQUIPMENT FOR SUGAR MAKING

- Bowl of cold water
- Bowl for glucose
- Paintbrush
- Stoppered bottle for acid

- 1 Skimmer
- Candy thermometer
- Gloves to avoid fingerprints and moisture

WHY DOES SUGAR CRYSTALLIZE?

- Repeated dipping of fork or utensil in sugar
- Not skimming during boiling
- Dirty marble
- Sweaty hands
- Overworking sugar
- Over-warming sugar in the microwave
- Using poor-quality sugar

Use cold water in the pot so the crystals have more time to become dissolved.

Use a paintbrush to wash down the crystals on the side of the pan and a sieve to skim off the scum from the top.

Before the sugar boils, it is very important that you remove the scum that forms on the surface.

Stir often, and skim as often as necessary.

Add glucose to the sugar and water mixture.

Add 10 drops of tartaric acid to the boiling sugar.

A Word on Isomalt

ISOMALT IS A TYPE OF SUCROSE produced through a rearrangement of certain enzymes. It is often used instead of granulated sugar for decorative sugar work. Though most of the procedures explained here apply to both granulated sugar and Isomalt, all of the procedures, unless otherwise noted, involve sugar.

If you use Isomalt for piping sugar and making cages, mix it with a little water, just enough to make it look like wet sand—about 10 percent water to Isomalt. Boil the mixture up to 340°F (170°C). If you are pulling the Isomalt to make flowers, for example, it is important that the Isomalt boil for only 15 minutes. Any longer, and the Isomalt releases more water, making it brittle and less pliable.

When deciding whether to use sugar or Isomalt for work, consider these points:

- Because Isomalt absorbs very little moisture and does not crystallize, it is preferred for small decorations for dessert. You just don't know how long the dessert will be on the plate.

- When you use Isomalt for spun sugar and cages, you can use it again. You can't do that with sugar; it will crystallize. Put the Isomalt scraps in a bag with some limestone, and reuse.

- A pound of Isomalt costs between three and four dollars. A pound of sugar costs about sixty cents. But because sugar crystallizes so easily, there is much waste, while Isomalt can be reused. For that reason—plus the fact that you can produce more in less time with Isomalt—the cost factor of Isomalt is reduced.

- There is a color difference between the two. Where white garnishes made from sugar are creamy, Isomalt garnishes are pure white. Isomalt is more brittle to work with. It takes more skill and practice to make a nice rose out of Isomalt than sugar, and it takes more skill to make it shiny.

Adding the Color

In general, light colors complement food; dark colors overwhelm the plate if overused and can take away from the focal point of the plate. This example features yellow, because it works well as a plate garnish and goes well with food.

The powdered color agent should be placed in a plastic cup, and water should be added with a paintbrush. It should be then be mixed until it has a smooth consistency and the color is completely dissolved. Color can be added at any time.

Place the powdered color agent in a plastic cup, add water, and mix with a paintbrush.

Once the sugar is boiling, the color can be added at any time.

Color tips

I NORMALLY USE POWDERED COLOR. It dissolves in water, and it can keep for years. Water-based color agents may contain a preservative (acid); this additional acid could throw off the sugar formula, resulting in sugar that is too soft.

It is difficult to get the same color from batch to batch, even if you count the drops. This is why you should finish a piece once you start it—not only because of matching colors, but because to attach a new piece of sugar to a cooled piece of sugar, you must use heat, and often the cooled sugar will crack.

Pulling Sugar

After the sugar is cooked, it is a good idea to pull it. If the cooked sugar is left as is, it will have no shine. Pulling incorporates air and gives the sugar a silky sheen. After pulling, segment the sugar and store it. The sugar segments can then be rewarmed relatively quickly and formed into the finished garnishes. Pieces of this kind can be stored for six months in an airtight container with limestone pellets. Other points worth mentioning:

- Pull sugar on a warm table. If the table is too cold, the sugar will get cold and break.

- Use your hands, rather than a scraper, to gather the sugar into a lump, but be careful not to have sweaty hands.

- When pulling sugar, be sure not to twist it like a braid.

- A heat lamp is better than a microwave for rewarming these sugar segments, because incorrect use of the microwave can cause crystallization.

Pour the sugar on a Silpat or oiled marble.

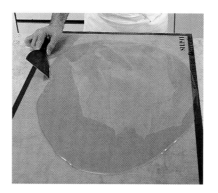

Start to fold the sugar from the edges to the inside.

Use your hand or a scraper to form the sugar into a lump.

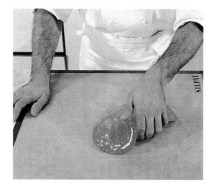

The cold side of the piece (marble side) is folded into the center. Repeat this process until the consistency starts to change; you can hear the sugar snap.

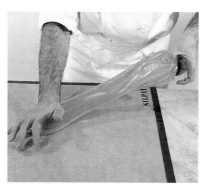

Begin to pull the sugar. Pull with one hand, stabilizing the piece with the heel of the other hand.

Loop one side over the other to incorporate air.

Once the sugar is cooled, stretch to approximately 1 inch thick.

Continue to pull the sugar until your sugar gets lighter and shinier.

Use a scissors to snip off approximately 8-inch pieces.

Bubble Sugar

Chefs use shards of bubble sugar to dress up plated desserts, as a backdrop or connective element. Bubble sugar offers intriguing visual texture as well as color splash. To make bubble sugar, use parchment paper. Keep in mind that every company's paper is coated differently. My best success is with recycled, or unbleached, parchment paper. Whatever paper you use, if the process isn't producing a garnish that you like (or if you want to use any paper you have around), you can wet the paper with a towel dipped in high-percentage alcohol (Everclear alcohol), and it should work.

Let the sugar cool on the paper. If you are not using the sugar immediately, don't release it from the paper; the bubble sugar can be stored as is, in a plastic container with limestone pellets.

Pour hot sugar (320°F [160°C]) in a line at the top of the parchment paper.

Pick the paper up and let the sugar flow to the bottom. Then pick the paper up by the other side and let the sugar flow back across the paper. Repeat the process.

Cages

Sugar cages are most often used to perk up a plate that is simple or minimally designed. They can enclose domes or discs of mousse or parfait, small portions of cake, sorbet presentations, and so on. The primary tools to make sugar cages are a ladle, and a fork or spoon.

Pick up the hot sugar with a fork and gently wave the fork over the ladle.

Start at the bottom of the ladle, go completely around the base, and create a lattice of diagonal lines.

Wait a few seconds, then remove the cage from the ladle.

Tips for making cages

LOOK FOR A ONE-PIECE LADLE—one that does not have welding at the joint of the handle and scoop. This way there will be no interruption in the cage structure.

The ladle must be cold and oiled. Any kind of oil will do, but it is not wise to make the ladle too cold. Dip it in cold water, not ice water, for production. Ice water can create condensation or sweat on the ladle even after it is wiped dry, causing the cages to stick to the ladle. Isomalt is a good choice for this process, as it does not crystallize like sugar, even with repetitive dipping of the fork in and out of the sugar.

There is no exact temperature to judge whether the hot sugar is ready for this process. Rather, examine the consistency. Dab some with the fork and pick it up; if it creates a thread it is ready, but if it drops it is too hot and the sugar needs to cool some more.

Generally, three forks of sugar are sufficient: one at the base and then two at most for lines.

When making more than 1 cage, dip the ladle in cold water, dry it, oil it, and continue. A person skilled with sugar can make one hundred cages in 3 hours, including the boiling and packing.

Fan

A sugar fan is most often propped upright off-center on a plate and serves as a backdrop to the dessert forms. The sugar glistens beautifully in any dining room. A proper surface for making a fan can be a cake plate, a marble slab, or the back of a sheetpan. Generally, 7 forks are sufficient for one fan. The fan can be sprayed with an airbrush for different colors and effects.

Using a fork, gently wave the sugar over the surface, all in one direction, but concentrating at a base point.

Fan out from the base point; this base point will be thicker with sugar and will stabilize the fan.

Use scissors to trim the fan while it is still warm and pliable.

Spun Sugar

Diners are always impressed with the lustre and texture of spun sugar. One of its most common uses is as a nest, which can be used to enclose scoops of ice cream or sorbet, a fruit dessert, or any simple form. Some additional notes:

One way to tell if the hot sugar is ready is to draw some out with a fork or whisk. If the sugar forms lumps, it is not ready. It should make threads.

Isomalt is much better for this technique than sugar because it can be rewarmed often without crystallizing. It also has a much longer working temperature than sugar.

The best method is to have 2 pans: you work with one, and when the sugar gets cold you put it on the stove to rewarm; the other you maintain at a warm temperature, then heat it when you are ready to use it.

Use a whisk or other device to test the sugar for readiness.

Dip the device into the sugar and let the sugar fall on your hand.

Gather the sugar in your hand and wrap it loosely around your widely splayed fingers.

Set the device aside and begin to form the nest.

To make a tighter weave, gently compress the sugar.

Allow some of the threads to form the bottom of the nest.

EWALD NOTTER CREATES HIS OWN DEVICE FOR SPUN SUGAR: He takes a metal plate and drives headed nails through it, and attaches the entirety to a handle. With this rather medieval device he makes beautiful sugar nests and other forms.

A whisk can also be used for this process, but requires a sideways motion. The one problem with the whisk is that it takes longer, and therefore the sugar can get too cold.

You can also make spun sugar between two dowels: you dip the whisk in the pan and with almost a throwing, paddling motion, you swing the whisk back and forth over the dowels.

Piping

This is the ideal, simple way to personalize a plate, whether for a birthday, corporate event, or other function. There is no limit to the numbers, letters, and abstract figures you can draw with sugar, in colors that are limited only by your own skill and imagination.

Drawing lines on a sheet of paper will guide you as you do the piping; this is to ensure that what you're producing is of a uniform size. (If your hand-eye skills still need polishing, you can draw the image on paper, put parchment paper over it, and virtually trace it with your piping bag.)

Pipe sugar using line guides or images traced on parchment paper.

As usual, boil the sugar to 320°F (160°C) (Isomalt, 340°F [171°C]) and shock the pan in ice water to stop the sugar from cooking further. Let the sugar rest and set a little bit, and then pour it into a double piping bag. Use a towel to cover the piping bag to protect your hands. Isomalt is more effective for this procedure.

Multicolored Ribbons

Ribbons can be used to create composition on a simple plate, to frame certain dessert forms, or to draw disparate forms together visually. Ribbons formed into a bow are pure ornament and a real crowd pleaser.

For sugar to be used in ribbons, Ewald Notter normally uses dark colors, because pulling the sugar makes it lighter. Also, you can add white to vary the color. If you want plenty of shine, pull the sugar and fold it, as demonstrated earlier, but if you want especially good shine, the sugar must be as cold as possible to work with.

When putting sugar pieces together to make ribbons, the darker colors are proportionately thinner, the lighter colors, thicker. Be sure that all the colors constituting a ribbon have the same consistency and temperature; they must have been boiled the same way. Otherwise, you will not be able to pull out a nice, even ribbon, because some colors may be too brittle. To assemble, he pulls the dark color thin so that it is the length of the light piece. Then he adheres a third color. For this ribbon there are 6 pieces: white, black, blue, green, yellow, then white again. The black is there to break up the color.

There are several ways of pulling ribbons, but the method shown here is best for restaurant production.

Under a heat lamp, cut hotdog-size pieces of the lighter colors and smaller pieces of the darker colors; flatten and adhere side by side.

Pull the ribbon material, snip, and repull until the ribbon reaches the desired thinness and color value.

Under the heat lamp, snip the ribbon into 4-inch pieces.

Fold a 4-inch portion around a dowel. Over a flame, crimp and pinch the end to a point.

Gather 6 of the larger pieces, heat the tips, and join the tips to form a circle.

On this base, create another tier of 4 pieces.

Clustered in this way, uniformity of individual ribbons is not so important.

Rose

To make the petals, form a flat circle of warm sugar. Then, with your thumb and index finger of both hands, work the sugar upward and pull a sharp border (or work space); then, with your thumb on top and index finger underneath, pull out a piece the size of a petal. After you pinch it off, form the petal with your thumb in the palm of your hand. You can then quickly rewarm the whole petal over the flame and crimp back the edges.

Heat the end of the petal and attach it upside down to the base. As you attach the petals, make sure they are all the same height but that the outside petals are a little lower, so you get the effect of an open rose.

A rose is put together with the following pieces: a tight inside roll for the stem, then 3 half petals arranged tightly to form the bud, then another 3 full petals to start your circle around the bud, and finally 5 full petals, or 6 to make a bigger rose.

To make the petals, form a flat circle of warm sugar.

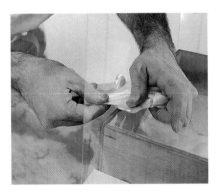

With the thumb and index finger of both hands, work the sugar out, away from the center. That center will form the base of the rose.

Pull out a piece the size of a petal, pinch off the end, then form the petal by pressing the sugar with your thumb into the palm of your hand. Quickly rewarm the petal and crimp back the edges.

Heat the end of the petal and attach it to the base.

A rose consists of the base, 3 half petals arranged tightly to form the bud, 3 full petals for the first circle around the bud, and 5 or 6 additional petals.

Thread

Sugar threads are the form of choice for subtle, light touches on a plate. They can be used flat on the plate to accent the dessert forms, or placed vertically in the dessert itself to add height.

Simply draw some hot sugar with a fork or whisk, and form into threads of any shape you desire. For coils, wind the sugar thread around a pen or other object. Plastic or metal is preferred over wood, because wood absorbs too much heat. The colder the item, the better.

For longer threads or threads that must maintain some structural integrity, use an air tube to inject some air, which adds stability.

To make thread coils, wrap a warm pulled sugar thread around a pen.

When the sugar thread is cool, slide it off the pen.

To make longer threads, place a glob of sugar on an air tube. Pump air into the sugar.

Pull the sugar into a thread.

Form the sugar into the desired shape.

Storage

Most chefs prefer to set aside time to produce simple garnishes once or twice a month, and then store the pieces for use as needed. The sugar pieces should be stored in plastic containers and kept dry with limestone pellets (or calcium carbonate or silica gel). Particularly delicate pieces can be stored on wire racks in these containers, with limestone crystals underneath. To pack pieces for travel, use 8 micron large-strength, high-density bags.

Store pieces in a plastic container.

Certain pieces can be stored on a rack.

Glossary of Classic Desserts and Pastries

It is a given that classic desserts are undergoing constant revision, across cultures and over time. Following are general descriptions of the classics, with an understandable bias toward the contemporary understanding of them. If a dessert's country of origin is known and generally accepted, it is noted. In some cases, more specific information about a dessert's genesis is also included; historians will admit that some of these are fable, some are fact.

ABOUKIR round, thin layers of sponge cake and chestnut/liqueur-flavored cream, drizzled with coffee-flavored fondant and sprinkled with pistachio nuts. (Switzerland)

ABOUKIR ALMOND a petit four consisting of a sphere of marzipan into which are pressed two whole, blanched, and roasted almonds; the entirety is then dipped in boiling sugar syrup.

AEBLESKIVER a cake or doughnut deep-fried in a pan of the same name. (Denmark)

AFGHAN a chocolate cookie filled with crushed cornflakes and dusted with icing or sugar.

AGRAZ a sorbet made from the juice of unripe grapes, almonds, sugar, and kirsch. (North Africa)

AKWADU a mixture of chopped bananas, butter, orange and lemon zests, brown and white sugars, and coconut, which is baked in a pie dish. Served hot or cold. (Ghana)

ALCAZAR an almond-and-egg-white meringue cake topped with a marzipan lattice; the gaps in the lattice are filled with strawberry jam or marmalade; the cake is flash-baked to brown the marzipan.

ALFAJORE sweet or flaky pastry circles that are baked, cooled, and joined, enclosing a cinnamon-flavored custard. (Peru)

ALLUMETTE a rectangle of puff pastry spread with royal icing and baked; once cooled, it is served plain or split and filled with a variety of fillings. Created by a chef named Planta, seeking a way to use up leftover pastry and icing. (Switzerland)

AMANDINE sweet pastry enclosing a creamy almond filling; it is baked, topped with flaked almonds and candied cherries, and apricot-glazed. (France)

AMARETTI macaroon-like cookies containing ground almonds, cinnamon, and lemon zest, and dusted with powdered sugar. (Italy)

ANGEL FOOD CAKE a light cake of flour, egg whites, cream of tartar, salt, sugar, and a flavoring, such as vanilla. (United States)

ANZAC a hard biscuit of whole wheat and plain flours, sugar, milk powder, and water. Contemporary versions are lighter, and can employ oats, butter, cinnamon, and other elements. (Australia)

AWWAM a yeast-risen, deep-fried sphere of pastry that is dipped in honey flavored with lemon and rosewater. (Lebanon)

BABA AU RHUM a light yeast cake with rum-soaked golden raisins, and soaked, after baking, in rum and sugar syrup. Invented by a seventeenth-century Polish pastry chef in honor of his king, Lesczyinski, who, when exiled to France, ordered that the recipe be made richer and sweeter. Named after the king's favorite fictional character, Ali Baba. (Poland/France)

BABKA a cake similar to baba au rhum, with egg whites but without yeast. (Poland)

BABOVKA a rich cake of alternating layers of dark, chocolate-flavored batter and light, vanilla batter, incorporating chopped hazelnuts and grated chocolate, dusted with powdered sugar. (Czechoslovakia)

BAGATELLE a genoise sponge cake that is split and filled with pastry cream, Diplomat cream, and strawberries; the cake is decorated with strawberries and marzipan. (France)

BAKED ALASKA a liqueur-soaked sponge cake encasing layers of ice cream, which is then completely covered with meringue; it is baked in a very hot oven, until the meringue is browned. The meringue insulates the ice cream and prevents melting. Inspired by a doctor experimenting with the heat conduction properties of meringue. (United States)

BAKEWELL TART puff pastry smeared with jelly enclosing an egg, butter, and almond filling. Named after the town where it was invented. (England)

BAKLAVA butter-drenched layers of phyllo and a mixture of sugar, cinnamon, and ground almonds, pistachios, and walnuts; after baking, it is glazed with a honey/sugar syrup, and served in triangles. (Greece)

BALKA a cone-shaped yeast cake. (Poland)

BALUSHAHI sweet pastry dough deep-fried in clarified butter, then dipped in a sugar syrup. (India)

BANANAS FOSTER a banana split lengthwise, sautéed in butter, rum, sugar, and spices, then flambéed and served with the sauce and vanilla ice cream. Created in honor of a regular customer at Brennan's restaurant in New Orleans, circa 1950. (United States)

BANANA SPLIT three scoops of ice cream, whipped cream, chocolate sauce, chopped nuts, and a cherry atop a banana split lengthwise, served in a boat-shaped glass dish. (United States)

BANBURY CAKE an oval cake of puff pastry filled with spiced dried fruits. Originated with soldiers returning from the Crusades, inspired by sweetmeats found in the Holy Land. (England)

BASBOOSA a semolina cake flavored with a syrup of lemon and rosewater. (Egypt)

BA-TA-CLAN an almond cake with a vanilla-flavored icing. (France)

BATTENBERG a sweet cake brushed with apricot jam and covered with marzipan; red-colored cake segments and neutral segments are arranged in a checkerboard fashion. Once known as Tennis Cake. Named after a German royal family. (England)

BAUMKUCHEN an almond cake that is prepared by placing batter on a rotating spit over a grill; once that layer is set, another is brushed on, continuing until the cake has many concentric ring layers. It is finished by being pierced all over with a comb, then covered with buttercream and cocoa powder. The German name translates as "Tree Cake," for the tree-ring-like layers. (Germany)

BEIGNET small pipings of choux pastry, deep-fried. The French fritter. (France)

BEIJOS DE ANJO a mixture of beaten egg yolk folded with whites, baked, then poached in a sugar syrup flavored with vanilla and cloves. (Brazil)

BETTLEMAN a bread pudding composed of milk-soaked stale bread or cake crumbs, sugar, spices, candied peels, and a meringue; topped with butter, it is baked. Also known as "beggar's pudding."

BIBER a honey cake with a spiced filling and covered with a potato glaze; traditionally decorated with a cookie or candy upright bear. (Switzerland)

BIENENSTICH a yeast cake filled with custard and topped with a honey, butter, and almond mixture. Name means "bee sting"—the topping is so sweet, it was said that it attracted bees. (Germany)

BIREWECK a spherical confection made of sweetened dough mixed with candied and fresh fruits macerated in kirsch. (France)

BISCOTTI a crisp, sweet, double-baked biscuit approximately 8″ [20.3 cm] in length, traditionally prepared with almonds in the batter; sometimes flavored and/or partially dipped in chocolate. (Italy)

BLACKBERRY PUDDING a bread pudding, composed of stewed, sweetened blackberries and breadcrumbs, served with cream.

BLACK BOTTOM PIE a crumb-crust-lined pie pan filled with a dark chocolate custard layer and a meringue-lightened vanilla- or rum-flavored custard layer, which is topped by whipped cream and chocolate shavings. (United States)

BLACK FOREST CAKE a triple-layer cake of genoise sponge soaked with kirsch-flavored simple syrup, filled with sweet whipped cream and cherries (sometimes macerated in kirsch), then covered with whipped cream, shaved chocolate, and cherries. (Germany)

BLANCMANGE an almond pudding, molded and served cold. (France)

BLINI a yeast pancake, primarily from buckwheat; traditionally served with caviar or smoked fish, it may also be served with a sweet or other savory ingredient. (Russia)

BLINTZ a very thin, crêpe-like pancake, browned on one side, topped with fruit, whipped cream, cottage cheese, and/or jam (or savory fillings), then folded into a rectangle and baked or browned; served with sour cream. (Eastern Europe)

BLITZEN KUCHEN an orange-flavored tea cake that rises quickly, due to its baking powder agent. (Germany)

BOMBE/BOMBE GLACÉE a two-layer frozen dessert formed in a demisphere mold, called a bombe. Most often, a demisphere of ice cream or sorbet containing a filling of custard, mousse, another sorbet flavor, or a mixture of cooked egg yolks and sugar syrup which is cooled and blended with whipped cream. After unmolding, a bombe glacée is garnished with nuts, shaved chocolate, candied fruits, etc. A bombe can also be a frozen dessert consisting of several layers of sorbet and/or ice cream. There are many bombes with their own distinct names (Diplomate, Succès, Cecilia, Cyrano). (France)

BOSTON CREAM PIE not, strictly speaking, a pie—two layers of sponge cake enclose rich vanilla pastry cream; the top is glazed with chocolate. (United States)

BOUCHÉE bite-size puff pastry (or pâte à choux) filled with a variety of sweet or savory ingredients.

BOULE DE NEIGE a term applying to either a petit four of meringue sandwiched around chocolate buttercream, enrobed in vanilla buttercream and chocolate flakes; or a spherical layer cake of vanilla genoise sponge and vanilla buttercream covered in buttercream and flaked coconut. (France)

BOURDALOUE a tart of wine-poached apples or pears, covered in crème frangipane. (France)

BOURDELOT a cored apple filled with a mixture of spices, breadcrumbs, butter, and golden raisins, enclosed in puff or shortcrust pastry and baked. (France)

BOUREK phyllo or puff pastry (in a rectangular, square, triangular, or roll shape), enclosing a sweet or savory filling, deep-fried then dipped in a sugar syrup; the sweet filling is often a mixture of eggs, brandy, and sugar. (Turkey)

BRANDY SNAP a batter flavored with brandy, molasses, and spices baked and wrapped around a dowel, forming it into a thin cylinder which is filled with flavored whipped cream, butter cream, or ice cream. (Great Britain)

BREAD PUDDING slices or cubes of bread soaked in a mixture of milk, eggs, vanilla, sugar, and spices, and then baked in a mold with, optionally, a mix of nuts, dried fruits, or candied fruits. (United States)

BRESTOIS a cake consisting of genoise sponge mixed with almonds and lemon and orange zest, baked in a brioche mold, filled with apricot jelly, covered in apricot glaze and roasted flaked almonds. (France)

BRIOUAT cylinders of phyllo pastry filled with a mixture of ground almonds, cinnamon, sugar, butter, and orange flower water, deep-fried or baked, then immersed in warm honey before serving. (Morocco)

BROWNIE a dense square of butter, chocolate, eggs, flour, and sugar, which is baked; sometimes incorporating nuts, sometimes featuring a flavor other than chocolate, such as butterscotch. (United States)

BROWN BETTY a fruit compote (usually apples) or stewed fruit base topped with a crumbly topping of breadcrumbs, brown sugar, and cinnamon. (United States)

BRUNE KAGER small, round cookies flavored with cinnamon, ginger, lemon, cloves, and corn syrup, decorated with almonds. (Denmark)

BUBLANINA sponge cake batter topped with cherries or plums, baked and decorated with vanilla sugar. (Czechoslovakia)

BÛCHE DE NOËL a genoise sponge cake rolled with chocolate or mocha buttercream and often frosted with buttercream, then decorated with mushrooms of meringue, leaves of marzipan, and berry-like candies, to resemble a wooden log. (France)

BUCHTELN a sweet bun containing jam. (Austria)

BUCKLE rich cake batter and fresh fruit baked together, until a crust forms on top; served warm with ice cream. (United States)

BUDINO DI RISO a rice pudding tart. (Italy)

BUNUELO a round of deep-fried pastry, dusted with cinnamon and sugar. (Mexico)

BURANELLI knot-shaped, deep-fried sweet cake rolled in superfine sugar, powdered sugar, or cinnamon. (Italy)

BUTTERFLY CAKE an individual serving of Patty Cake (or Queen Cake); a cone-shaped piece is removed from the top of the cake, whipped cream is piped into the crater, and the cone piece is halved and placed in the cream to resemble wings. (England)

BUTTER TART a rectangular or round tart of sweet pastry dough enclosing a rich filling flavored with vanilla and brown sugar and dense with raisins. (Canada)

CABINET PUDDING the English version of a Diplomat Pudding: a baked (or steamed) dessert of breadcrumbs, eggs, and dried fruit; sometimes served frozen. (England)

CAFÉ LIÈGEOIS coffee ice cream whipped with coffee, served with crème Chantilly and chopped nuts. (Belgium)

CANNELON a puff pastry cylinder most often filled with two fillings, either mousses or ice creams, and dusted with powdered sugar.

CANNOLI a cylinder of deep-fried sweet pastry filled with whipped sweetened ricotta cheese, sometimes incorporating chopped pistachio nuts, chocolate bits, or candied citrus peel. (Italy)

CARAC a tartlet consisting of sweet pastry filled with chocolate ganache, characterized by a single dot of melted chocolate at the center of the crown.

CARROT CAKE a sweet cake incorporating finely grated carrots and nuts, traditionally frosted with a cream cheese icing.

CASSADEILLES puff pastry filled with anise-flavored walnuts.

CASSATA a term referring to two desserts: Cassata alla Siciliana is a rectangle (or dome) of liqueur-soaked sponge cake enclosing a mixture of ricotta cheese, shaved chocolate, and candied fruits, glazed with chocolate ganache. Cassata Gelata is an oval of ice cream with the same, or a similar, filling. (Italy)

CASSE MUSEAU hard cookies of almond and cheese; the name, translated as "jaw breaker," refers to their origin—during a traditional French festival, revelers threw the biscuits at each others' mouths, sometimes breaking jaws in the process. (France)

CASTAGNACCIO a thin chestnut cake flavored with rosemary, incorporating dark and golden raisins and pine nuts. (Italy)

CASTLE PUDDING a steamed or baked pudding prepared with jam or jelly at the base of a dariole mold; inverted, and served.

CAT'S TONGUE long, thin, sweet butter cookies, characterized by the mold in which they are baked. (France)

CENCI brandy- or rum-flavored dough formed into knots and deep-fried, served warm dusted with confectioners' sugar. Name translates as "rags and tatters," though they have earned the nickname "lovers' knots." (Italy)

CHARLOTTE RUSSE a large yield of a mousse or light bavarois entirely surrounded by ladyfingers or sponge cake. It was invented by Antonin Carême, somewhat by accident, and named Charlotte à la Parisienne; years later the second term was added because all things Russian were fashionable. (France)

CHARLOTTE any of a number of desserts that are molded or baked with cake or bread forming the outer circumference. Usually, a charlotte is prepared in a special deep, cylindrical, tapered mold and unmolded before portioning for serving; a mousse, bavarois, or custard holds a dense suspension of fruit, with ladyfingers, brioche, or cake lining the mold. Served warm or cold. Created in the eighteenth century and named for the wife of King George III of England, it was originally an apple compote baked in a round mold lined with toast slices; crucial adaptations by Carême and others have given it a French identity. (England)

CHECKERBOARD cookies consisting of a cinnamon-flavored white dough and a lemon-scented chocolate dough; the doughs are layered in an alternating fashion prior to baking. (Holland)

CHEESECAKE over a crust of graham crackers, gingersnaps, or wafers, a dense cake of sweetened cream cheese, eggs, and cream. Sometimes incorporating sour cream, and sometimes flavored with chocolate, mocha, strawberry, etc. Adapted by the ancient Romans, inspired by foods they encountered when warring with the Greeks. (Italy)

CHEESE STRAWS long, slender reeds of puff pastry with a cheese, usually Parmesan, patina.

CHELSEA BUN a baked yeast dough incorporating fruits and spices glazed with jam. (England)

CHESS PIE an open pie crust supports a rich filling of butter, eggs, sugar, and a small portion of flour. (United States)

CHERRIES JUBILEE cherries that have been macerated in a kirsch syrup are flambéed at the service table with the use of kirsch and served with vanilla ice cream.

CHICHIFREGI fluted servings of fried yeast dough coated in sugar. (France)

CHIFFON CAKE a richer, less sweet version of an angel food cake leavened with whipped egg whites and baking powder, and using vegetable oil; the cake can be flavored and/or incorporate nuts and dried fruit, and is often glazed with a sugar icing. (United States)

CHIFFON PIE a sweet pastry shell encloses a light filling created by folding stiffly beaten egg whites or whipped cream into egg yolks, with gelatin sometimes added. The pie can accommodate many flavorings and additions. (United States)

CHOCART fruit purée-filled puff pastry, served hot. (France)

CHOCOLATE TRUFFLES small spheres of chocolate ganache (chocolate melted with cream), sometimes flavored, either dusted with cocoa powder or enrobed in a thin chocolate shell.

CHRABELI a biscuit made from meringue and flour, intended to be dry on the outside and soft on the inside.

CHRISTMAS CAKE a dense, sweet cake incorporating candied fruits and nuts, covered with marzipan and royal icing.

CHRISTMAS PUDDING a cinnamon-flavored bread pudding with raisins, dates, currants, candied peels, and almonds. It is traditionally bound in cheesecloth and suspended to air for 6 weeks to develop its flavor, then boiled again for 2 hours before serving.

CHURRO twisted strands of a pâte à choux are deep fried, then rolled in cinnamon and sugar. (Mexico)

CIAMBELLA a lemon-flavored pound cake, baked in a tube or bundt pan, sometimes incorporating brandy-soaked raisins. (Italy)

CLAFOUTIS sour cherries, or other fruits, are topped by a thick, custardy batter, which puffs and forms a crust when baked together in a flan dish. Served warm, with ice cream or whipped cream. (France)

COBBLER fruit topped with scone or other rich dough that is often dolloped with butter and drizzled with sugar prior to baking. Prepared in a deep, rectangular pan; portions are often served warm, with ice cream. (United States)

COLIFICHET a dry, crisp cookie, served as a petit four. (France)

COLOMBO DI PASQUALE a sweet yeasted bread with cherries and almonds, traditionally shaped in the form of 2 doves, but now often as a twist, glazed with sugar. Invented by a slave girl who won her freedom by giving the King (circa 1170) this dove-shaped bread. (Italy)

CONCORD CAKE layers of chocolate meringue are covered with chocolate mousse then topped with strips of more chocolate meringue. Invented by Gaston Lenôtre. (France)

CONDÉ a term used to describe a cake of puff pastry, royal icing, and almonds, served hot; also, a cold dessert of gelatin, rice, milk, and poached fruit, served on fruit purée; it is also used as a term of praise—à la Condé (referring to an esteemed French general) indicates quality, an item in pastry prepared as perfectly as possible. (France)

CONGRESS TART a sweet pastry brushed with jam at the base and filled with an almond mixture; diagonal slices of pastry crisscross the top, with an apricot glaze and kirsch-flavored fondant.

CONVERSATION CAKE the French version of the Congress Tart—puff pastry with an almond filling and crossed lines of pastry and royal icing decorating the lid; named for a play, *Les Conversations d'Emilie*. (France)

COUPE any combination of fruit, ice cream, and sauce, often topped with a flavored whipped cream, served in a tall glass of the same name.

COUER À LA CRÈME prepared in either a basket lined with cheesecloth or a porcelain mold with bottom holes (for drainage), a mixture of cream cheese and whipped cream or crème fraîche with lemon juice, vanilla, salt, and sugar is chilled for several hours, portioned, and served with berries. (France)

CREAM PUFF a rounded portion of choux pastry dough is baked and, when cooled, split and filled with a creme or custard. A profiterole is a miniature cream puff. (France)

CRÈME BAVAROIS (BAVARIAN CREAM) a custard composed of egg yolks, sugar, milk, fresh whipped cream, and a small measure of gelatin, flavored with fruit purées, coffee, or chocolate.

CRÈME BEAU RIVAGE a baked custard flavored with powdered praline. (England)

CRÈME BRÛLÉE a lightly baked custard that is cooled, then topped with an even layer of sugar which is flamed under a broiler, blowtorch, or iron until it caramelizes. Some trace the origins of this dessert to Cambridge. (England)

CRÈME CARAMEL an egg custard is placed in a mold lined with caramel, and baked in a water bath; when it is cooled and unmolded, the caramel acts as a sauce. (France)

CRÈME CHIBOUST a custard folded with meringue and set with gelatin. Invented by Chiboust, a patissier circa 1846. (France)

CRÊPE a thin, unleavened pancake, served brushed with jelly, citrus juice, or sugar; rolled and filled with thick sauces and/or fruits; or stacked and layered with chocolate. (France)

CRÊPES SUZETTE sweet crêpes brushed with a sauce of butter, sugar, orange juice, and orange zest, topped with an orange liqueur and flamed. First served in a Paris restaurant, circa 1900, but perhaps named for Princess Suzette of France who was dining with the King of England when chef Henri Carpentiere accidentally set their dessert afire and served it as such. (France)

CROISSANT a buttery, rich yeasted dough that is laminated, giving it a light and flaky texture. Baked in crescent form, served plain or slathered with jelly or sometimes filled. Legend has it that, during the siege of Budapest by the Turks in 1686, a potentially disastrous tunnel assault by the Turks was detected by bakers and pastry chefs who were working all night; they alerted the army, and thus the attack was defeated. The bakers were honored by being allowed to use the crescent symbol of the Ottoman Empire, and created this pastry. (Hungary)

CROQUEMBOUCHE a pyramidal celebration cake consisting of stacks of pastry-cream-filled profiteroles joined together with caramel and decorated with spun sugar. The name means "crack-in-the-mouth." (France)

CROUSTADE a baked square of puff pastry that encloses a filling, either sweet or savory. (France)

CRULLER doughnut-type dough is formed into a log, twisted, and deep-fried. The name is from the Dutch "krulle," meaning "twisted cake." (United States)

CRUMBLE stewed fruits topped with a mixture of flour, butter, and sugar.

CRUMPET a round tea cake; yeast batter is placed in a ring and fried in a pan or on a griddle on one side only. (Great Britain)

CUPCAKE an individual sweet cake baked in paper enclosures in muffin tins, and usually topped with an icing of chocolate or other flavors. (United States)

CUSTARD a smooth, thick mixture of sugar, eggs, and milk or cream cooked in a double boiler or in the oven at low heat, until firm; it is served in a bowl, or used as an ingredient in other desserts. (France)

DACQUOISE a cake consisting of three layers of crisp almond or hazelnut meringue filled and frosted with flavored (usually coffee) buttercream, dusted with powdered sugar, and decorated with toasted hazelnuts and shaved chocolate. (France)

DADAR rice flour and coconut milk crêpes are rolled with a filling of grated coconut, cinnamon, brown sugar, and vanilla; served warm. (Indonesia)

DANISH a term that encompasses some 100 different pastries (butter-rich, laminated yeast doughs), filled with sweet fillings and/or dusted with sugar/cinnamon, etc. (Denmark)

DARTOIS rectangles of puff pastry enclose an almond cream—or jam, fresh fruit, or other cream—filling. (France)

DAY/NIGHT MOUSSE CAKE a cake in which layers of genoise sponge enclose alternating layers of white and dark chocolate mousses; sometimes chocolate-iced.

DEATH BY CHOCOLATE a term used to denote a variety of ultra-rich chocolate desserts; perhaps the most famous is Marcel Desaulniers'—a cake consisting of layers of chocolate brownie, cocoa meringue, and mocha mousse is frosted with ganache, topped with chocolate mousse, and sits in a pool of mocha rum sauce. (United States)

DESDEMONA a small, round cake served for tea or as a petit four; two 3″ [7.6 cm] rounds of Othello sponge cake sandwich a vanilla-flavored whipped cream, and the sandwich is brushed with apricot glaze and covered in fondant. (Great Britain)

DEVIL'S FOOD CAKE a two-layer cake of rich, moist cake leavened with baking soda (which imparts the characteristic auburn coloring in the dark crumb) filled and covered with chocolate frosting. (United States)

DIPLOMAT PUDDING a mold is lined with kirsch-soaked brioche segments or ladyfingers and filled with layers of Bavarian cream, apricot jam, candied fruits, cherries, and currants. (France)

DOBOS TORTE a seven-layer cake of very thin rounds of chocolate genoise or sponge-cake filled with chocolate buttercream; the torte is covered with buttercream and a shiny caramel glaze. Created by Chef Josef Dobos, circa 1890. (Hungary)

DOCINHOS DE AMENDOIM a mixture of roasted peanuts, coconut, sugar, and eggs is slow-cooked, cooled, dusted with confectioners' sugar, and cut into squares. (Brazil)

DOLLY VARDEN CAKE a cake (of any flavor) baked in a special tin (or pudding bowl); after baking, a doll is placed on the cake and the entirety is decorated to resemble a woman in a long hooped dress. (Great Britain)

DOUGHNUT an individual serving of yeast- or baking powder-leavened, sweetened dough shaped into an oval with its center cut out with a special cutter, then deep-fried or baked; while cooling, they can be dusted with various sugars or nuts, or glazed with chocolate, etc. (United States)

DUAL TORTE chocolate and white mixtures, both flavored with almonds, are baked together and covered with flaked almonds.

DUCAT a yeast-risen butter cake sprinkled with cinnamon sugar, served with custard. (Austria)

DUMPLING a mixture of bread, butter, eggs, cream cheese, sugar, and zest is shaped into crescents, boiled, then rolled in sweet cookie crumbs. An apple dumpling, on the other hand, consists of a pastry or biscuit crust wrapped around a whole apple, and baked. (England)

DUNDEE CAKE a fruit cake brushed with apricot glaze and decorated with blanched almonds. Originated in the town of Dundee. (Scotland)

DUTCH APPLE TORTE a shortbread-like shell encloses a filling of apples, almonds, and coconut, often crowned with an apricot glaze.

EASTER BREAD individual, round yeast buns with raisins. (England)

ECCLES CAKE two individual-serving shortcrust pastry ovals, joined in a characteristic twist, containing a currant mixture. (England)

ÉCLAIR a pâte à choux cylinder containing a flavored pastry cream (usually vanilla, but also coffee or chocolate) and topped with a glaze of chocolate, or a flavor matching the filling. (France)

ENGADINER a tart containing a mixture of walnuts caramelized in cream, sugar, and honey, and sometimes chocolate. (Switzerland)

ENGLISH PLUM CAKE a rich, yeasted fruit cake. (England)

FAR BRETON a baked dish similar to a Bread Pudding, featuring pitted prunes as well as golden raisins. (France)

FARAREER phyllo dough arranged in bird's nest fashion, baked, and soaked in a flavored honey syrup. (Greece)

FASCHINGSKRAPFEN a ball of fried yeast dough, filled with jam, and rolled in vanilla sugar. (Germany)

FAT RASCAL a large scone filled with a spiced mixture of candied cherries, citrus peels, and almonds; served hot. (England)

FINANCIER similar to sponge cake, a baked mixture of ground almonds, egg whites, flour, sugar, and melted butter, often with sliced almonds in the batter; can be served as is, or brushed with apricot glaze and decorated with strawberries, or glazed with fondant, or used as a base element in other desserts. (France)

FLAN a term used to denote a pastry shell open at the top (as opposed to a pie shell); also a custard dessert topped with caramel. (France/Spain)

FLOATING ISLAND mounds of sweetened, beaten egg whites poached in milk or water are "floated" in a thin crème anglaise and topped with crushed praline or caramel. (France)

FLORENTINE a thin cookie of caramelized butter, sugar, and cream incorporating dried nuts and fruit, and coated in combed chocolate at the base. (France)

FLORENTINE TORTE layers of sponge cake and buttercream topped with a praline or caramel base incorporating dried fruits and nuts.

FLUMMERY a fruit gelatin dessert folded with a whipped mixture of egg whites and cream. (Wales)

FOGUETE sweet pastry cylinders deep-fried and filled with a mixture of pineapple, raisins, and cashews; dipped in a sweet syrup and dusted with confectioners' sugar before serving. (Portugal)

FONDUE sweet or savory, a thick mixture presented in a pot over mild, continuous heat and used as a dipping liquid for fruits, cookies, etc.; the traditional sweet fondue is melted chocolate with cream and an optional liqueur. (France)

FOOL a fruit purée or fresh fruit folded with whipped cream, served chilled, parfait-style. (Great Britain)

FRAISIER a sponge cake filled with crème Chantilly, decorated with fresh strawberries, melted chocolate, and royal icing.

FRENCH TOAST thick, buttered bread slices dipped in an egg/milk mixture, cooked in a frying pan until browned, and served with maple syrup, whipped cream, ice cream, or fruit.

FRIANDISES an assortment of small, light pastries or confections served with coffee or tea, or as an alternative to dessert; the petit four, which is a small pastry of a specific size, is a type of friandise. (France)

FRITTER any of a variety of batters and doughs in individual servings—or fruit dipped in a batter or dough—which is fried and served hot, usually rolled or dusted in sugar. An American beignet. (United States)

FRUITCAKE a butter-rich, dense cake, containing a high density of dried fruits and nuts that have (optionally) been macerated in liquor; normally baked in a loaf or tube pan and drenched in a liquor such as brandy. (England)

FUDGE a rich, sweet mixture of sugar, butter, cream, and a flavor, usually chocolate, as well as optional mix-ins such as nuts; the mixture achieves its smooth, soft texture when cooked to the soft ball stage; once cooled, it is cut into squares. (United States)

FUNNEL CAKE batter is poured through a funnel into a deep container of hot oil; this process yields swirling, crisp spirals, which are served hot with sugar and maple syrup. Originated in the Dutch communities of Pennsylvania. (United States)

GALETTE a flat, round cake, a descendant of the traditional Twelfth Night Cake. The type of dough and toppings vary from region to region. (France)

GALICIEN a sponge cake filled with nut-flavored buttercream, traditionally finished in pistachio icing. (France)

GAUFRETTE a thin Belgian waffle, consisting of four heart-shaped pieces arranged to form a clover. Served with cream, syrup, and ice cream.

GELATO ice cream, Italian-style. The gelato served in an Italian gelaterie is light and airy due to low fat content and relatively high holding temperature, but exports and American-style gelatos contain less air than American ice creams, and so are quite rich and dense. (Italy)

GENOA CAKE a buttery fruit cake containing ground almonds and dried fruit. (Italy)

GINGERBREAD any of a variety of bread-like, cake-like, or cookie-like baked goods, highly spiced. Probably originating in the Middle East, and brought to Europe via the Crusades.

GOD CAKE triangular puff pastry tartlets filled with fruit. Traditionally given by god-parents to their godchildren at Easter time. (England)

GRANITA an iced treat made from sugar, water, and a flavoring, such as fruit juice or coffee; due to its high water content, and by frequent stirring of the mixture as it freezes, it achieves its characteristic grainy/shard texture. (Italy)

GRUNT fresh fruit and a quantity of water topped with pastry dough and sugar, steamed in a closed kettle over an open fire, or baked; served warm with ice cream. The name supposedly derives from the sound the fruit makes in the kettle. (United States)

GULAB JAMUN a cinnamon-flavored sweetmeat soaked in rosewater. (India)

HAARLEM a sponge cake soaked with lemon syrup, filled and iced with buttercream. (Denmark)

HAMANTASCHEN a triangular pastry filled with a mixture of poppy seeds and honey and (optionally) almonds, raisins, prunes, or apricots; it is deep-fried or baked and dusted with confectioners' sugar. (Israel)

HARLEQUIN CAKE a cookie baked with apricot and strawberry jams, covered with a water icing.

HEDGEHOG a mixture of sugar, coconut, cocoa, eggs, and crumbled cookies is placed in a jellyroll pan and refrigerated; it is served in squares, often iced or topped with chocolate chips and/or nuts.

HEFETEIG a rich yeast cake topped with apricots, and served with an apricot glaze and flaked almonds. (Germany/Austria)

HERALDIC DEVICE a collection of four small tarts, each filled with a different jelly or fruit.

HOLLANDER a walnut torte filled with a sweet walnut filling and topped with a strawberry glaze.

HONIG CAKE a honey-glazed honey cake incorporating ground almonds. (Germany)

HOT CROSS BUNS small, sweet yeasted buns containing raisins or other dried fruit that are topped, before baking, with a cross made of flour paste and brushed with a sugar glaze after baking. The traditional cross mark is said to be a leftover from the medieval custom of placing crosses on bread to protect against evil spirits.

HUMMINGBIRD CAKE a layer cake incorporating crushed pineapples and mashed bananas, with a cream cheese frosting.

HUTZELBROT a rich, spicy yeasted cake filled with dried fruits, dates, and pears. Traditionally served at Christmas.

IAGO two discs of a 3″ [7.6 cm] round sponge cake are filled with coffee buttercream, brushed with apricot glaze, and coated with coffee-flavored fondant. Named for the villain in Shakespeare's *Othello*, this petit four is often accompanied by others, similarly named: Othello, Desdemona, Rosalind. (England)

INDIANER an individual portion of baked or fried dough filled with cream and crowned with chocolate. Said to have been inspired by a marital spat between a Viennese baker and his wife (circa 1850); he accused her of amorous attentions to a tightrope walker (indianer), and in a rage she threw a wad of dough at her husband which missed him, but fell in a fire. (Austria)

ISCHL two round cookies made from a cinnamon-flavored, ground almond cookie dough are joined with raspberry, strawberry, or apricot jam; one cookie has a hole cut to display the jam, and is dusted with confectioners' sugar. (Austria)

JACOB'S BATON a cylinder of pâte à choux, no more than 1¼″ [3 cm] long, filled with vanilla cream and topped with chocolate. A small-portion éclair.

JALEBIS batter is piped into twists, fried, crisped, soaked in a sweet syrup, and served immediately. (India)

JALOUSIE a puff pastry rectangle is slit several times lengthwise to display the filling, which is either frangipane cream, a light almond cake mixture, or fresh or poached fruit. The name translates as "Venetian blind," inspired by its appearance. (France)

JELLY CAKE a small sponge cake slathered with jelly and dried coconut, sometimes filled with cream.

JESUITE triangular puff pastry cases filled with almond paste and covered with royal icing prior to baking. Named for its resemblance to a Jesuit priest's hat.

JUNKET a light pudding made from a milk, sugar, and a flavor tablet gelled with rennet, which is formed from stomach acids of calves. (Great Britain)

KAAK a sweet pastry is formed into delicate rings and baked; still hot, the rings are dipped in a milk/sugar glaze. (Lebanon)

KAB EL GHZAL crescents of sweet pastry dough flavored with orange flower water are filled with a cinnamon-flavored ground almond mixture. (Morocco)

KALTSCHALE fresh fruits macerated in a sweet wine sauce covered with a red berry purée and served in a bowl set in ice. (Russia)

KATAIFI layers of dough formed into strands are filled with either a spicy nut mixture or a creamy rice mixture, baked with butter, then soaked in a citrus-flavored sugar syrup. (Greece)

KIPFERLN a shortbread-like cookie bent in a horn or horseshoe shape. (Austria)

KISSEL a dessert similar to Kaltschale, but with a purée thickened with cornstarch. (Russia)

KLOBEN a yeast cake, usually crescent-shaped, filled with a sweet mixture of dried fruits and peel, coated with an apricot glaze.

KLUAY BUDT CHEE sliced bananas are stewed in a mixture of sugar, coconut milk, and salt, then sprinkled with chopped, peeled mung beans; served hot or cold. (Thailand)

KOUNAFA strips of buttered phyllo layered with a sweetened mixture of nuts and spices (and sometimes ricotta or cream cheese), baked, and then soaked in a citrus syrup. (Arabia)

KOURAMBEITHES a cinnamon-flavored hazelnut shortbread, either baked or fried, then rolled in sugar, served warm. (Arabia)

KRANSEKAGE a large, round, celebration cake "wreath" composed of different applications of marzipan, decorated with royal icing. Name translates as "wreath cake." (Denmark)

KRAPFEN yeasted dough, similar to doughnut dough, fried in such a way that a white band remains in the center; filled with jelly and dusted with sugar. (Germany)

KUCHEN a breakfast cake or individual pastry made of sweet, yeast-risen dough, sometimes incorporating fruit or nuts, which is glazed after baking with a sugar icing and nuts; also, the German term for cake, or pastry. (Germany)

KUGELHUPF a cake baked in a special fluted ring mold that is buttered and lined with sliced almonds; after baking it is dusted with confectioners' sugar. Many countries claim this as their own, though it appears to have originated in Austria. In Austria, it is understood to be a pound cake with plain vanilla or marbled batter, or a sweet yeast cake incorporating kirsch-soaked raisins. In Germany, it is a pound cake with a sandy texture lightened with egg whites. Antonin Carême contributed to France's version, which is also the most widely known—a sweet yeast bread with dried fruits. (Austria)

KULITCH a yeast-risen cake—baked in a cylindrical mold or kugelhupf pan—consisting of brioche dough incorporating dried fruit macerated in wine or vodka, topped with a white icing or fondant, and a sprinkling of nuts, traditionally served at Easter. (Russia)

LADY BALTIMORE CAKE a moist three-layer cake made from a batter employing egg whites, with a filling of chopped pecans and dried fruits, and a white frosting of boiled icing. (United States)

LADYFINGERS light, oblong, cake-like cookies with a soft interior and a somewhat crisp exterior, used as an element in many desserts. (France)

LAMINGTON a square of buttercake glazed with chocolate and coconut; created by the chef of Lord Lamington, circa 1900. (Australia)

LANCASHIRE CAKE a fruit-filled, yeast-risen bun. (England)

LANE CAKE a white layer cake with a custard filling incorporating dried fruits, nuts, and coconut, covered with boiled icing. (United States)

LARDY CAKE a rich, sweet cake of sugar, lard (or butter), and flour filled with dried fruit. (England)

LAS PALMAS a rich buttery cake topped with a coconut-sugar glaze and melted chocolate.

LEBKUCHEN a German gingerbread that is thick, almost cake-like, honey-sweetened, and spiced. The cookies made from the dough are shaped or molded, and the dough often incorporates almonds and candied citrus peel. The dough is also used to make gingerbread houses, ring cakes, heart cakes, etc. (Austria/Germany)

LECHE FRITA a lemon- and cinnamon-flavored custard is baked, cooled, and cut into squares; the squares are then deep-fried and dusted with cinnamon and confectioners' sugar. (Spain)

LEMON MERINGUE PIE a sweet pastry base, sometimes chocolate-coated, supports a rich lemon custard topped with browned meringue. (United States)

LEMON POSSIT sweetened cream is boiled and flavored with lemons until it reaches a smooth, creamy texture. (England)

LIGHTNING CAKE the American version of the German Blitzen Kuchen, this is a buttercake flavored with orange and incorporating nuts.

LINZERTORTE a thin, spicy, ground-almond-based sweet pastry layer is filled with raspberry jam and topped with a lattice of the pastry dough; the top is dusted with confectioners' sugar. (Austria)

LORD BALTIMORE CAKE a three-layer golden cake filled with boiled icing suspending candied cherries, chopped nuts, and crushed macaroons; it is topped with more boiled icing. Possibly created to use up egg yolks left over from Lady Baltimore Cakes. (United States)

LUCULLUS a rich, sweet pastry layer and a liqueur-soaked savarin base enclose a raspberry soufflé mixture; the entirety is baked and served with a raspberry sauce. Named for a general of the Roman Empire.

MACAROONS a cookie of sugar, egg whites, and almond paste which is warmed, formed into small rounds, and baked, ideally so that the outside is crisp and the inside is chewy. A popular variation substitutes coconut for the almond paste, though other flavorings are possible. The name is derived from the Greek "makaria," or pleasure. (Italy)

MADELEINE a cookie of flour, butter, eggs, sugar, and a flavor agent, traditionally lemon, baked in a special, scalloped mold. Said to be named after a young girl who brought them to Stanislas, the Duke of Lorraine, (circa 1730) and thus to the court of Louis XV. (France)

MAI LANDERLI star-shaped, lemon-flavored butter cookies, traditionally served at Christmas. (Germany)

MALAKOFF TORTE a torte of japonaise meringue layered with coffee cream and topped with hazelnuts.

MALTAIS thin discs of a dried paste, composed of candied fruit peel and almond meal, topped with two flavored (kirsch and orange blossom) fondants. (France)

MANDELBROT a cookie made from an almond bread that is baked, cut into slices, and baked again. (Germany/Israel)

MANJAR BLANCO a thick, sweet, cinnamon-flavored milk pudding. (Peru)

MARGUERITE CAKE a dense orange-flavored cake prepared in a round cake tin or springform pan.

MARJOLAINE traditionally, a rectangular cake of alternating layers of almond meringue, chocolate buttercream, and praline cream. There are many variations, but all are extremely chocolaty. (France)

MARQUISE a coffee-flavored genoise cake topped with chocolate fondant encloses a thick whipped filling of chocolate and cream. The term also applies to the filling itself, to a chocolate dacquoise, and may also be used to describe a dessert of fruit ice and cream. (France)

MAZURKA an individual cake of eggs, honey, lemon, and lemon zest, plus ground hazelnuts or almonds, usually baked in a muffin pan or in paper baking cups; served with whipped cream. (Russia)

MELTING MOMENT a star-shaped butter cookie, sometimes rolled in coconut and topped with a cherry prior to baking. (Great Britain)

MEN'S TORTE a chocolate marzipan shell encloses a white-wine custard.

M'HENCHA a phyllo roll encloses a nut filling flavored with orange flower water. The roll is formed into a coil, and baked. The name means "serpent." (Morocco)

MIMOSA CAKE an unleavened cake layered with buttercream, covered with sugar, piped chocolate, and marzipan decorations.

MISSISSIPPI MUD CAKE a dense chocolate cake with a chocolate ganache icing. (United States)

MONKEY FACE butter cookies sandwich a jelly center, and the entirety is glazed with lemon icing; three small holes are cut in one face of the sandwich cookie to form the monkey face.

MONT BLANC a mound of sweetened chestnut purée is topped with crème Chantilly and decorated with chocolate shavings; sometimes flavored with brandy. Named for the mountain on the border of Italy and France. (France/Italy)

MONTMORENCY a term that applies to any dessert that depends for its flavor primarily on cherries; the Montmorency cake is genoise sponge crowned, and sometimes filled, with cherries, topped with Italian meringue, and flambéed.

MOUSSE a light but creamy dessert of beaten egg whites and whipped cream with a flavoring, such as chocolate or fruit purée; a chocolate mousse may also contain butter and egg yolks, while the fruit mousses may contain gelatin; served chilled. The methods of making savory and sweet mousses vary greatly; not all preparations contain either eggs or butter. The name translates as "foam" or "froth." (France)

MUFFIN in the United States, a small, mushroom-shaped sweet cake baked in a muffin tin, risen with baking powder, often incorporating dried fruits and/or nuts; in England, a yeast-risen flatbread. (United States)

NAPOLEON three layers of puff pastry sandwich a sweet mixture of pastry cream and crème Chantilly, or sweetened whipped cream and jam; it is often crowned with white fondant drizzled with chocolate fondant, or confectioners' sugar; also known as millefeuille. (France)

NAPOLITAIN discs of sweet hazelnut or almond pastry sandwich layers of jelly, crowned with fondant. (France)

NAVETTE a buttercake soaked in orange flower water, baked in a barquette mold to resemble a boat hull. Though the recipe is French, it is thought to descend from ancient Egypt. (France)

NEGERKUSSE a chocolate-coated cookie sandwiching buttercream.

NELUSKO a pitted cherry soaked in kirsch, dipped in fondant, and often bottom-dipped in chocolate as a base, served as a petit four.

NERO ROSETTE a rich cookie piped into a rosette, its base dipped in chocolate.

NESSELRODE PUDDING a light custard that incorporates chestnut purée, candied fruits, nuts, and liqueur; it is either set with gelatin or frozen. (France)

NOCKERLN a layer of milk flavored with vanilla topped with a soufflé mixture; the entirety is baked. Served in small portions, usually on a pastry serving piece. (Austria)

OBSTTORTE on a sponge cake base placed in crème patissiere incorporating candied fruits, the entirety decorated with roasted flaked almonds. (Denmark)

OEUFS À LA NEIGE mounds of sweetened egg whites that have been poached in water or milk are topped with praline or a caramel drizzle and floated in a pool of (often lemon-flavored) crème anglaise. If the meringues are formed into flatter rounds, the dessert is called "Ile Flottante"—in English, "Floating Island." (France)

OLIEBOLLEN spiced fried dough filled with fresh or candied fruits, rolled in sugar.

OMELETTE SURPRISE an oval of sponge cake (or a cookie) soaked in syrup is topped with ice cream, and the entirety is covered with Italian meringue; after a dusting with sugar, the omelette is baked (or blowtorched) until browned, about 2 minutes.

OPERA CAKE a rectangular cake consisting of three slender layers of almond genoise or biscuit soaked in sugar syrup, alternating with distinct layers of ganache and coffee buttercream; typically, the side is not frosted, but the top is glazed with ganache, decorated with gold leaf and a chocolate piping of "Opera." Created in honor of the Paris Opera. (France)

OTHELLO two small semicircular sponge cakes are joined with chocolate pastry cream (or jam), and the entirety is brushed with apricot glaze and covered with chocolate fondant. Created by a pastry chef to honor the major characters of Shakespeare's *Othello*—the title character plus Iago and Desdemona—and Rosalind from Shakespeare's *As You Like It*. All use Othello sponge as a base, but the fillings differ, the color of the fondant changes, and the form changes: they are commonly made to resemble peaches, plums, or potatoes. (Great Britain)

OVERFLODIGSHORN various-sized rings of marzipan joined with melted chocolate and arranged to form a horn of plenty; candies and gifts are placed in the horn, which is a traditional wedding cake. (Denmark)

PAIN AU CHOCOLAT a rectangle or square of either croissant or Danish pastry dough wrapped around a chocolate stick and baked. (France)

PAIN D'EPICES risen with baking powder, this cinnamon and mixed-spice bread also incorporates honey and mixed candied peel. (France)

PALET DE DAME a small, crisp cookie of egg whites, butter, sugar, and flour; sometimes flavored; served as a petit four. (France)

PALMIER a thin-rolled rectangular sheet of puff pastry is folded over itself several times, with granulated sugar between each layer; the short ends are folded in towards the center twice; the pastry is then cut into strips which are laid on their side; the sugar caramelizes during baking. Can be served as a petit four or to sandwich mousse, crèmes, or whipped cream and fruit. Also known as "Elephant Ears" and "Palm Leaves." (France)

PANCAKE a batter of flour, eggs, and milk is cooked on a griddle; the thin round cakes are treated in different ways in various cultures, both as a sweet and savory course. In the United States, they are served with butter and syrup and/or fruit.

PANAMA CAKE a three-layer cake consisting of sweet cake incorporating sponge crumbs, ground hazelnuts, and almonds layered with chocolate buttercream and flaked almonds.

PANDOWDY spiced fruit which is tossed with spices and butter and sweetened with molasses topped with a crumbly dough and baked; during baking, the crust is pushed into the fruit—a process called "dowdying;" served warm with cream or sauce. (United States)

PANETTONE A rich bread incorporating dried fruits and nuts, baked in a tall cylindrical mold. Name means "Bread of Toni," in honor of the man who invented it (circa A.D. 200); by developing a bread that made him rich and famous, Toni made it possible for his daughter to marry the (wealthy) man she loved. (Italy)

PANFORTE DI SIENA a rich and spicy bread/cake incorporating honey and dried fruits, heavily dusted with confectioners' sugar. (Italy)

PANNA COTTA a gelled custard dessert, often with caramel sauce lining the mold; served with chocolate sauce, fruit purée, or fresh fruit. (Italy)

PA-PAO-FAN a rice pudding decorated with eight dried or candied fruits or nuts; the name translates as "treasure of eight." (China)

PARFAIT a term referring to the traditional French dessert of a custard or fruit ice frozen in a tall cylindrical mold and, unmolded, served with whipped cream (contemporary versions are in rectangular form); or a light dessert consisting of whipped egg yolks, cream, egg whites, and a flavoring; or a dessert served in a tall fluted glass consisting of several layers of mousse, pudding, whipped cream, and/or ice cream served with fruits, sauces, and nuts. (France)

PARIS BREST a baked ring of choux pastry is split and filled with a mixture of praline buttercream, pastry cream, and Italian meringue. Invented in 1891 by Pierre Gâteau to honor the annual bicycle race from Paris to Brest; the shape is intended to simulate a wheel. (France)

PARIS STICK a shortbread cookie half-dipped in chocolate.

PARKIN a sweetened oatcake, served in slices. (Scotland)

PASHKA a pyramidal cake of cottage cheese, sour cream, butter, and sugar, suspending nuts and dried fruits, decorated on each face with XB ("Christ is Risen") in dried fruit. (Russia)

PATTY CAKE an individual buttercake, baked in a special tin, filled with a crème or jelly.

PAVLOVA a large, crisp meringue shell encloses a filling of crème Chantilly (or plain whipped cream) and fresh fruit. Created, circa 1930, to honor Anna Pavlova, the Russian ballerina. (Australia)

PEACH MELBA A peach poached in spicy syrup is served over ice cream, drizzled with a Melba sauce (raspberry purée), and decorated with sliced almonds and whipped cream. Invented by Auguste Escoffier, to honor Dame Nellie Melba, an opera diva. (France)

PEAR BELLE HÉLÈNE a poached pear served with vanilla ice cream and chocolate sauce. Invented by Escoffier to celebrate the opera *La Belle Hélène*. (France)

PECAN PIE an open pie shell holds a filling of pecans, butter, eggs, molasses, and brown sugar; served warm or cold, with ice cream or whipped cream. (United States)

PETIT FOUR a small, baked (or flamed) pastry item of two types: a petit four sec ("dry") is one that is served without embellishment as it came from the oven; a petit four glacé ("iced") is one that is finished with a glaze, fondant, chocolate, etc. The term most particularly applies to single-serving, small, elaborately decorated and iced cakes, though small tartlets, chocolates, and coated fruits also fall under this term. The name most probably stems from the literal meaning, "small oven," or, by extension, the low temperature at which these items were baked, after the large cakes were done and the ovens were slowly cooling. (France)

PFEFFERNUSSE a cookie sweetened with honey, flavored with pepper and other spices, glazed with lemon icing. (Germany)

PISCHINGER TORTE layers of sponge, japonaise, and a chocolate buttercream with crushed pralines are covered with buttercream, hazelnuts, and confectioners' sugar. (Austria)

PITHIVIER a cake consisting of two rounds of puff pastry encasing a filling of frangipane cream; prior to baking, the circumference is cut into a scallop pattern, creating the characteristic sunburst effect. (France)

POLKA a cake with a sweet pastry base on which is placed baked choux pastry filled with a crème patissiere and fresh cream mixture. Traditionally, lines of caramelized sugar decorate the top, once thought to delineate the steps of the polka dance.

PONT-NEUF a sweet tartlet encloses a filling of crème frangipane topped with crushed macaroons. First served in a patisserie adjoining the famous Parisian bridge. (France)

POPOVER a small pastry fried in a gem iron at such intense heat that the dough quickly rises; filled with crème or jam. (United States)

POUND CAKE a rich cake baked in a loaf pan; typically flavored with vanilla, though other flavors are possible, as is the addition of nuts; served sliced, with fruit, or fruit purées, ice cream, or whipped cream. So named because the original recipe called for a pound each of sugar, butter, eggs, and flour; contemporary versions are lighter, often employing baking powder to thin the batter. (Great Britain)

PRINCESS CAKE a layer cake of sponge and a custard/crème Chantilly filling, which is also heaped on top to form a dome; drizzled with marzipan and melted chocolate. (Denmark)

PROFITEROLE a small sphere of baked pâte à choux filled with ice cream, mousse, or pastry cream and/or a sauce. Eaten individually or stacked in a pyramid and drizzled with chocolate sauce. The name translates as "small gift." (France)

PUMPKIN PIE a pie shell supports a spicy (usually cinnamon, ginger, brown sugar), creamy filling of puréed pumpkin, eggs, and cream; served warm or room temperature, with whipped cream. (United States)

QUEEN CAKE a small, round individual buttercake, dusted with confectioners' sugar and served with whipped cream.

QUEEN OF PUDDINGS an egg custard poured over sponge cake crumbs and baked, then glazed with strawberry jam and topped with meringue. (Great Britain)

QUEEN OF SHEBA an almond-chocolate cake with many variations. These may be as simple as a moist, rich, rum-soaked cake with almonds that is glazed with chocolate ganache, or as complex as a chocolate almond rum cake that is soaked in an orange juice/orange liqueur mixture, filled and frosted with a chocolate ganache-vanilla buttercream mixture, topped with a thin round of marzipan, and glazed with ganache. (France)

QUILTERS' CAKE a version of pound cake with walnuts, created circa 1870 and popularized through farmland barn-raising and quilter bees. (United States)

REHRUCKEN a chocolate/almond cake baked in a special, curved, oblong mold, covered in a chocolate glaze. (Austria)

RELIGIEUSE puffs of choux pastry filled with chocolate (or vanilla or coffee) pastry cream, stacked and frosted with chocolate (or coffee) icing. The name translates as "nun," whose mode of dress the dessert—either individual serving or large size—somewhat resembles. (France)

RIGO JANCSI a two-layer chocolate cake with an orange-flavored, rum-tinged whipped chocolate ganache filling and chocolate glaze; served in squares. Created to honor a nineteenth-century philandering, violin-playing gypsy. (Hungary)

RIGODON a bread pudding of brioche dough incorporating nuts and dried fruits, soaked in milk, and baked.

RIZ À L'IMPERATICE a dessert of sweetened milk, rice, and cream (Riz à la Condé) with gelatin and poached fruit, served with fruit purée, produced in a savarin mold or in individual servings.

ROSALIND a petit four consisting of two Othello sponge circles joined with raspberry jam and coated with cherry-flavored fondant. Although considered in a group with Iago, Othello, and Desdemona, Rosalind is a character in Shakespeare's *As You Like It*.

ROULADE a sponge cake or genoise batter minus the butter but with egg whites, baked in a jelly roll pan and rolled while still warm; unrolled, the cake is spread with a filling (buttercream, jam, whipped ganache, etc.) and rolled again, then covered with buttercream, whipped cream, etc., or dusted with confectioners' sugar. (France)

RUGELACH small drums or crescents of a cream-cheese-based dough rolled around a filling, either cinnamon-flavored chopped nuts and raisins, poppy seeds, chocolate, or jam. (Poland)

RUIFARD a yeast dough tart supports a filling of sliced apples and quinces topped with a buttered crumble of streusel and golden raisins. (France)

SABLÉ a gritty-textured shortbread cookie, flavored with orange or lemon and sometimes incorporating ground nuts, topped with a dollop of jelly. The dough is also used as a tartlet base. (France)

SACHER TORTE a rich, slender chocolate cake filled with apricot preserves and iced with a smooth, shiny chocolate glaze; the word "Sacher" is piped in chocolate script on top. Devised by Royal Pastry Chef Franz Sacher circa 1830 for the Congress of Vienna, later the signature dessert at his hotel; still later (1950s), the subject of a recipe ownership/authenticity dispute with a Viennese pastry shop, settled in favor of the Hotel Sacher (thus the signature). (Austria)

SACRISTAIN puff pastry strips are brushed with an egg wash, formed into twists, covered with flaked almonds, and baked, then sprinkled with sugar.

SAFRA a semolina cake filled with a spicy date mixture is soaked, after baking, in a warm syrup of sugar, honey, water, and lemon. (Libya)

ST. HONORÉ on a circular base of puff pastry, four concentric rings and puffs of pâte à choux are piped; the cake is brushed with egg wash and baked. When cooled, the puffs are filled with crème chiboust and topped with caramel, and the cake is topped with crème chiboust and fresh fruits. Invented circa 1845 by Chiboust, a French pastry chef, to honor the patron saint of pastry cooks and chefs. (France)

SALAMMBO a choux pastry puff filled with orange-flavored crème, covered with caramel, with chopped pistachio nuts arranged on either side, leaving a clean line of caramel across the top. Named after a late-nineteenth-century opera.

SALLY LUNN a yeast-risen flavored sweetbun, served warm, split, and spread with butter or whipped cream. (Great Britain)

SAND CAKE a moist loaf-cake made with potato flour, rich with butter and eggs, and flavored with brandy; outside Denmark, the term applies to a leavened cake incorporating cherries and ground almonds, with the almonds (or as an addition, ground rice) retaining a gritty quality; served warm. (Denmark)

SARAH BERNHARDT an individual serving of a chocolate-enrobed chocolate ganache cone atop an almond macaroon. (Denmark)

SAVARIN a ring-shaped, yeast-risen cake soaked in a rum syrup, filled with pastry cream or crème Chantilly or, less commonly, ice cream, fruit, berries, or mousse. Invented by August Julien, a nineteenth-century pastry-making Parisian, it was named after Brillat-Savarin, the famous gourmet and writer. (France)

SAVOIARDI cylindrical, sponge-based cookies, often used as components of desserts, such as charlottes. Also known as ladyfingers.

SAXONY PUDDING a sponge pudding.

SCHLOTFEGER a rectangular tuile cookie baked then quickly wrapped around a dowel; the cylindrical cookie is served as a petit four as is, or dipped in chocolate or filled with a mousse or whipped cream.

SCONE a light, individual round cake of butter, wheat flour, water, and baking powder; when baked correctly, it should be browned at the top and bottom, but white on the sides, with a soft, white interior; served hot, split, and spread with jam or butter. (Scotland)

SCROLL danish or puff pastry is rolled with ground cinnamon or custard, cut into slices, and baked.

SEMIFREDDO a creamy, iced, molded dessert containing whipped cream, meringue, or whipped eggs and layers or clusters of nuts, fruit, chocolate, or cookie crumbs; semi-frozen, it is served with a sauce or used as a filling for a meringue-shell cake. (Italy)

SHERBET a frozen dessert similar to ices and sorbets except that it contains milk. From "sharbart," a drink containing fruit juice, sugar, spices, and milk.

SHOE SOLE a small, thin portion of puff pastry that is tight-rolled, then rolled in confectioners' sugar and baked until the sugar caramelizes, turning so the caramelization is even; served as a petit four.

SHOO-FLY PIE a biscuit crumb crust filled with molasses, brown sugar, and spices. (United States)

SHORTBREAD a cookie or biscuit composed of butter, flour, sugar, salt, and sometimes a flavoring; it is baked slowly so that the finished product is melt-in-the-mouth buttery. (Scotland)

SHORTCAKE a mixture of butter, flour, baking soda, sugar, and a liquid of milk, water, and eggs, lightly baked until the product is dense and cakey. Served with fruit and whipped cream. (United States)

SHREWSBURY a sandwich cookie consisting of 2 pieces of shortbread surrounding jam, with a hole cut in the top layer. (England)

SIMNEL CAKE a spicy fruit cake partially filled, and glazed, with marzipan. (Great Britain)

SINGAPOUR a genoise sponge cake filled with macerated fruit and decorated with candied fruits and an apricot glaze.

SNICKERDOODLE a butter cookie flavored with cinnamon or nutmeg or other spices, incorporating nuts and dried fruit; a dusting of sugar and cinnamon prior to baking creates a crunchy top. (United States)

SNOW PUDDING a fruit jelly or fruit-flavored (usually lemon or apple) cream is warmed and folded with egg whites, and allowed to set.

SOCKERSTRUYOR a deep-fried, flower-shaped fritter. (Sweden)

SOPAIPILLAS strips of pastry dough deep-fried, drained, and dusted with confectioners' sugar. (Argentina)

SORBET a frozen dessert of water, sugar, and a flavoring ingredient, such as fruit purée, fruit juice, or a liqueur. The Italian name, sorbetto, translates as "water ice," but the dessert originated in China.

SOUFFLÉ beaten or whipped egg whites folded through a flavored pastry cream or other egg custard placed in a ramekin that has been coated with butter and sugar, and baked; the air in the egg whites expands with the heat, the steam is contained by the forming crust, and the dessert rises, sometimes to twice its original size; the result is a meringue-like shell encasing a warm liquid. From the verb "souffler": to blow or to breathe. (France)

SOUPIR-DE-NONNE a quenelle of a choux-pastry-based mixture deep-fried and served with fruit sauce. Translated as "nun's sigh," a contemporary variant of the original, quite vulgar, label. (France)

SPECULAA a thin spice cookie (brown sugar, cinnamon, cloves, brandy) made in the shape of Santa Claus. (Holland)

SPRINGERLE a cookie flavored with anise seed and lemon, embossed with elaborate Christmas-theme pictures or designs by using a springerle rolling pin or individual, carved wooden molds. (Germany)

SPUMONE 1 or 2 layers of ice cream enclose a filling of semifreddo, zabaglione, or brandy-flavored whipped cream with dried fruits and nuts. Slices are taken from a log-shaped whole and served with a sauce. (Italy)

STOLLEN a firm, somewhat dry yeast-risen bread filled with dried fruits and nuts. (Germany)

STRAWBERRIES ROMANOFF chopped strawberries macerated in orange juice or orange liqueur, served in a bed of whipped cream.

STRUDEL a rectangular dessert composed of a sheet of dough that is stretched thin, brushed with butter, and rolled around a filling of fruit and fried breadcrumbs; after baking, portions are served plain or with whipped cream or ice cream. The name is German ("whirlwind"), the dessert is Hungarian, the refinement and popularization is Austrian. (Hungary)

SUCCÈS a cake consisting of layers of almond meringue alternating with layers of praline or chocolate buttercream; chopped hazelnuts or sliced almonds are pressed into the side, and the top is dusted with confectioners' sugar; the term also applies to the crisp meringue itself. (France)

SUMMER PUDDING crustless bread slices enclosing a sweetened, cooked berry mixture. (Great Britain)

SUNDAE served in a bowl or glass, scoops of ice cream topped with a combination of syrups, sauces, purées, nuts, fruit, or sweet condiments. In turn-of-the-century America, "sodas" were prohibited from being served on Sundays; a soda shoppe owner simply eliminated the soda water and named the result a sundae. (United States)

SWISS ROLL sponge cake thickened with marzipan rolled into a log with a slathering of jam. (Great Britain)

SYLLABUB a creamy dessert—also used as a filling for other desserts—made from cream or milk beaten with white wine, sugar, lemon juice, and, optionally, brandy or sherry. (Great Britain)

TALIBUR an apple is cored and stuffed with a spiced mixture of almonds and dried fruit, then wrapped in puff pastry and baked.

TAPIOCA a pudding using the tapioca starch (derived from the root of the cassava plant) as a thickener.

TARTE TATIN caramelized apples served on a puff (or other) pastry base; prepared in a deep frypan, the pastry tops the filling until, after baking, the tart is turned right-side-up. Created by the Tatin sisters, turn-of-the-century hoteliers, as a way of using up spare pastry. (France)

TEA CAKE a yeast-risen bun incorporating dried fruits and a sugar glaze baked into the surface.

TERRINE layers of mousse, ice cream, or a crème are molded in a deep rectangular pan or are encased in an oblong or rectangular pastry case, often baked in a water bath.

TÊTE DE NEGRE a petit four consisting of two domes of meringue joined with chocolate buttercream, the entirety covered in buttercream and grated chocolate. (France)

TIFFANY CAKE an extremely rich, dense fruit cake. (United States)

TIPPALEIVAT yeast batter is formed into a cruller shape, fried, and rolled in sugar. (Sweden)

TIPSY CAKE a sponge layer cake with sherry custard, glazed with whipped cream and the sherry custard. (Great Britain)

TIRAMISÙ a deep bowl contains layers of spongecake or ladyfingers that have been soaked in coffee and brandy alternating with a custardy filling of zabaglione, coffee-flavored mascarpone, and grated chocolate. The name translates as "pick me up" and legendarily was created in a bordello, to restimulate the clients. (Italy)

TOLLHOUSE COOKIES a buttery chocolate chip and (optional) nut cookie. Created circa 1933 by the Tollhouse restaurant. (United States)

TONKINOIS an almond cake filled with a praline-flavored buttercream and glazed with orange fondant, grated roasted almonds, or shredded coconut. (France)

TORTA DI MANDORLE a sweet pastry shell filled with frangipane and unblanched almonds is baked, cooled, and dusted with confectioners' sugar. (Italy)

TORTONI a mixture of ice cream or sweetened whipped cream and crushed macaroons is garnished with shaved chocolate and served frozen in individual paper cups. (Italy)

TOT-FAIT a pound cake incorporating nuts and candied fruit peel; cut in half, it is filled with poached fruits and whipped cream.

TRIFLE stale breadcrumbs soaked in port, or a fortified wine, form the base for a layer of fresh fruits, a sweet custard, and other optional garnishes. (Great Britain)

TROIS-FRÈRES a mixture of eggs, butter, rice flour, sugar, and maraschino cherries baked in a savarin mold, poured onto a circle of sweet pastry and decorated with cherries. Created by the three Julien brothers (1800s), one of whom also invented the Savarin.

TRUFFLE a round petit four, usually chocolate ganache dusted with cocoa, though other flavors and garnishes are possible.

TURKISH DELIGHT a gelatin dessert flavored with citrus or rosewater, and sometimes dusted in confectioners' sugar.

TURNOVER a disc of puff pastry dough is topped with a fruit filling, then the edges are brushed with egg yolk and brought together to form a half-circle pocket; after a dusting with sugar, it is baked.

TWELFTH NIGHT CAKE a general term for cakes that are traditionally made and exchanged on January 6, which marks the day the Three Wise Men visited the Baby Jesus.

Sometimes a bean is inserted in the dough, and whoever finds the bean in a finished slice is hailed as the Bean King.

UPSIDE-DOWN CAKE in a saucepan, cake batter is poured over pineapples that have been sautéed with brown sugar and butter; during baking (or frying), the bottom layer caramelizes. The cake is inverted and served. May be made with other fruits and/or baked in a cake pan. (United States)

VACHERIN a "basket" of meringue (either a continuous spiral or rings stacked atop one another) contains ice cream, mousse, or crème Chantilly and fresh fruit. (France)

VATROUCHKA a cake of curd cheese and dried fruits on a sablé base, covered with a lattice of sweet pastry. (Russia)

VATROUCHKI spherical turnovers made from brioche dough filled with curd cheese and fruit, either baked or fried.

VETTALAPAM a cinnamon- and cardamom-flavored coconut custard. (Sri Lanka)

VICTORIA SANDWICH CAKE 2 layers of sponge cake sandwich raspberry (or strawberry) jam and sweetened whipped cream (or buttercream). (Great Britain)

VISITANDINE a boat-shaped cake of sweet pastry enclosing a mixture of ground almonds, butter, sugar, and egg whites. (France)

VOL-AU-VENT 2 or 3 discs of puff pastry placed atop one another (the topmost with their centers removed), then baked and the center filled with mousse or fruit. Created by Antonin Carême, trying to lighten a dessert he'd served for years with sweet pastry. (France)

WAFFLE a thin batter leavened with baking powder or yeast is placed in a waffle iron (a 2-sided, hinged, ribbed iron) and cooked; the resulting crisp cake is served with a combination of butter, fruit, or syrup. (United States)

WUCHTELN a butter-rich yeast cake filled with plums, served with a crème anglaise or custard. (Austria)

YORKSHIRE PUDDING a simple pudding (composed of flour, eggs, and water) baked in small containers with a preheated fat or oil. Before the nineteenth century, an additional step was involved: placing the pudding under a roast meat spit to catch the dripping juices. (Great Britain)

ZABAGLIONE a mixture of egg yolks, sugar, and marsala wine whisked over heat until foamy and served as is, in a glass or bowl, or it may be used as a garnish to a mousse or frozen and eaten in slices. The difference between zabaglione and France's sabayon is the substitution of dry white white or champagne for the marsala. (Italy)

ZITRON a small sweet pastry tartlet filled with lemon butter and topped with lemon fondant. (Switzerland)

ZUCCOTO a dome of liqueur-soaked sponge cake encloses a chocolate and fruit ice cream center; decorated with whipped cream and flaked chocolate. (Italy)

ZUG TORTE a top and bottom layer of japonaise sandwiches and a kirsch-soaked layer of sponge cake and buttercream; the entirety is glazed with buttercream and cherries. (Switzerland)

ZUPPA INGLESE in a deep bowl, sponge cake soaked in a rum or kirsch is layered with pastry cream, toasted almonds, and candied fruit, the entirety covered with Italian meringue, which is browned in the oven or under a salamander. Created by Italian pastry chefs in the nineteenth century to mimic English puddings, which were popular in Italy at the time; the name translates as "English soup." (Italy)

Source List

Valrhona
LMC 73rd, Inc.
Valrhona Chocolates Division
1901 Avenue of the Stars
Suite 1800
Los Angeles, CA 90067
310-277-0401

Van Leer Chocolate Corporation
110 Hoboken Ave.
Jersey City, NY 07302
201-798-8080

Wilbur's Chocolate Co.
48 N. Broad St.
Lititz, PA 17543
800-233-0139
717-626-1131

World's Finest Chocolate
4801 S. Lawndale
Chicago, IL 60632-3062
800-366-2462
773-847-4600

ACMC Table Top Temperer
3194 Lawson Blvd.
Oceanside, NY 11572
516-766-1414

The Sinsation Chocolate Maker
Chandré LLC
14 Catharine St.
Poughkeepsie, NY 12601
800-3-CHOCLA

Hilliard's Chocolate System
Hilliard's
275 E. Center St.
West Bridgewater, MA 02379-1813
508-587-3666

ABC Emballuxe, Inc.
650 Crémanzie Est
Montréal, QC H2P 1E9 CANADA
514-381-6978
individual pastry molds, demisphere molds, acetates, custom transfer sheets and silkscreens

Albert Uster
9211 Gaither Rd.
Gaithersburg, MD 20877
800-231-8154
Swiss baking and confectionery products and professional tools, including orange compound, transfer sheets, clear gel, soft gel, dextrose, ice cream and sorbet stabilizers, coconut purée, yellow and orange chocolates, macadamia paste, almond paste, lemon rappé, cherries in kirsch, Tahitian Gold vanilla beans, invert sugar (trimoline), fondant patissier

Assouline & Ting
314 Brown St.
Philadelphia, PA 19123
800-521-4491
215-627-3000
chocolate, fruit purées, extracts, nut pastes, flours

The Baker's Catalogue
King Arthur Flour
P.O. Box 876
Norwich, VT 05055-0876
800-827-6836
specialty flours, sugars, chocolates, salts, purées, including praline paste, equipment

Barry Callebaut
St. Albans Town Industrial Park
RD #2, Box 7
St. Albans, VT 05478-9126
800-556-8845
imported and domestic chocolate couvertures, praline paste, molds, plus feuilletine, cocoa bean nibs, Krem d'Arome cocoa paste

Beryl's Cake Decorating Equipment
P.O. Box 1584
N. Springfield, VA 22151
800-488-2749
703-256-6951
tools for wedding cakes, chocolate work,
confectionery work

Braun Brush Company
43 Albertson Ave.
Albertson, NY 11507
800-645-4111
516-741-6000
extensive line of brushes for the baking industry,
custom-made brushes

Bridge Kitchenware Corp.
214 E. 52nd St.
New York, NY 10022
800-274-3435
212-838-6746
$3 for catalogue, refundable with first purchase;
bakeware, pastry equipment, molds, cake rings

The Candy Factory
12530 Riverside Dr.
N. Hollywood CA 91607
818-766-8220
$5 for catalogue, refundable with first purchase;
candy molds, custom molds, flavoring oils, colors

The Chef's Collection
10631 S.W. 146th Pl.
Miami, FL 33186
800-590-CHEF
brand-name professional cookware, cutlery,
gourmet accessories

Chocolates à la Carte
13190 Telfair Ave.
Sylmar, CA 91342
800-808-2263
818-364-6777
chocolate forms, signature chocolates

Chocolate Tree Ltd.
1048 N. Old World
Third St.
Milwaukee, WI 53203
414-271-5774
ambrosia and other chocolates

Cuisina
1701 E. 123rd St.
Olathe, KS 66061
800-345-1543
pastry ingredients, including Triquel instant thickener,
Boiron Kalamansi lemon purée

A Cook's Wares
211 37th Street
Beaver Falls, PA 15010
412-846-9490
chocolate, extracts, bakeware

Creative Culinary Tools
264 S.E. 46th Terrace
Cape Coral, FL 33904
800-340-7278
813-549-7715
custom silkscreens, molds, grilles, mold-making
compound

Dairy Fresh Chocolate
57 Salem St.
Boston, MA 02113
800-336-5536
617-742-2639
Callebaut, Lindt, Peter's, Valrhona chocolates

DeChoix Specialty Foods
58-25 52nd Ave.
Woodside, NY 11377
800-834-6881
718-507-8080
chocolate, fruit purées and pastes, nuts and nut products

Demarle, Inc., USA
2666-B Rte. 130 N
Cranbury, NJ 08512
609-395-0219
silpats, Flexipan, custom Flexipans, bread mats, forms

Easy Leaf Products
6001 Santa Monica Blvd.
Los Angeles, CA 90038
800-569-5323
213-469-0856
23-karat edible patent gold leaf

European Connection Inc.
313 Mount Vernon Pl.
Rockville, MD 20852-1118
301-838-0335
transfer sheets, flavoring oils

Ferncliff House
P.O. Box 177
Tremont City, OH 45372
937-390-6420
Van Leer, Guittard, Merckens, Nestle chocolates,
candy- and pastry-making supplies

Gourmail
126A Pleasant Valley, #401
Methuen, MA 01844
800-366-5900, ext. 96
Valrhona chocolate couverture; Cocoa Barry chocolate
couverture

Gourmand
2869 Towerview Rd.
Herndon, VA 22071
800-627-7272
703-708-0000
chocolate, flavorings, extracts, pastes

Harry Wils and Co, Inc.
182 Duane St.
New York, NY 10013
212-431-9731
fruit purées, IQF fruit, chocolate, extracts, nuts,
nut products

Holcraft Collection
P.O. Box 792
211 El Cajon Ave.
Davis, CA 95616
916-756-3023
chocolate molds, antique molds

Hygo
P.O. Box 267
Lyndhurst, NJ 07071
800-672-9727
201-507-0447
disposable pastry bags for cold and hot fillings

Industrial Plastics Supply Co.
309 Canal St.
New York, NY 10013
212-226-2010
plastic demispheres, tubing, grilles

International School of Confectionery Arts
9290 Gaither Rd.
Gaithersburg, MD 20877
301-963-9077
sugar-, candy-, and chocolate-making equipment,
Isomalt, glucose, powdered vegetable dyes

Istanbul Express
2434 Durant Ave.
Berkeley, CA 94704
510-848-3723
Ghirardelli, Guittard, Merckens, McLindon chocolates, chocolate molds

J. B. Prince Company
36 E. 31st St., 11th Floor
New York, NY 10016
212-683-3553
Flexipans, cake rings, molds, stencil grilles, silpats,
baking tools and equipment

Kerekes
7107 13th Ave.
Brooklyn, NY 11228
800-525-5556
718-232-7044
molds, baking tools and equipment

Kitchen Witch Gourmet Shop
127 N. El Camino Real, Suite D
Encinitas, CA 92024
760-942-3228
Cocoa Barry chocolate

La Cuisine
323 Cameron St.
Alexandria, VA 22314
800-521-1176
bakeware, molds, cake rings, silicon sheets, Flexipans,
chocolate, pastes, Tahitian vanilla beans

Maison Glass
P.O. Box 317H
Scarsdale, NY 10583
800-822-5564
914-725-1662
nut pastes

Matfer Kitchen and Bakery Supplies
16249 Stagg St.
Van Nuys, CA 91406
800-766-0799
818-782-0792

Metropolitan Cutlery, Inc.
649 Morris Turnpike
Springfield, NJ 07081
888-886-6083
201-467-4222
professional bakeware, butane stoves

The Modern Chef
P.O. Box 163
Little Falls, NJ 07424
201-338-0639

New York Cake and Baking Distributors
56 W. 22nd St.
New York, NY 10010
800-94-CAKE-9
212-675-CAKE
airbrushes, cake-decorating supplies, gum paste supplies

Steven M. Palumbo
145 Ferncrest Ave.
Cranston, RI 02905-2620
401-461-8020
1322 10th N.W.
Washington, DC 20001-4216
202-232-2264
silicone for mold making

Paradigm
5775 S.W. Jean Rd., Suite 106A
Lake Oswego, OR 97035
800-234-0250
503-636-4880
Ghirardelli, Guittard, Lindt, Merckens, Peter's
chocolates, dessert sauces

Patisfrance
161 E. Union Ave.
E. Rutherford, NJ 07073
1-800-PASTRY-1
fruit purées, chocolate, transfer sheets, nut products,
flavoring pastes, extracts, and essences, plus Kataifi,
powdered glucose, pastry cream powder

Pearl Paint
308 Canal St.
New York, NY 10013
800-221-6845, ext. 2297
212-431-7932, ext. 2297
acetate, custom silkscreens, airbrushes, art supplies

Penzeys Ltd.
P.O. Box 933
Muskego, WI 53150
414-679-7207
spices, including cassina (Indian cinnamon)

Previn Inc.
2044 Rittenhouse Square
Philadelphia, PA 19103
215-985-1996
digital pocket thermometer, chocolate molds, candy-
making supplies

Rafal Spice Company
2521 Russell
Detroit MI 48207
800-228-4276
313-259-6373
essential oils, extracts, flavorings

SCI Cuisine International
P.O. Box 659
Camarillo, CA 93011
800-966-5489
805-482-0791

Sweet Celebrations (formerly Maid of Scandinavia)
7009 Washington Ave. S.
Edina, MN 55439
800-328-6722
chocolate, cake-decorating and gum paste supplies,
chocolate- and candy-making supplies, molds, baking
supplies and equipment

The Sweet Shop
P.O. Box 573
Ft. Worth, TX 76101
800-222-2269
817-332-7941
Peter's chocolates

Sparrow
59 Waters Ave.
Everett, MA 02149
800-783-4116
617-389-4115
Cote d'Or, Valrhona, Schokinag, Callebaut chocolates

Swiss Connection
501 First St.
Orlando, FL 32824
800-LE-SWISS
407-857-9195
Lindt, Barry Callebaut, Braun (coating) chocolates,
molds, mixes, ingredients, supplies

Swiss Chalet Fine Foods, Inc.
9455 N.W. 40th St.
Miami, FL 33178-2941
Miami (headquarters): 305-592-0008
Houston: 713-868-9505
Los Angeles: 562-946-6816
marmalades, fruit compounds, chocolate, flavorings

Tomric Plastics
136 Broadway
Buffalo, NY 14203
716-854-6050
chocolate molds, candy-making supplies

Tropical Nut & Fruit
P.O. Box 7507
1100 Continental Blvd.
Charlotte, NC 28273
800-438-4470
704-588-0400
Ambrosia, Baker's, Blommer, Guittard, Merckens,
Peter's and more chocolates, dried fruits and nuts

White Toque, Inc.
536 Fayette Street
Perth Amboy, NJ 08861
800-237-6936
fruit purées, IQF wild berries, shelf-stable fruit,
chocolate sauces

Williams-Sonoma
P.O. Box 7456
San Francisco, CA 94120-7456
800-541-2233
chocolate, flours, baking pans and equipment

The Wilton School of Cake Decorating and Confectionary Art
2240 W. 75th St.
Woodridge, IL 60517
630-963-7100
cake-decorating supplies

Zabar's
2245 Broadway
New York, NY 10024
212-496-1234

Bibliography

Bloom, Carole. *The International Dictionary of Desserts, Pastries and Confections.* New York: Hearst Books, 1995.

Curnonsky. *Larousse: Traditional French Cooking.* New York: Doubleday, 1989.

Friberg, Bo. *The Professional Pastry Chef.* 3rd edition. New York: Van Nostrand Reinhold, 1996.

Herbst, Sharon Tyler. *Food Lover's Companion.* New York: Barron's, 1990.

Maree, Aaron. *Patisserie.* Sydney, Australia: Angus & Robertson, (a division of HarperCollins Publishers, New York), 1994.

Tannahill, Reay. *Food in History.* New York: Crown Publishers, 1989.

Index